AMERICAN DEMOCRACY IN ENGLISH POLITICS
1815-1850

AMERICAN DEMOCRACY
IN ENGLISH POLITICS
1815–1850

DAVID PAUL CROOK

CLARENDON PRESS · OXFORD
1965

Oxford University Press, Amen House, London E.C.4

GLASGOW   NEW YORK   TORONTO   MELBOURNE   WELLINGTON
BOMBAY   CALCUTTA   MADRAS   KARACHI   LAHORE   DACCA
CAPE TOWN   SALISBURY   NAIROBI   IBADAN   ACCRA
KUALA LUMPUR   HONG KONG

PRINTED IN GREAT BRITAIN BY
PITMAN PRESS, BATH

TO

MONICA AND MY MOTHER

FOREWORD
by BERNARD CRICK

HERE IS a fascinating monograph which deserves close study from at least
five different points of view. It is bold enough to cross frontiers which
seldom seem natural enough to be worth the stubborn defences put up
around them; but it is modest enough not to claim any new Imperial
authority of discipline or method, but simply to try to dismantle some of
the barbed wire. Perhaps I stray into military metaphor because it is almost
as dangerous for a political scientist to introduce something historical
as it was for Dr. Crook, as an historian, to study among political scientists.

Firstly, and most obviously, here is a contribution to Anglo-American
history. This is so in a double sense: it provides further evidence for the
need to treat Britain and the United States as part of a single Atlantic
economy, not merely of commerce, but of ideas and even styles of
politics—certainly until the American Civil War; and, more conven-
tionally, it shows the formation of opinion about the United States which
was to have some influence, both direct and indirect, upon British diplo-
macy. As America attracted more and more immigrants from outside
Great Britain, as she looked more and more inwards to the continent
through railroads and less and less outwards through the Atlantic ports,
and as other great powers industrialized, the peculiar intimacies of
tradition and commercial relationships between the two countries (of
which Mr. Frank Thistlethwaite wrote so suggestively in his *The Anglo-
American Connection in the Early Nineteenth Century*) grew less. But in the
period under consideration, just as immediately before, it is almost ludicrous to ignore the pull of American in English economic and social
history; still more so it is to have ignored the colonial style of politics,
and its close connections with the City of London, the Middlesex and the
Yorkshire style, in accounts of English politics in the 1760s and 1770s.
But what is good for the goose is good for the gander. American historians have rarely been completely candid about how much both the
style and the doctrine of American politics before the Civil War were
English, more specifically Whig, or rather characteristic of the whole
range of alternatives that could be characterized by that party label and
intellectual concept. No less than that, but certainly no more. It is hard
to know who has neglected the factor of the other's existence the more

—though Dr. Crook does not waste time on this kind of speculation. But I am fascinated in a rather simple way to discover that nearly all present-day formulations of High Tory anti-Americanism, and intellectual generalities about politics and society in the United States (for the United States has always attracted generalizations), find some clear precedent in the English and Scottish publicists of the 1830s and 1840s. Only the extreme and uncritical pro-Americanism typical of the Benthamites and the Radicals is now missing (except among a few university teachers and a slightly larger number of popular entertainers). Dr. Crook rightly passes lightly over the relatively well known and almost wholly predictable views of the out-and-out pro-Americans; he concentrates on a wholly original analysis of the far more subtle and complex views found in the Whig and Tory journals.

This book's second contribution is to a more purely British history. There are occasions when pitched battles are fought, as part of the continuous campaign of politics, on some at first sight strangely irrelevant site, some foreign field. Parties take their stand and close their ranks by their attitudes to a foreign country, be it—at different times—France, the United States, Russia, or Spain. The most practical of politicians then reveal not merely prejudices but reasonably systematic (if often highly irrational) doctrines. The reasons why the battle takes place at all may be purely domestic and may have little to do with the choice or the accident of the field on which it is fought. But then the actual topography of the field may have some tactical effect on at least the temporary outcome of the struggle. Plainly the mere occurrence of the American Civil War was to temper Radical enthusiasm for all things American, just as its outcome, its revelation of such economic and military strength, was to impress Conservative opinion in Britain. To tie one's claims to prescience and wisdom to foreign interests and events, over which one has no control at all, is at least to run tactical risks. The doctrinaire character of High Toryism, almost as great as that of Benthamism, is revealed in the debate over America. Dr. Crook is shrewd and commonsensical to be able to insist on the great importance of this debate, while not, even when showing its astonishing ubiquity, exaggerating its importance. He offers no facile case, as there have been some (on whom the author's comments, while firm, are yet more polite than mine would be), for the causal influence of 'the idea of America' and American ideas on British politics. I am of the opinion that it is far more revealing to treat all American politics, at least until the mid nineteenth century, as an extension of the politics of one section of British society, than to claim that Radical and Chartist movements depended on American example and influence—as does

Dr. G. D. Lillybridge in his *Beacon of Freedom: The Impact of American Democracy upon Great Britain, 1830–1870*. Rather Dr. Crook shows what a unique and revealing catalyst the debate proved for political opinion in Britain: 'The comparison tells us', he writes, 'more about Toryism in the Victorian age than about the real United States.' But this is in itself valuable, particularly when we are trying to understand a politics normally so tacit and unexplicit as English Conservatism. And it is interesting to see, when so many attempts are being made to dissolve away all distinctions into a maze of contradictory events, how clearly a Benthamite position distinguishes itself from a Whig and a Whig from a Tory. Indeed, the author surprises one by the great variety and often subtlety of viewpoint he has discovered among the opponents of Radicalism: there are, certainly by comparison, too few studies of Conservative opinion in Britain.

The third contribution is to a purely American history (if such an abstraction is allowable). For it is impossible even to begin to treat the history of the United States in the purely empirical manner in which it is now the fashion to treat English eighteenth- and nineteenth-century history—a corrective method now itself in danger of turning rigid, of narrowing, rather than ever extending, the range of factors involved in historical explanation. Part of American history is the constant absorption both with their own image of themselves and with the views of others. The prevalence of intellectual and of social history as subjects in American universities is a witness to this. Put it this way, somewhat impudently and imprudently: an American Namier would at least have to allow a greater causal effect for the lenses through which practical men look at reality than would British historians—of certain periods. (Do general ideas influence men in political action? Of course they do, sometimes and to some extent. If we are to be ruthlessly empirical, let us at least be thoroughly eclectic.) Two points of substance emerge here, one very familiar: the high degree of sensitivity shown by Americans as to what foreigners, particularly the British, said about them. But the less familiar point that emerges is how very Whiggish American politics appear—and the Whigs were the British commentators who, by and large, understood America best and could achieve the most objectivity. The idea that citizenship is based on property (the leisure, independence and concern that it creates) remained important even when it was held, as the Americans held, that all men (save the dissolute, the idle, the Indian and the Negro) could gain by their honest Lockeian labours the necessary minimum of property to be a citizen. Too often 'democracy' is a misleading anachronism when applied sweepingly to characterize American society at this period, unless the concept is used (as it was indeed at the Philadelphia Convention) to point to one element in what the English Whigs correctly saw as a 'mixed constitution'. This was, indeed, what was meant by the late-eighteenth-century usage of 'Republic' and 'Republican'. For the debate about the virtues of Republican government or 'democracy in America' has its real roots in the decade that followed the Stamp Act crisis of 1764. Then 'the Patriots' on both sides of the water were patriots of 'Republican principles', commercial connections, and middling status.' Patriot' was part of the rhetoric of Republican and reformist Whiggish, not of purely aristocratic, Tory (or later, Conservative) politics. (I think Dr. Johnson was plainly referring to these men in his celebrated aphorism, to the scoundrels of the Wilkite 'patriot gang' who were the 'Friends of America', those would-be Roman *citizens* who loved their *Patria*, and not to those loyal men who respected the 'Ranks and Orders' of feudal society and tried to revere the semi-alien dynasty.)

The fourth contribution of this book is to the history of political thought. There are a few precious books that, either consciously or unconsciously, bridge the gap between history and political theory—I would almost say, if I were not frightened of getting the author into trouble, between observation and generalization. Both seem to have grown excessively introspective and narrowly concerned with particular sources as Source of Very Source. The archive and the philosophical book alike are arrogated to be everything, instead of something. (Yet there is a large measure of agreement between the school of Namier and that of Oakeshott: philosophical books seem only to be studied to show that they mislead quite as much, are just as much mere ideology, as the pamphlets detested by the purely archival historians.) But there has been little study of what is probably the most important subject-matter of the history of political thought, and a neglected aspect of historical explanation: the theories of the untheoretical—something of what Collingwood meant by 'presuppositions', or the general prejudices or principles by which even the most practical men, consciously or unconsciously, select from the infinity of possible facts to make some order out of their environment. It is archly partisan to think that if the concept of 'tradition' is added to that of 'practice', then there is no problem; and that we can then simply proceed to describe what in fact people do, how in fact things work. For tradition is never a unity, or if it is, then there may be several traditions within one society, certainly within one unit under common rule (such as Empire, or a Federal State); and new and unexpected events do occur, which call for invention as well as adjustment. So every practical politician in fact holds, at some level of explicitness, theories both about how things work (and he may often be wrong: parts of government are secret, even deliberately deceptive), and about what things should happen. (Political principles are inherently both descriptive and prescriptive: it is asserted or felt that something which can or does work should be the general rule.) It is usually very hard and notoriously speculative to try to uncover this shaping level of doctrinal subjectivity and theoretical belief. People do exaggerate and, worse still, in seeking to deceive others by books and pamphlets, they commonly deceive themselves. But the fact that statesmen do not talk of principles in their correspondences is not evidence that they do not pursue principles, or that their thoughts and perceptions are not given order by them; it is only evidence that they are normally writing to people of roughly the same principles among whom such things are taken for granted. Rarely if ever do they need to be made explicit, for the people concerned are living in what Mr. Peter Laslett in a brilliant essay has termed 'face to face' societies. But a dispute about the character of some foreign country, when that country does not *immediately* touch domestic politics, and when the dispute is nominally, in form at least, conducted on a literary and intellectual level, does reveal what may be called the doctrines of the anti-doctrinaires (just as the study of behaviour by itself does reveal the *element* of interest in those who positively revel in moral explicitness). This Dr. Crook has done. I would point to this book, though this is not the author's main intention, as contrary evidence whenever it is said that the study of political ideas is irrelevant to historical explanation. But it also shows political theorists where their main sources should lie if they are to be relevant to anything.

The fifth contribution is to something little studied in this country, either by historians or philosophers: what one may call, in the manner of the work of Max Weber and Karl Mannheim, 'the sociology of knowledge'. This I take to be a study of the circumstances associated with the existence and importance of particular ideas. Such a study has often been held in low repute because of the intellectual and political fanaticism of its founder's insistence that *all* ideas and doctrines are *determined* by circumstance and social structure. But that is no reason why we should not attempt to discover *how much* certain ideas are 'determined', or simply to study ideas as social functions (without presuming to judge whether that is all or only part of what they are). Yet many empiricist historians who have little time not merely for Marx, but for all such 'holist theorists' (as both Sir Isaiah Berlin and Professor Karl Popper have put it), in fact share Marx's fundamental conviction that all ideas are the epiphenomena of interests, that and nothing else. Dr. Crook does not plunge into these troubled waters. I should not appear to suggest that he does. Rightly, his purposes are both more modest and more concrete. But he does present, as it were, a rare and fully documented 'case study' of the relationship between perception and interest in politics. There is much theory on this, but few hard cases: mostly there are just random examples, to show that explanation is plausible (not that it is true), or—worse still—hypothetical, invented examples to show that an explanation is logically tenable. There must be a lot of logically tenable explanations. If this book is more purely descriptive and down-to-earth than I might seem to suggest, it does its job so well that these more general problems become both quite unavoidable and also highly specific: in this way it is something of a quiet protest against the pedagogic separation of history from the other social sciences. In this context the chapter on the reception of Tocqueville's masterpiece is of special relevance.

When the author reflects on the variety of viewpoints on things American in the journals of the period, even over what might naïvely seem quite simple issues of fact, he comments: 'what is interesting and important to my mind, is the subjectivity of the appraisal.' I am sure that he is right. The very reason that some give for ignoring such events, or for thinking that their study is not a part of true historical research, gives them their true importance: their subjectivity. For comparison is mostly a valuable way of knowing ourselves. And if we have internal differences—well, we have internal differences (why we have them is not the issue here). But when publicists debate the 'real nature' of some foreign country with a passionate intensity, or with all sorts of pretentious claims to exhaustive objectivity, they are at least revealing the doctrinal consistency of their own domestic politics—hedged with compromises though it must be at every actual step. This is not to say that doctrine is all; just that it is often far from negligible. It is interesting that the publicists of the second quarter of the nineteenth century reached out instinctively for a comparative method to help clarify their own problems and convince their opponents, just as historians in the last quarter of the century tried to make 'the comparative method' *the* method of a true history, though it was not, as many thought, a purely objective history, but the history of the rise of scientific learning and of free political institutions. Even this was too narrow: it tended to be, explicitly even and with great precision, Anglo-Saxon. But perhaps we have lost something in suspecting the very scale of all such enterprises. That is why I make these remarks. Otherwise it is not easy to put this book into the wider context its merits deserve. For its demonstration of the intensity of the debate about America among English publicists does challenge the meaningfulness of what too often

seems to be purely national history. I do not think that it is always a
'purely intellectual exercise' to ask our students to 'Compare and contrast
. . .' such and such in the United States and Great Britain: there are
obvious historical reasons why, almost apart from the actual existence of
great similarities (in any comparison of relativities), we do go on asking
such questions, privately and in politics, as well as in such odd things as
examinations; and in any case even contrasts between things flagrantly
unconnected may illuminate. If I am guilty of taking advantage of Dr.
Crook's admirably careful and balanced thesis for the sake of a polemic
that is really a plea for more histories of the actual ideas of politicians and
publicists, I can only plead in mitigation for someone to explain why the
American connection has been so neglected in standard histories of this
period, but not by the political writers of the day. Perhaps such an explanation would take the form of a study similar to Dr. Crook's of attitudes to
America in our times—not neglecting those of historians. And again it
might take an Australian not so much to achieve, as to possess, the
necessary dispassion.

PREFACE

COMPARATIVE POLITICS have fascinated thinkers and polemicists since at least the time of Aristotle and Plato. It has seemed an obvious and natural thing for men to look out of themselves and their homeland to see how things are done better or worse elsewhere. Foreign stereotypes have thus been constantly deployed in domestic politics. This study is an attempt to show the use to which ideas about one country—the United States of America—were put in the politics of another—England in the early nineteenth century. The French and American Revolutions had captured the world's attention: both events were pictured as radical in the popular mythology of the time, and conservatives everywhere struggled to prevent emulation. As a result, comparison involving America (and France, until the Terror) aroused stronger emotions in Britain than comparison usually evoked, because, for reasons which I will set out, the fate of America came to be identified with the fate of Democracy. America was at the very knuckle of the English political situation; it was as natural for men to be as committed about America as about English politics.

Perhaps the progress of science also encouraged comparison. Englishmen in the nineteenth century were possibly more willing than men of earlier times to supplement arguments resting on moral absolutes by arguments resting upon systematic comparison supposed to be divorced from subjectivity. (Such comparative techniques were then of course becoming popular in natural history and geology.) Certainly, the pragmatic English were readier to make this concession to science than to countenance any Hegelian dialectic which should make an alternative bridge between science and ethics. Thus while nineteenth-century Europeans were beginning to fight their political battles by reference to dialectical materialism and philosophies of history, the English quarrelled over the meaning of American history.

The wish to be scientific, however, was not father to the deed. In too many cases needs prevailed over scientific objectivity, and comparison became a very subjective process, sometimes even a wall-eyed process of verifying preconceived ideas. Nevertheless, we may gain an insight into English predicaments by studying the meaning which Englishmen assigned to American history. The verdicts which they passed upon America, and American solutions to universal problems, were used to interpret and meet their own situation. Where their assessments involved a shift of interpretation away from the dominant legends current in America itself, this elucidates English history. As we know, in the United States new political legends were built up and subtle changes of spirit occurred within the law as a new society evolved in the nineteenth and twentieth centuries. The formal principles of American politics, which crossed the Atlantic as myths after 1776, underwent other mutations in an England with separate values and history. There was, for example, a world of difference between the stereotype of American democracy believed in by followers of Andrew Jackson, and that accepted by English Tories; and the comparison tells us much more about Toryism in the Victorian Age than about the real United States.

ACKNOWLEDGEMENTS

THE PRESENT study has grown out of the work done for a Ph.D. degree at the London School of Economics and Political Science. I am grateful to many people for their kind encouragement, and above all to Bernard Crick, who was always erudite, stimulating, and a good friend, and who generously led an Australian through the labyrinth of English scholarship. Ken Minogue of the London School of Economics, Professor D. W. Brogan of Cambridge, Frank Thistlethwaite, now Vice-Chancellor of the University of East Anglia, and Charles Grimshaw and Damodar Singhal of Queensland also gave valuable assistance and suggested improvements. I was enabled to carry out my studies by a scholarship awarded by the University of Queensland, Australia. The Commonwealth Public Service of Australia kindly granted me leave of absence for three years. To the Graduate School of the London School of Economics, and in particular to Dr. Ann Bohm, its Secretary, I am thankful for much friendly assistance. The library staff at the British Library of Political and Economic Science and the British Museum were unfailingly helpful. Finally, I have an especially personal debt to my teachers, and now colleagues, in the History Department of the University of Queensland, who first helped me along the road of scholarship.

St. Lucia,
  Brisbane.

CONTENTS

More powerful than the eloquence of Mirabeau or
the sword of Napoleon, the democratic government
of America has struck far and wide into the minds
of the European people. . . .

Archibald Alison, 1833

CHAPTER I

INTRODUCTORY: THE FRIENDS OF AMERICA

IT IS now accepted that the American Revolution was, from its occurrence, a stimulus to liberal movements in Europe. John Adams, towards the close of his life, wrote of the Independence: 'Its effects and consequences have already been awful over a great part of the Globe; and when and where are they to cease?' Eighteenth-century France was the most obvious beneficiary of the 'awful' influence of American ideas, but Britain also felt their effect. From the days of Wilkes and the Rockingham Whigs, a close association and sympathy existed between English Radicals and American democrats.[1] After 1789, with the upheaval in France, American ideas were often dubbed jacobinical, but they continued to sustain those who fought against the Tory Reaction and for a new, and more liberal, society in England. Until quite late in the nineteenth century the American democratic experience was believed to be closely relevant to British political issues. Whether one ought to acquiesce in, or oppose, the 'Americanization' of Britain was a common form of stating the political problem of the age.

What was the American appeal? The Republic had most of the liberal virtues—apparently free institutions, a rule of law, the constitutional protection of individual rights and liberties, religious toleration, and minimal government. The events of 1776 were a commendation of revolution in the good old Whig tradition; even the terrors of the French Revolution failed to obliterate the fact. The American secession had quite clearly been engineered and consolidated by responsible men who thought like Englishmen, not like Jacobins—1776 was more akin to 1688 than to 1789. The continued stability of the Union also resolved a long-standing debate whether a republic was conceivable for a large territory, or was only suited to small states. As Hume had foretold, the fruitful combination of the ideas of representation and federation had enabled popular government to adapt itself to a vast continent.

[1] See Michael Kraus, *The Atlantic Civilization: Eighteenth Century Origins* (New York, 1949), especially Ch. X.

Radicals drew more extreme deductions from the success of a specifically democratic experiment—as it seemed after the Jeffersonians got
power. They would have agreed with Daniel Webster's view of the
Union's role in the great drama of human affairs:

We are placed at the head of popular governments. Thus far, our example shows
that such governments are compatible, not only with respectability and power, but
with repose, with peace, with security of personal rights, with good laws, and a
just administration. . . . Our history proves that the popular form is practicable,
and that, with wisdom and knowledge, men may govern themselves.

As long as America seemed to show these things, it was assured of sym-
bolic importance to the idealists and utopians, the reformers and the
aspirant classes of Europe—for all indeed who believed that in political
action and constitutional change lay a chance of bettering society and
themselves. America had enormous appeal, especially, to those who had
claims to the tradition of the Enlightenment, to the optimists with a wide
love for mankind and confidence in man's rationality. These people
praised America's non-corporate, non-customary society, and its constitution, which they said rested on reason and was framed in a modern
age for modern men. From the days of Thomas Paine to those of Richard
Cobden, such men found particular gratification in surveying the public
conduct of the Union. In the words of one:

How calm and reasonable is its language; always addressing itself to the understanding and the solid interests of the people, never to their passions or prejudices.
It seeks no aid from superstition, supports no gainful impostures, and uses none of
that disquieting cant with which the old governments of Europe varnish over the
degradation of the people. It is a stranger to state-craft and mystery. All its acts
are done in the face of day. It promotes knowledge, religion, and learning, without
the preference of particular sects, and without debasing them by falsehoods
beneficial to the ruling powers. It is the only government in the world that dares
to put arms freely in the hands of all its citizens. From Maine to Mississippi, it
commands a prompt and ready obedience without any other weapons than a
constable's staff. In a word, it secures property, satisfies opinion, promotes the
development of industry and talent with a rapidity hitherto unexampled, and
with the smallest sacrifice of individual rights and property on the part of the
people, it accomplishes all that the most expensive and powerful governments
pretend to.[2]

It is tempting to think that radicals and idealists historically have been
lukewarm patriots. (Not always of course—they have sometimes, as in

[2] D. B. Warden, *Statistical, Political, and Historical Account of the United States*;
quoted, with relish, by James Mill in *Westminster Review*, Vol. 1, No. 1, Jan. 1824,
p. 268.

France, stood for the nation against the dynastic system.) Their vision has usually been far-ranging, and their faith has been in mankind rather than the nation. Their instinct has been, very often, for abstract and comparative arguments rather than for domestic ones. Conservatives have, on the other hand, eschewed extravagant faiths, theory, and utopianism. Wisely, as far as their own interest is concerned, they have tried to restrict debate within a national framework, for comparison has, on the whole, encouraged change and questioning. Radicals have been everlastingly seeking utopias, investing in them their hopes and aspirations, and then resisting the sceptics and disenchanters. As Russia was the utopia of Socialists after 1917, and fulfilled some emotional need, the United States was the ideal commonwealth of nineteenth-century Radicals in Britain. Both resisted disillusion for many years. Utopianism, by its very nature, seems perpetually doomed to disappointment, because of the inevitable discovery that peoples and systems are never perfect. Nor are they usually wholly bad, so that the extravagant scepticism of conservatives regarding extra-national experience must also be modified. Thus during the first half of the nineteenth century, as information about the new world increased, many erstwhile friends of America became disappointed with it, while Tory attitudes mellowed.

The importance of the American example in English politics has only recently received scholarly attention. Most interest has centred upon the Radicals and friends of America, who used that example in the cause of change in Britain. Frank Thistlethwaite has analysed with insight the psychology of such men.[3] He describes them as the 'outsiders' of English society, as new men of the Industrial Revolution who resented their exclusion from power and privilege inside the Establishment. Among them were manufacturers and traders, middle-class Dissenters, Bentha-mites, Cobdenites, intellectuals, artisans, and Chartists. Although, as Thistlethwaite emphasizes, there was no unanimity in the domestic political interests of this 'nation' of Englishmen, they shared a common outlook. All were, for their own reasons, dissatisfied with the existing political order. The industrialists and advocates of 'laissez faire et laissez passer' wanted to dismantle the restrictive corporate order, to open the way for new wealth and new technology. Working-men and factory-owners, for quite separate reasons, opposed the rule of land and status. Most important, the 'outsiders' were essentially non-conformist in politics, as well as in religion; and for that reason 'understood vicariously' the

[3] See his *The Anglo-American Connection in the Early Nineteenth Century* (Philadelphia, 1959), Ch. 2; and 'America and Two Nations of Englishmen', *Virginia Quarterly Review*, XXXI (1955).

American experience, which was one of uprooting, dissent, and rebellion. It was seen that transatlantic society did without what Bentham called the dross of established aristocracy and prelacy; it was dynamic and progressive, a land of economic opportunity, and therefore vastly encouraging to those struggling for a society open to all talents in England. The working-class attributed America's high wages and social equality to universal suffrage; Benthamites praised the efficiency and utility of republican institutions; Dissenters admired the voluntary system in religion; and Chartists fought for the American representative system in Britain. Thistlethwaite traces in compelling detail the inter-relationship of reform movements in England and the United States, showing convincingly the importance of transatlantic links, especially between the political radicals and humanitarians of both worlds. Abolitionists, feminists, educationists, Dissenters, temperance advocates, zealots of international peace—crusaders of all colours drew material and moral support, as well as propaganda, from the new world. For the 'insiders' of the Establishment, however, the American example was 'a subversive influence deeply to be feared'.

Further documentation of America's compelling attraction for British Radicals has been provided by an American historian, G. D. Lillibridge.[4] He deals shortly, and much too abruptly, with conservative opinion, but gives valuable and concentrated attention to the working-class Radicals and Chartists. He shows graphically how they welcomed and used American propaganda in a series of campaigns—for universal suffrage and the ballot; for cheap government; for free and secular education; for a free press; for the separation of church and state; and for land reform. Indeed, so tediously was the American theme repeated and exploited that it 'bore a strong resemblance to accepted ritual'. The chief priests were able Radical journalists and agitators such as Henry Hetherington, Richard Carlile, William Carpenter, and the irrepressible William Cobbett, who edited the numberless cheap and usually illegal Radical papers and pamphlets of the time: Hetherington's *Poor Man's Guardian*, Carlile's *Gauntlet* and *Prompter*, Beaumont's *London Dispatch*, Carpenter's *Political Letters and Pamphlets*, Cobbett's *Political Register*, together with *The True Sun*, and the *Working Man's Friend*. The working men's associations were other theatres of agitation. From 1830 to 1832, during the fight for the Reform Bill, resolutions praising American republicanism were passed by such bodies as the National Union of the Working Classes and the National Political Union. Here is not the place to re-tell this tale

---

[4] See *Beacon of Freedom: The Impact of American Democracy upon Great Britain 1830–1870* (Pennsylvania, 1954).

of admiration, but it is clear that such sentiments approached the revolutionary. In the troubled weeks following the Lords' rejection of the Reform Bill in October 1831, for instance, Hetherington exhorted the readers of his *Poor Man's Guardian* to look to the American Revolution as 'the best precedent and guide to the oppressed and enslaved people of England'. Radical groups in February 1832 celebrated Tom Paine's birthday at Temple Bar, and drank their toasts to 'The U.S.A.—may her republican institutions be imitated all over the world!' The same enthusiasm was revived during the Chartist crisis of the forties: the Stars and Stripes was regularly unfurled at Chartist meetings; long panegyrics on the American constitution appeared in the Chartist press;[5] and at one stage in 1840—not long after Parliament's rejection of the People's Charter— the Metropolitan Charter Union seriously considered an extraordinary proposal that President Tyler of the U.S.A. should be asked to intercede with the British Government on behalf of England's wretched working classes. The plan came to nothing, but thoughts of America continued to sustain the Chartists even during the twilight years of their movement.

Lillibridge, precisely because he has focused his gaze upon the Radicals and Ultra-Radicals, believes that American ideas (as moral force) had a 'momentous influence' upon British history—especially important because it was exerted during 'the crucial formative years of the democratic movement in both Europe and the United States':

. . . in the nineteenth century [he says] the American destiny to lead the world up out of the desperate jungles of ignorance and misery and onto the high plateaus of human happiness was not only accepted in confident grace by most Americans, but was welcomed with hosannas by innumerable Europeans who were rotting in those very jungles.[6]

On the other hand, the defenders of established interests—the Tories in England—are said to have consistently opposed such ideas in a frenzy of anti-Americanism. About 'the rising industrial business interests' (amongst whom he somewhat strangely includes the Whigs), Lillibridge is more cautious. He suggests, although he does not investigate the suggestion very deeply, that such interests used the American example only so long as it was convenient to do so, i.e. until their own enfranchisement in 1832. After that date, he thinks, they rejected American arguments which might have strengthened the claim to power of their erstwhile allies the working-class. Middle-class opinion, according to Lillibridge, remained cool towards America until after 1850, when Cobden

[5] See, e.g., *Chartist Circular*, 30.1.1841. Lillibridge, in Chs. 1 and 2, gives a very full account of what is merely outlined above.
[6] Lillibridge, p. xii.

and Bright—'the two members for the United States'—appealed to the American model to justify further reform of the franchise.

About Lillibridge's main theme—that American ideas exerted a 'momentous influence' in favour of change in Britain—I have some serious misgivings. The American theme is set in better perspective by looking at a wider spectrum of opinion. My conclusion, reached after surveying moderate and conservative opinion, is that historians have underestimated the capacity of some really influential groups to resist the more radical lessons of America, to accommodate facts about America to their own safe and pragmatic traditions. The revolutionary and more theoretical groups were, in this period, forced upon the defensive; doctrinaire solutions to problems were decisively repudiated. The exponents of moderation were ascendant, and they were capable both of discrediting the undeniably radical aspects of America and of asserting that country's (very real) undoctrinaire aspects. For some purposes, that is, they accepted and fought, but on other occasions they discounted, the idea of America as a symbol of revolution and democratic radicalism.

Their resistance sprang from feelings of disquiet about many qualities in American life. British and American civilizations were very close, indeed blood relations in many respects, but were profoundly warring in other respects. Those who emphasized the dissenting nature of America (and the friends of America) were right in doing so; and it was precisely the gulf between the psychology of challenging Dissent and that of ruling Establishment in England that prevented dominant opinion there from wholeheartedly countenancing America. Democracy was, in English memories, the politics of Civil War Puritanism, a theory which had been decisively rejected during the aristocratic age of Walpole, George III, and Edmund Burke. Even after the revival of radical reformism in the late eighteenth and early nineteenth century, there remained a continuing tension between the dominant political values of England and the United States: as I shall try to show, different concepts were in existence respecting the nature of man and the masses, natural laws and rights, and the proper use and end of power. The study of America in English politics is thus, at one level, the study of the clash and interaction of political philosophies. Imitation of America, which was predominantly a spur to change and accommodation of new forces to an old situation, was undoubtedly important; but to suggest that it was the crucial factor is to neglect those who, out of belief or inertia, were wedded to an older style of politics.

Resistance to the alien aspects of America was of course compatible with approval of the non-alien. Thus we frequently find the new world pictured in the image of the old. Surprisingly often men of the centre in

Britain referred to American society as an experiment in compromise and conciliation, liberal rather than majoritarian, concerned less with dogma than with order, and founded on a Revolution which was national-ist rather than ideological. There they found little to convince them that their own pragmatic approach to politics was unsound.

As the above remarks suggest, it is not my intention to duplicate modern studies of what might be called the British 'Left' of that time, but rather to add to the existing knowledge about political groups whose reaction to transatlantic influence has been only cursorily studied. As far as I am aware, no separate study has been made of the Benthamites in this respect during the years in which they spearheaded Radical opinion and were a very real force in politics. Again, despite some interesting comments made *en passant*, little attempt has been made to investigate in depth the impact of America upon British Conservatism and Whiggism. This study will try to set out a spectrum of opinion ranging from the intellec-tual Radicalism of Jeremy Bentham and John Stuart Mill, through the widespread and informed Whiggery of the centre, to the established Toryism of the right. There will be found here no attempt to measure American influences in each and every field of day-to-day politics. I have been concerned primarily to reconstruct the theoretical climate of the time, and have therefore confined my attention mainly to the response of articulate thinkers. What will emerge, I hope, is a sense of the com-plexity, and often ambivalence, of opinion about America that existed in groups whose political interests were not always served by uncritical admiration of transatlantic society and politics. What is interesting and important, to my mind, is the subjectivity of the appraisal; stereotypes about the new world in all groups were related to, and illustrated quite fascinatingly, the historical traditions, the political philosophy, the immediate political interests, and the temperaments of the people involved. The publicists of the parties, in particular, are open to the charge that they adjusted the 'facts' about America, even when they were ascertain-able, to a propagandist framework. This was at times—as in the case of Bentham and his followers—an iron framework which positively dis-couraged objective studies. The simplest stereotypes were accepted by the Ultra-Radicals, the Chartists and working-men, whose aspirations and ideals were closely bound up with a utopian vision of the United States. They held out the longest against evidence, sometimes overwhelming evidence, about American delinquencies. It was the interest of the Radicals to do a good public relations job for America, because they wanted the British customer to buy its main product (in their eyes), political democracy. And, like many P.R.O.'s, they did not hesitate to conceal the truth when it was unpalatable, or, at best, to give a very subjective and selective version of the facts. The Ultra-Tories, on the other hand, wanted America to have a bad press, and used similar means to this completely different end. The most objective impression of America often came from the Whigs; partly, it would seem, from temperament—the Whig tradition was a pragmatic one which rarely countenanced eulogy—but also for political reasons, for objectivity did no obvious harm to Whig interests.

From what I have been saying it follows that one ought to be suspicious of any attempt to divide opinion about America into two armed camps—into a protest movement of the Left, which was favourable, and an upperclass Establishment which was hostile. Although broadly valid, this analysis has outlived much of its usefulness, and is particularly inadequate as it applies to centre opinion about the Republic. That opinion is best considered in its own right. The Benthamites are a case in point. As Thistlethwaite is aware,[7] it is a simplification to regard them as typical 'outsiders'. Their Radicalism was not of the extreme Lockeian tradition favoured by American liberals; they were upper-middle-class professional men who were ready to join the Establishment once they had reformed it; and ultimately their belief was in a democracy run by the middle class. They made uneasy bedfellows with the Chartists, and during the late thirties and forties separated themselves from working-class political movements. Even their enthusiasm for things transatlantic was relatively short-lived, as Chapter II of this study will attempt to show. The Whig appraisal of the United States was, again, quite distinct from that of either Benthamites, Radicals, or Tories: it warrants separate treatment.

Conservative opinion was also more varied than has been suggested. It consisted of more than upper-class dislike of a vulgar and licentious democracy; it was more than resistance to the 'subversive' Americophilia of Radical opponents, although both sources were very important. For the Tories, the United States provided an argument against the philosophy of *laissez faire*, which posed a greater threat to the power of the aristocracy than did political Radicalism. There were bonds of sympathy, and exchanges of ideas, between British and American conservatives, and this provided some counterbalance to supra-national, transatlantic reform movements. The Tories were in many ways, particularly in their appreciation of America history, more realistic about the Republic than the Radicals. They were more aware of the non-democratic, the conservative

---

[7] Thistlethwaite, *Anglo-American Connection*, pp. 73–74. (This book is referred to hereafter as 'Thistlethwaite'.)

elements in transatlantic society and politics than has usually been allowed them by historians, although they were divided about their importance.

A final chapter is devoted to the great influence upon informed opinion in Britain of Alexis de Tocqueville's *Democracy in America*.

There is a compelling tendency, in a subject such as this, to look at American influence with hind-knowledge about the triumph of liberalism and American-type democracy in the West. Moral judgements may easily be made against middle- and upper-class attitudes because they have not received the plaudits of posterity. At the time, however, the future of American republicanism, and the theory of democracy, was by no means certain. Many of the qualifications and misgivings of Whigs and Tories were eminently reasonable. They deserve to be regarded as legitimate political thinking. In the following pages I have tried to explain, not to pass judgement upon, the beliefs of individuals and groups.

Finally, no attempt has been made in this book to debate at length the exact influence of American comparison, as contrasted with local factors, in shaping English developments. Such an occupation is a barren one at this stage of knowledge. Comparison was almost certainly a minor and tangential influence when viewed as part of the whole mosaic of the history of the time. To this extent I believe that Lillibridge has exaggerated the importance of the America example,[8] perhaps as a corrective to the fact that most English historians have underestimated or ignored its effect. Thistlethwaite rightly insists upon recognizing the limits of Atlantic influences and connections.[9] The Americophiles, he indicates, were a minority in Britain; while their American supporters frequently harboured sentiments not conducive to the birth of an Atlantic community. Radicals sometimes developed loyalties to un-American ideas, and later in the century this was to lead them far away from the new world. Most important, the Establishment ultimately absorbed the rebels, resisted fundamental changes, and rendered the American example obsolescent. National problems were finally solved in a peculiarly national way. And yet . . . many 'and yets' spring to mind. American influence is not to be traced solely by the empirical changes it produced in government and social relations. It affected the political thought of men with mountainous intellectual influence such as Tocqueville and John Stuart Mill. American experience acted as a catalyst, enabling men of all

[8] For F. H. Herrick's criticisms of Lillibridge in this respect, see *Am. Hist. Rev.* LXI (1955), 174–5. 'If he had studied men and the shaping of their minds more directly through letters, diaries, and memoirs he would have seen how little the reforms achieved in the 'thirties were determined by American democracy, how secondary American influence was on the Chartists. . . .'

[9] See Thistlethwaite, op. cit., pp. 172–6.

parties to distil their ideas about the democratic process. In so far as their response was very often a critical one, do we discount this as an Atlantic influence? There are other difficulties. One of them is that the example of the United States was inextricably bound up with political ideas which themselves sprang from European tradition, and that tradition continued independently to inspire English thinkers. How are the two influences to be unscrambled and measured? This study stresses the subjective nature of perceptions about the Republic. America exerted no 'pure' influence at all, so how is it to be assessed, except in terms of the needs and beliefs of Englishmen?—and these are notoriously slippery concepts to examine scientifically.

It is also true that American influence varied enormously on individuals as well as on groups. It is for this reason that I have attached so much importance to identifying the authors of writings about America in the periodical literature, for the knowledge adds significantly to an understanding of the forces at work. For some men America seems to have been a major source of inspiration. Richard Cobden, to take but one example, apparently arrived at most of the leading principles to which he devoted his public life—his internationalism, his pacifism, his anti-colonialism, his opposition to customary economic controls, his ideas on education, etc.—by a shrewd combination of deduction from first principles and deduction from American practice. At the other pole, a crucially important reformer such as Edwin Chadwick was completely uninterested in the United States, as were many Whig and Tory states-men. Conservative and Whig impressions of the Republic were, indeed, highly idiosyncratic. Croker's opinions were very different from those of Gifford or Egerton; Jeffrey's from those of Merivale or Greg. American example, moreover, seemed to be more effective as propaganda in some campaigns than in others. It was employed with greater success in the fight for law reform than in the agitation for the ballot. It is debatable whether America's ideological influence is an imponderable, but it is certainly difficult to estimate it exactly, or to make final generalizations about it, whilst studies of the Anglo-American connection are still in this early stage.

CHAPTER II

THE BENTHAMITE MILLENNIUM

AT TIMES in the early nineteenth century it is difficult to distinguish the very warm regard of English Benthamites for the United States from that of their political allies, the Radicals and Ultra-Radicals. Each group had a simple and idealistic stereotype of transatlantic democracy which could be used to support the campaign for Radical Reform in Britain, although the Benthamite vision owed much more to doctrinaire utilitarianism. The near-identity persisted as long as the Benthamites provided the intellectual leadership of Radicalism, as long as the interest of Benthamism and working-class Radicalism ran on a parallel course. Jeremy Bentham's longevity also played a part, for he created the essentials of the utilitarian image of America, and as long as he lived it remained the current interpretation amongst his followers.

During the 1830's there was a reaction against the pro-Americanism of the previous decade. Only the die-hards continued to be apologists of the American system; Bentham's ideas were supplanted by the more serious and critical interpretations of Alexis de Tocqueville and John Stuart Mill. The sensitivity of the Benthamites about their exclusion from power and prestige was appeased after 1832. Their political interests began to diverge from those of working-men and Chartists, whose good, it was felt, would be best promoted by a numerous and enlightened middle class (an attitude equivalent to 'the great betrayal' in the artisan mind). Even the most dedicated reformers began to feel that their best chance of pushing through Bentham's ideas of legal and administrative reform was to infiltrate existing institutions. The United States was still vastly attractive to such men, but less in its political than in its economic and social aspects. John Stuart Mill's conception of the Republic as the political organization of an essentially middle-class community, not a working-men's millennium, now had greater appeal.

1. *The Influence of Jeremy Bentham*

Jeremy Bentham was for most of his life an ardent admirer of the United States, then in its first phase of national development. This fact had significant implications for his political thought, implications which have not however received much attention from scholars of utilitarianism.

Bentham died in 1832, the year of the Reform Bill and the high point of liberal enthusiasm for transatlantic democracy. He was thus spared the painful sight of the growing liberal disillusionment about American politics that characterized the later thirties and forties. He remained ever, as he wrote of himself to John Adams Smith in 1817, a 'Philo-Yankee' in his writings. In his old age he informed Andrew Jackson that he was actually more of a 'United States man' than an Englishman, an attitude of moderate disloyalty which became entirely characteristic of the utilitarian press in the 1820's.[1]

Bentham was originally attracted to the United States as a vast experimental field for his ideas upon codification of the law.[2] He sent his *Fragment on Government* to Franklin in 1780, and later offered his services to President Madison, and the various State governors, as their codifier of laws and constitutional architect.[3] In Edward Livingston, author of the penal code for Louisiana, Bentham believed that he had both an admirer and disciple (which is perhaps one reason why Livingston was so handsomely treated in the Benthamite *Westminster Review* in the 1820's).[4] Through his interest in law reform, Bentham became acquainted with a number of leading Americans, and collected a good deal of information on American topics. He corresponded during his long life (1748–1832) with Franklin and Madison, Governor Plumer of New Hampshire, John Quincy Adams and Richard Rush (American Ministers to England), and John Adams Smith (nephew of John Quincy Adams). Bentham met Aaron Burr in London in 1807, and invited another American, John Neal—a contributor to the *Westminster Review*, and a later propagator of utilitarianism in America—to live with him in the 1820's.[5] From the many works he acquired upon the United States, Bentham set up an American 'Collecteana', including, besides printed books and legal commentaries, newspaper clippings and sets of the *North American Review* and *Niles Weekly Register*.

[1] Bentham to John Adams Smith, 22.12.1817, letter in Bentham MSS, University College, London, XII. 18; and Bentham to Jackson, in J. S. Bassett, ed., *Correspondence of Andrew Jackson* (Washington, 1926–31), IV. 46. Part of this chapter has already appeared in the author's 'The United States in Bentham's Thought', *Aust. J. Politics & Hist.*, Vol. X, No. 2, Aug. 1964, 196–204.

[2] A useful account of Bentham's dealings with Americans, and his interest in law reform in the Union, is given in Chilton Williamson, 'Bentham Looks at America', *Pol. Sc. Quart.*, LXX (Dec. 1955), 543–51. I have drawn upon some of this information in the following paragraphs.

[3] *The Works of Jeremy Bentham, published under the superintendence of his executor, J. Bowring*, 11 vols. (London, 1838–43), IV. 454–67, 478–508. Hereafter cited as *Works*.

[4] *Works*, X. 558–9.

[5] *Works*, X. 555–6. See also John Neal, *Wandering Recollections of a Somewhat Busy Life* (Boston, 1869).

Bentham's first interest was to emancipate the Americans from the yoke of an irrational common law derived from England, but he became aware of American successes in social and political fields. In 1788 Bentham advised the French to look at American models, in his *Essai sur la Représentation*, prepared for the information of the French Estates, due to meet in 1789.[6] He advised the French democrats, if they wished to be true to their principles, to implement virtual manhood suffrage and secret voting. He was not yet approving democracy, but simply indicating where democratic premises should logically end.

As Bentham became increasingly sympathetic to the democratic idea after 1807, he began energetically collecting more data about the only practical democracy then in existence. He studied American libel law, religion, and the religious tests required for office. The state constitutions attracted his main interest, and he subjected to close scrutiny the Massachusetts Constitution of 1820 and the New York Constitution of 1821. Bentham was particularly impressed by the working of popular suffrages, and by the responsibility shown by ordinary people when assembled in electoral conventions.[7] The healthy state of America, he felt, confirmed his radical theories, and was ammunition to be used in the liberal struggle against the Tory Reaction.

By 1817 Bentham was constantly exhorting the readers of his pamphlets to consult the American example. He did so in the important *Plan of Parliamentary Reform in the Form of a Catechism*, etc. (London, 1817); in his *Radicalism Not Dangerous* (1820) and the address to his *Fellow Citizens of France*[8] (1830); and in the first volume of the *Constitutional Code*, published in 1830.[9] He was writing and thinking about the United States, therefore, in the very years in which Benthamism acquired the *Westminster Review* and in which an increasing number of able and Radical intellectuals gathered round him. It was hardly surprising that the master's ideas about the United States were taken up in the utilitarian journalism of the time; and they retained an hegemony in Philosophical

---

[6] John Plamenatz, *The English Utilitarians* (London, 1949), p. 61.

[7] Williamson discovered among Bentham's papers a press report of the 1820 Massachusetts Convention, which emphasized the orderliness of proceedings although there was no disqualification for voting except 'absolute pauperism'.

[8] *Jeremy Bentham to his Fellow-citizens of France, on Houses of Peers and Senates* (London, 1830), in *Works*, IV. 449ff.

[9] Bentham, *Constitutional Code: for the use of all nations and all Governments professing Liberal opinions*, vol. I (London, 1830, published separately); the complete work is in *Works*, IX. 1–662. The ideal state pictured in the *Code* is, in its constitutional and administrative aspects, very reminiscent of the United States. Part III of the *Radicalism Not Dangerous* is entitled 'Defence from Experience in the Case of the United States', *Works*, III. 612–13.

Radicalism until after Reform had been won, and John Stuart Mill began to challenge them after reading Tocqueville.

To understand Bentham's regard for America, his political philosophy must be examined, for that philosophy almost predetermined his admiration. It was the fact that Americans enjoyed a high degree of felicity under a democratic government that impressed Bentham. Only in a democracy, he came to believe, could some approximation be contrived between the 'here and now' and an ideal state. It was axiomatic to him that the proper end of government should always be the great happiness of the greatest number of individuals of which the community was made up. But men, and especially in groups, were usually motivated by selfish interests, seeking always that course of action which would promote their own greatest happiness. The *actual* end of government in any political system, therefore, must be the greatest happiness of the governors.[10] The only form of government which served the common rather than a minority interest was consequently one in which there was a contrived identification of interest between rulers and ruled; in which institutions were so arranged that the governors, in seeking their own felicity, could not avoid serving the cause of the greatest happiness. Only a democratic form of government, Bentham believed, satisfied these requirements. Only in such a political system was the majority—whose interest must be in fact to obtain the greatest happiness for the greatest number—enabled to choose its own representatives. As it was in their interest to do so, they would naturally try to select members who would serve the universal rather than any particular interest. This identity of interests would be safeguarded by devices which would aim at ensuring that representatives acted as true agents of the people; by a virtual universality of suffrage, and by elections held annually in which voting was by secret ballot in roughly equal electoral districts.[11] Bentham also wanted representatives to be legally responsible for their legislative behaviour, and subject to recall by the electorate should the people think that their trust had been forfeited. To the end of greatest happiness, it was also necessary, he believed, that the Legislature should be fully sovereign, virtually unlimited in power except for the checks of a vigilant public opinion.

Apparently most of these ideas were conceived, or received, by Bentham independently of his awareness of American political experience. But the spectacular success of the Revolutionary settlement in America

---

[10] *Constitutional Code*, in *Works*, IX. 5.

[11] See *Plan of Parliamentary Reform, etc.* (London, 1817), in *Works*, III. 452, 459 (universal suffrage); 453, 562 (ballot); 521, 562 (annual elections); 452 (equal electorates).

appeared to vindicate them. There it seemed to him that the political omnipotence of the majority had ensured an identification of interests between the rulers and the community.[12] Because universal manhood suffrage, the secret ballot, and frequent elections had been largely conceded in the United States—because that country was in Bentham's view a total democracy[13]—the nation flourished and order prevailed.[14] Bentham believed America to be the land of efficient public administration,[15] of governmental economy and budget surpluses,[16] of liberty of the press[17] and liberty of religion, of progress in education,[18] and ability in law and the assembly. 'There they are', he wrote of the United States, 'with their prosperity the effect: there they are, with their good government—their matchless good government—the cause of it.'[19] Bentham was as rigid as any Ultra-Radical in his belief, illustrated in the new world, that the political principle of democracy *per se* made possible a thoroughgoing social transformation beneficial to mankind. He differed from most of the Radicals, however, in deriving this belief from the utilitarian premise.

Bentham's ideal *polis*, moreover, was a republic. This conclusion, too, he derived from his utilitarianism, and not direct from any transatlantic experience. A monarch, he argued, had few strong motives to act in the general interest. He was too insulated from the people either to feel an association of their interests with his, or even to acquire competent judgement on political questions. Finally, his abilities hung upon the chances of heredity. It was for these reasons that Bentham compiled his *Constitutional Code*, 'having for its object the bettering of this wicked world, by covering it over with Republics'.[20] Little wonder that he congratulated the Americans on emancipating themselves from the 'galling yoke' of English monarchy,[21] and rejoiced more than once in the 'illegitimacy' of their Republican government. For tactical reasons this strand of Bentham's thought was not ardently taken up by utilitarian reformers. James Mill, in fact, in a *London Review* article of 1836, suggested rather

---

[12] Bentham asserted this in *Constitutional Code, Works*, IX. 9.
[13] *Works*, III. 447, 562.
[14] Bentham was inexhaustible on this theme. See *Works*, III. 612–13, 437, 447, 472, 492, 494, 560, 562; and IX. 100.
[15] Bentham asked whether 'in the habitable globe, there exists anywhere so *regular*, so *well-regulated* a government'. *Works*, III. 447.
[16] He remarked in 1817 that America was paying off her public debt faster than England contracted hers. Ibid. 437.
[17] *Works*, II. 277.
[18] *Works*, IV. 531.
[19] *Works*, III. 437; see also 612–13.
[20] Bentham in a letter to Mordvinoff, *Works*, X. 542.
[21] *Works*, IV. 503–4, in a letter to Madison.

3

mildly the possibility of a Disraelian association of the popular and monarchical interests.[22] (Mill, who disapproved of an elected Executive on the American line, was willing to retain an hereditary monarch as head of the Executive, provided the legislature was properly representative of the people.)

The aristocracy and the Establishment, however, received a barrage of criticism from Bentham and the Philosophic Radicals after him. Bentham's democratic bent probably owed more, it seems, to his hatred of the few than to his love of the many, for it was the rejection of his Panopticon scheme by an aristocratic government that set him on the radical path. Aristocratic government became, for Bentham, government by and for selfish and sinister interests. Under no circumstances could it be expected to act according to the greatest happiness principle.[23] He consequently welcomed the appearance of a political system in America which repudiated the aristocratic principle of government and all forms of established privilege; and which triumphantly survived the repudiation:

There you have [he wrote]—not merely democratic ascendancy—democratic ascendancy in a mixed government—but democracy—pure democracy and nothing else. There you have not one democracy only, but a whole cluster of democracies: there, all is democracy; all is regularity, tranquility, prosperity, security: continual security, and with it continually increasing, though with practical equality divided, opulence. All, all is democracy; no aristocracy; no monarchy; all that dross evaporated.[24]

The Americans, he believed, were without 'useless place', unmerited pensions and sinecures, without peerages. Thus they enjoyed order without force: 'In republican America there are no dungeoning acts, no gagging acts, no riot acts; accordingly there are no riots.'[25] Free inquiry was not persecuted in the pretence of opposing sedition, and there was therefore no sedition. American education was superior to that of England because it was for the benefit of all and did not serve the 'separate and sinister interests of the few'.[26] Only the common interests were pursued in the United States, and these were the proper end of government—'the maximisation of subsistence, abundance, security and equality'.[27]

For these very reasons, Bentham exulted, the English upper classes feared the example of the United States. That country existed as the

---

[22] Vol. 2, No. 4, Jan. 1836, Art. 1 (Aristocracy). See also James Mill, *Essay on Government* (London, 1937, reprinted), pp. 60ff.
[23] *Works*, III. 446.
[24] Ibid. 447.
[25] Ibid. 562.
[26] *Works*, IV. 531.
[27] *Works*, IX. 63–64.

model of democratical prosperity at a time (1817) when England was helping to stifle popular movements in Europe, and to uphold absolute and illiberal governments there. He parodied the conservative reaction in these words:

There they are—but happily with the Atlantic between us and them—the never-sufficiently-accursed United States. There they are—living, and (oh horror!) flourishing—and so flourishing! flourishing under a government so essentially *illegitimate*! Oh what a reproach to legitimacy! Oh what a reproach, a never-to-be-expunged reproach, to our own Matchless Constitution—matchless in rotten boroughs and sinecures! Oh! had they but one neck—these miscreants! . . .[28]

Bentham, however, appreciated the impracticability, given the state of public opinion in England before 1830, of advocating total abolition of aristocracy and established prelacy. He pointed to the American ideal of twenty-six states, with democratic constitutions, eliciting as punctual an obedience to the law as any other government;[29] but after 1817 he contented himself with urging a 'democratic ascendancy' in Britain, to be attained by means of a Radical parliamentary reform.[30]

Let us look more closely at Bentham's conception of the nature of misgovernment by minorities, because his taste for American comparisons originated here. Bentham was aware of America as a model for reformers, as an absolute standard to be aimed at; but he also drew upon its example to undermine the psychological supports of oligarchical government in England. As Thomas Peardon has shown, Bentham was something of a pioneer in analysing 'the sanctions, promises, myths, symbols, and slogans' which enabled the few to retain power, at the expense of the many, even when government was corrupt and oppressive.[31] In his *Constitutional Code*, Bentham discerned four such props of misrule—corruption, 'delusion', fiction and 'factitious honour'. In each case, the American example could be used to dispel current myths, and to clear the way for a more rational and moral form of government.

Corruption was, in Bentham's eyes, an instrument of demoralization, by whose means an *élite* was recruited to aid the minority in the administration of power. He defined corruption widely to include not only bribery in money, offices, and honours, but all the laws and institutions of a country which were corruptive in effect. In an England headed by the

---

[28] *Works*, III. 437.
[29] *Fellow-Citizens of France, etc.* (London, 1830), in *Works*, IV. 449.
[30] *Works*, III. 446.
[31] Thomas P. Peardon, 'Bentham's Ideal Republic', *Canadian J. of Econ. and Pol., Sc.* XVII (May 1951), 184–203. The article is an analysis of the political ideas of the *Constitutional Code*.

Corruptioner-General and Company (as he irreverently called the King and his cohorts), he asserted that the institution of aristocracy itself, and all the paraphernalia of the Establishment, were inducements to corruption. Yet in republican America, where there was a contrived identification of the interests of rulers and governed, there was no need for corruption in any form. No group had to be bribed to help a minority to govern, to buy support, for government was the voluntary creation of a willing majority. Bentham was quite uncritical on this point, declaring for example in his *Plan of Parliamentary Reform* (1817) that the American Congress was entirely free of bribery and corruption.[32] And of course, the United States was emancipated too from the more subtle corruption of institutions, for its people had succeeded in shaking off 'the yoke of English monarchy—the yoke of English aristocracy—the yoke of English prelacy —all those galling yokes . . .'[33]

'Delusive' techniques were chief among the myths which Bentham discerned as protecting the existing constitution. The ruling *élite* used such devices to gain the acquiescence of the people in minority government. An impression of grandeur and omnipotence was created by display of the pageantry and trappings of monarchy, by the titles and wealth of aristocracy. The few controlled the vital channels of information and opinion and employed propaganda in support of the rulers. For example, they used 'fictitious entities', that is abstract terms such as Crown, Throne, Church, Law, and Property, instead of the concrete terms King, Churchmen, Lawyers, and the Rich, in order to clothe the ruling group in artificial respect and veneration and render criticism 'bad taste'. Fiction played a large part in law and government, but its only practical use was to buttress traditionalism and legitimacy. Aristocratic titles of rank were signs of 'factitious honour' that were delusive and artificial, for they were marks of privilege that had not been earned; their corruptive effect was more persuasive than offers of money or office.[34]

Bentham did much to knock away these props of aristocracy by rational enquiry, scepticism, and abuse; but a comparative argument enjoyed peculiar advantages. Bentham could appeal effectively to the analogy of a country such as the United States which had no need for the devious propaganda and fictions used in England.[35] The analogy, moreover, encouraged a questioning of the 'eternal verities' of oligarchy, and threatened the theory of the 'matchless constitution' revered by Blackstone and Burke. The success of an alternative social system, more

---

[32] *Works*, III. 494.   [33] *Works*, IV. 503-4.
[34] Peardon, op. cit., pp. 188ff; and *Works*, IX. 46ff.
[35] For instance, *Works*, IX. 64; and II. 481-2.

egalitarian than the English, cut at the roots of popular veneration for the upper classes. Crown, Throne and Altar inevitably lost some of their air of 'clouded majesty' when it became apparent, by comparison with Republic, Voluntary System, etc., in the United States, that other social and political forms might exist and prosper—might, indeed, be superior. Caste and hierarchy had been repudiated in the Republic, and replaced by a system of 'natural honour' which rewarded only those whose merit deserved recognition. By employing such comparisons, the reformer evaded many difficulties that faced domestic arguments. He was in effect attacking the English King, Nobility and Church, but with much less danger of pro- voking popular hostility ('deluded' by aristocratic propaganda) or of ending in jail as a 'traitor' or 'atheist'. Comparison, as Bentham stated more than once, was a short-cut to true opinion. He did not consider the possibility that deviant conclusions might be drawn from American experience, or that the observer of the democratic scene might be faced simply with a new set of myths. It was not until later that such doubts began to arise in the camp of utilitarianism.

America, had he realized it, was Bentham's dilemma as well as his utopia. There existed a deep schism between American liberalism (as distinct from American radicalism) and Benthamite utilitarianism, a schism of which Bentham himself was only dimly aware. Indeed this dim awareness of difference has been perpetuated by a whole school of writers who view Benthamism as essentially individualistic and find in it affinities with the approach to politics which the Americans derived from Locke (inter alia). Bentham has been far too often misrepresented as the essential liberal. He is, if anything, more inclined to accept anti-individua- list arguments, to fix his gaze on the individual-in-society, the individual as a unit of the greatest number, than is quite respectable for a liberal. Utility, rather than the liberty or the dignity of the individual, is his primary value. His early reliance on the benevolent despot; his subsequent replacement of king by the majority (which has something suspiciously like a Rousseauistic 'general will', to be defied by the dissident only at some risk), strengthen our suspicions of Bentham. He is to be placed rather with the Jacksonian democrats than with the Fathers of the Consti- tution. His claim to be an individualist rests largely on his acceptance of the maxim that 'each is the best judge of his own interest', which implies the inviolability of the individual. But, as the more perceptive scholars have pointed out,[36] this is secondary in his thought to, and does not really depend upon, the concept of 'the greatest happiness of the greatest

---

[36] See, e.g., M. J. P. Plamenatz, 'The Legacy of Philosophical Radicalism' in M. Ginsberg (ed.), Law and Opinion in the 20th Century (London, 1959), pp. 35–36.

number'. Should state interference (even authoritarianism) be shown to be more efficient means to his basic ends, then Bentham would logically have been forced to abandon his individualism (just as John Stuart Mill was forced to modify his utilitarianism to remain a liberal), and such a change is intimated in Bentham's later writings. In the *Constitutional Code*, he envisaged complex and powerful administrative departments whose activities would have wide social ramifications. He was determined to grant all-pervasive powers to his ideal, and democratic, Legislature, a body which has subsequently been regarded as anticipating the positive state of the twentieth century. In the interest of effective government directed toward the general good, he was willing to eschew constitutional checks and balances restraining authority.[37] Hence there was implied in his thought an antagonism to many basic political forms in America—to 'fundamental' constitutions overriding statutory law, to bills of rights, and to the separation of powers—to most of the devices which Americans believed protected the individual against the oppressions of authority, but which Bentham believed hamstrung government.[38] In his theory total democracies could not be dangerous, for they represented the greatest good. It was pernicious therefore for a majority to shackle itself unnecessarily, out of a chimerical regard for the rights of man or the individual (although it might legitimately shackle its representatives to itself).

The doctrine of natural rights and the contract theory of government— both of which were enshrined in American liberalism—Bentham explicitly denounced as incompatible with utilitarianism. He wrote of the Declaration of Independence that it was 'a hodge podge of confusion and absurdity in which the theory to be proved is all along taken for granted', and opposed the Americans in the first stages of their Revolution because of the weaknesses of their arguments in this respect.[39] He ridiculed the inclusion of lists of natural rights in American state constitutions, and once regretted 'that so rational a cause should be rested upon reasons, so much fitter to raise objections than to remove them'.[40] Whereas the Americans

---

[37] Both Bentham and James Mills, of course, approved all manner of checks aimed at ensuring that representatives pursued the common rather than their own selfish interests; and Mill once said that 'upon the right constitution of checks, all goodness of government depends'. (*Essay on Government*, pp. 33–34.) Bentham, however, discountenanced all checks which hindered effective government without corresponding advantages in binding representatives to the people.

[38] These devices he almost certainly included among the imperfections of the American political system, as part of that 'quantity of useless and hence mischievous complication, by which the transparency of the system still continues to be disturbed'. *Constitutional Code*, in *Works*, IX. 63.

[39] *Works*, X. 63. See also IX. 122–3, on natural rights.

[40] *Works*, I. 154n.

THE INFLUENCE OF JEREMY BENTHAM

21

had, in the Revolution, forcibly rejected legal authority as the sole
source of legal rights, Bentham always asserted government to be
the only source of rights. His differences from the Americans, like his
admiration for them, were based upon a utilitarian rather than a liberal
value.

That this contradiction between Benthamism and American liberalism
never became very prominent in Benthamite thinking about American
politics was due to a number of causes. Bentham—like most English
observers—tended to see what he wanted to see in the United States;
and it was clearly in the interests of Radicalism that a positive rather than
a negative image of American democracy should be projected for the
benefit of English public opinion. It was perhaps significant in this respect
that Bentham's American dislikes tended to appear in his less public
writings and, in any case, often took the form of recommendations for
even greater measures of democratization. Thus he criticized bi-cameralism
in America as an unnecessary restriction upon the popular will[41] and disapproved of the militia qualification for voting in some states as inconsistent with the principle of universal manhood suffrage.[42] In the same way
he reproached the Americans for retaining the body of English common
law, thus placing themselves under the dead hand of English legitimacy,
disguised as judicial precedent.[43] Bentham believed that most of these
defects would eventually be remedied in the Republic; and other factors
obscured the differences between his and the American styles of political
speculation. There was a strong pragmatic and utilitarian streak in the
American political make-up, despite their language of Lockeian liberalism.
Tocqueville was to note the existence of majoritarianism there, which had
dangerously little sympathy with liberal values. On the other hand,
Bentham's lack of sympathy with the categories of liberal thought was
obscured by his practical concern for advancing many unmistakably
liberal measures in England, such as the struggle for a free press, religious
freedom, and wider franchises.

Perhaps the primary reason for Bentham's unity of vision respecting
democracy in America, however, was the superficial and rigidly doctrinaire
nature of his analysis of the new world. Despite his knowledge of American law and constitutional forms, and despite his collection of works
upon the United States, Bentham never acquired a deep understanding of
the spirit of American politics, or indeed, a precise technical knowledge

[41] *Works*, IV. 448.
[42] Ibid. 348n.
[43] See Bentham to Madison, 1811, *Works*, IV. 453, 459–61. Bentham's views on
law reform are treated below, pp. 48ff.

of the American political process.[44] Thus he never fully appreciated the schism between his style of thought and that of most American liberals.

2. *Grote and Mackintosh*

George Grote, one of the younger group of Bentham's followers, was amongst the first to defend Bentham's view of new-world democracy against the questionings of traditional Whiggism. His defence was, in the first instance, an attempt to answer some of the objections put forward by Sir James Mackintosh, who had, in an important article in the *Edinburgh Review* of December, 1818, subjected Bentham's *Plan of Parliamentary Reform* to a searching analysis and criticism.[45] Mackintosh, who admired Bacon, Cicero, and Burke, was an old opponent of democracy. He criticized the doctrine of the ballot, questioned the principle of universal suffrage, and proposed, in opposition to the suggestions of Bentham, a doctrine of varied suffrage and representation of group interests. The severity of his attack provoked the writing in retaliation of some of the more significant Benthamite tracts of the times—including James Mill's article on *Government* for the *Encyclopaedia Britannica* in 1820, and Grote's first political pamphlet, in 1821.[46]

Amidst his other arguments, Mackintosh had attempted to disqualify the example of America as an argument for universal suffrage (a subject, he noted, 'to which Mr. Bentham has frequently adverted').[47] Mackintosh maintained that if universal suffrage should prevail amongst the labouring classes in England, 'a permanent animosity between opinion and property must be the consequence'.[48] Spoliation of the rich by the poor would be an ever-present prospect wherever the many were supreme; and the resultant class conflict would encourage the creation of absolute governments which would secure order by suspending the ancient safeguards of liberty. The validity of this conclusion was apparently contradicted, however, by the actual experience of the United States. There the system of universal suffrage was established, together with other devices advocated by Bentham—for example, frequent elections and secrecy of voting—and there,

[44] Williamson notes that Bentham more than once referred to the American Secretary of State as the 'Home Secretary' in his letters to Americans. Williamson, op. cit., p. 548. There is an interesting discussion of Bentham's criticisms of American institutions, from which I have drawn some of the above references, on pp. 549ff.

[45] *Edinburgh Review* (hereinafter *ER*), No. 61, Dec. 1818, Art. VIII (Universal Suffrage).

[46] George Grote, *Statement of the Question of Parliamentary Reform with a Reply to the Objections of the Edinburgh Review, Number LXI* (London, 1821).

[47] *ER*, No. 61, Dec. 1818, p. 199.

[48] Ibid. p. 172.

it was said, no such mischievous effects as Mackintosh predicted were in existence.

Mackintosh rejected this argument on two counts. He maintained, first, that universal suffrage was not completely established in America, since twelve out of its nineteen states debarred slaves from the franchise (as from the enjoyment of basic human rights). 'Democracy' in the slave states was merely another name for the universal distribution of privileges amongst a ruling caste, as in classical slave systems.[49] Moreover, even this privileged class had to satisfy a property qualification in Virginia; and similar restrictions were enforced in New England, the acknowledged seed-bed of American liberties. Again, he argued, it was doubtful how far the use of the ballot in many states demonstrated the advantages of secret voting, when secrecy was not obtained by its means (as was acknowledged to be the case in Pennsylvania).

In the second place, Mackintosh maintained that the undeniable success of America's system of popular government was the product of mitigating factors peculiar to the circumstances of the new world. His exposition of this doctrine of 'propitious circumstances' was indeed a classic of its kind, and many arguments were borrowed from it by Whigs, Tories, and utilitarians in the decades which followed. Universal suffrage was less dangerous in the United States, he contended, because the people were agricultural and isolated; because there were few large towns, and thus no inflammable industrial proletariat. Property was safe from attack because the majority of the people were either landowners, 'or have that immediate expectation of becoming proprietors, which produces nearly the same effect on character with the possession of property'.[50] The idea that American democracy was conservative because America society was a society of 'expectant capitalists' with a vested interest in the security of property was to become a popular concept amongst an English middle class attaining the heights of economic power. Precisely because this expectancy was absent in the psychology of the English lower classes, any measure of full democracy was likely to be accompanied by irresponsible confiscation—so ran the Whig argument.

Mackintosh also suggested a frontier hypothesis to explain the moderation of American democracy:

Adventurers [he wrote] who, in other countries, disturb society, are there naturally attracted towards the frontier, where they pave the way for industry, and become

[49] Mackintosh, though he regarded slavery as an abominable institution, approved the principle of apportioning state representation according to total (negro plus white) population. This, he felt, recognized a just principle 'that property is one of the elements of every wise representation'. Ibid. p. 200.

[50] Ibid. p. 200.

the pioneers of civilization. There is no part of their people in the situation where democracy is dangerous, or even usually powerful. The dispersion of the inhabitants, their distance from the scene of great affairs, are perhaps likely rather to make the spirit of liberty among them languid, than to rouse it to excess. The majority are in the condition which is elsewhere considered as a pledge of independence, and a qualification for the suffrage.[51]

Mackintosh was concerned to labour the distinction between the national circumstances of England and the United States as an argument against precipitous democratization. There was no ready land in England to propitiate the swollen town populations; no agrarian frontier to absorb the malcontents of society and turn them into a safe middle class with a 'stake in the country'. Therefore power ought prudently to be withheld from the grasp of the poorer sections, and their interests should be represented by some more responsible group.

Mackintosh's discussion of democracy in America repeated quite clearly the belief common among British Whigs, that universal suffrage was, at best, barely compatible with advanced industrialization. He predicted trouble for the United States when it too had 'the crowded cities and unequal fortunes of Europe'. It might be that, from the present unparalleled situation, popular usages and national habits would quietly prevail for so long as to become insensibly adapted to gradual changes in the national condition. Votes might then be safely used by the industrial populace.[52] But, he maintained, the popular system of election could not be suddenly imposed upon an advanced industrial society without disruption.[53] Even in the United States such a system, he felt, might prove too weak ultimately to counterbalance the growing influence of wealth in the South 'and the tendencies towards Toryism which are of late perceptible in New England'.[54]

George Grote, in typical Radical fashion, denied the 'propitious circumstances' doctrine and asserted the universal nature of democratic principles. His answer to Mackintosh was a vindication of Bentham's general theories and depended on the proposition that it was *never* the interest of the many—whatever the circumstances—to despoil the few or to desire a relaxation of the laws of property. Thus, he argued, Mackintosh

[51] Ibid. pp. 200–1.

[52] I.e., after it had been safely exercised for long years in the thinly-peopled states of the West—'In that long tranquility it may languish into forms, and these forms may soon follow the spirit'. Ibid. p. 201.

[53] Popular usages, he declared, were 'irreconcilably adverse' to an industrial condition.

[54] Ibid. p. 201. Mackintosh obtained most of his information on America from Henry Fearon, *Sketches of America, etc.* (London, 1818).

had offered a valid description of the success of universal suffrage in America, but was mistaken in suggesting that it was an exception to the general rule. America was, in fact, a genuine illustration of it. In this Grote was following Bentham, who had denied (in his *Radicalism Not Dangerous* (1820)) that any peculiarity of conditions in the new world operated to safeguard property there.[55] Grote's argument was as follows:

If representatives were chosen by the majority, they would pursue the universal interest, i.e. the interest which the many have in common with the few. This applied to questions of property. The many had an interest in maintaining the rights of property of *all*. As a class, the many respected the personal and proprietary rights of each other, including the rights of the wealthiest amongst their own ranks ('for without this mutual renunciation, it is idle to talk of the existence of a class and of a common interest').[56] Why then should they not treat the few in the same way? Indeed, when the many were incorporated with the few into a whole in a democratic system, the personal and proprietary rights of each member would be treated with due reverence—'for the separate interest of each individual among the many has already undergone so ample a reduction, in order to attain the point of coincidence with the interests of his numerous class-brethren, that it needs no farther sacrifice in order to adapt it to a slight increase of number'.[57] Confiscation would result in only infinitesimal gain for each individual amongst the many. At the same time, if all public protection of property were removed, every person would be threatened by the far greater danger of personal spoliation attendant on the loss of individual class rights. The English labourer possessed less property than his American counterpart, but he had an equally strong desire to retain what he did possess—and he could do this only by maintaining property laws. In their absence 'the rich man immediately finds himself at the head of an association, whose interest leads them to respect proprietary rules among themselves, and to violate them with regard to every one else'.[58] The poor man, however, could not make it the interest of any body to maintain its laws towards him—'He is perfectly isolated and defenceless, and stands exposed to plunder and slavery, from the powerful associations

[55] Bentham, *Works*, IX. 612–13. The likelihood of a general subversion of property rights, he declared, was as great in the natural condition of the United States as in that of England. He then vindicated the 'undangerousness' of democracy in general by referring to the perfect order, tranquillity, and respect for property which prevailed under popular government in America.
[56] Grote, *Statement of the Question of Parliamentary Reform, etc.*, p. 65.
[57] Ibid. p. 66.
[58] Ibid. p. 70.

in his neighbourhood.'[59] Under universal suffrage, therefore, the interest of the majority in the public protection of property would be safeguarded; and the few would enjoy as effective a security for justice as any other equal number amongst the many.[60] The American respect for property, which surprised so many critics of democracy, sprang not from any peculiar situation in the new world but out of motives which were universal in the democratic condition.

This was orthodox Benthamite reasoning on Grote's part, and his pamphlet found favour in the ranks of radicalism at the time. The attempt to annul any doctrine of 'propitious circumstances', and to ascribe as many as possible of the virtues of America to the operation of democratic principles, became, indeed, a characteristic endeavour of the utilitarians before 1832. Only afterwards did they extend sympathy to the view (inherent in Mackintosh) that different orders of democracy might be produced according to the womb of circumstances in which they were enclosed; and that democrats might profitably study these conditions. Once the dynamics of democratic societies began to be probed, the stiff orthodoxies of the twenties fell to the ground.

3. The 'Westminster Review' in the Twenties

Bentham's pro-Americanism was hammered out into an orthodoxy of Benthamite Radicalism during the 1820's. This was the decade during which Bentham's general theories were being simplified and popularized by his followers to serve the cause of Parliamentary Reform. Facts about the United States were culled by Benthamites from the travel accounts of liberals, or directly from Bentham's pamphlets and collection of Americana, so that there was little encouragement for more discriminating attitudes. The period was to seem, in retrospect, a dream time in which a Radical legend about the new world was consolidated.

The legend was set out in the pages of the *Westminster Review*, which was created, with capital supplied by Jeremy Bentham, to be the great Benthamite rival to the Whig *Edinburgh Review* and the Tory *Quarterly*. There were also references to America in the other newspapers and journals used by the utilitarians. These included the *Morning Chronicle*,

---

[59] Ibid. p. 70. In short, he concluded, where there is no law of property 'the rich man is a despot and the poor man a slave'.

[60] Only minority interests *separate* from the general interest would be disregarded; e.g. a popular legislature would refrain from bestowing monopolies or exclusive privileges enriching the few at the expense of the many. Popular government was thus to be favourably compared with government by the few, wherein only those interests which the few shared with each other were promoted.

edited by John Black (a friend of James Mill) from 1823;[61] the weekly
Examiner, edited by Albany Fonblanque from September 1830;[62] John
Arthur Roebuck's *Pamphlets for the People*, published from June 1835 until
February 1836; *Tait's Edinburgh Magazine*;[63] W. J. Fox's *Monthly Reposi-
tory*;[64] and the specialist journals, largely controlled by the Benthamites, the
Parliamentary History and Review, edited by Peregrine Bingham from
1826 to 1828, and the *Jurist*, published between 1827 and 1833 and largely
managed by Joseph Parkes of Birmingham.[65]

It was the *Westminster Review*, however, which published a great spate
of comment about transatlantic politics. Eight articles in the first year's
issues referred to American affairs, an indication of the utility of such
allusions to the new and enthusiastic group of reformers.

The Benthamites, with great confidence, drew extremely radical
lessons from the American scene. Unembarrassed by qualifications or
hesitations, they commended full-blooded democracy, having at that
stage apparently no doubts that the Republic was such a system. The
institutions of an absolutist Europe, on the other hand, were dismissed
as unworthy of investigation:

America is the only country which has presented us with the spectacle of a people
governed by a system of genuine representation; the spectacle, not of a nominal,
but of an actual republic, and an entire democratic ascendancy. . . .[66]

(France was no model, for her democrats had weakly allowed a despotism,
and then a monarchy, to be set up.) The Benthamites were nevertheless

---

[61] Black, according to J. S. Mill, was imbued with many of Bentham's ideas,
especially upon law reform, and for ten years after 1823 the *Chronicle* 'became to a
considerable extent a vehicle of the opinions of the utilitarian Radicals'. J. S. Mill,
Autobiography (London, 1924 ed.), p. 75.

[62] J. S. Mill and W. J. Fox contributed regularly to the *Examiner*, and it enjoyed
the reputation of being 'the chief organ of high-class intellectual radicalism'. (Richard
Garnier on Fonblanque in the *D.N.B.*) Fonblanque was an intimate of Bentham, the
Mills, and other leading utilitarians, contributed to the *Morning Chronicle* and *The
Times*, was leader-writer on the *Examiner* from 1826, and wrote for the *Westminster*.
See *Life and Labours of Albany Fonblanque*, ed. E. B. Fonblanque (London, 1874).

[63] To which both J. S. Mill and Roebuck contributed, and which was generally
known as a liberal journal.

[64] A Unitarian organ, independently owned by Fox and reformist after 1831.
Fox, a Unitarian preacher, had Benthamite leanings, was a friend of Bulwer-Lytton
and J. S. Mill, and wrote for the *Westminster*. Contributors to the *Repository* included
Mill, Harriet Martineau, and W. Bridges Adams.

[65] The *Jurist* was a law journal featuring Benthamite propaganda for legal reforms.
Parkes often included articles upon American jurisprudence in it. See, e.g., Parkes to
Bentham, 4.5.1828; B.M. Add. MS. 33, 546/213. The *PH & R* printed parliamentary
reports with Benthamite criticisms. It was an organ of the younger philosophical
radicals.

[66] *Westminster Review* (hereafter *WR*), Vol. 1, No. 1, Jan. 1824, p. 102.

exasperated by the 'imperfect and apparently conflicting' evidence in existence about the Republic. They appealed for a traveller who 'possesses a knowledge of the leading principles of legislation and political economy', i.e. a Benthamite, to provide the right answers. Impartial scrutiny, they were sure, would reveal utilitarian truths.[67]

In the meantime, they countered the abusive anti-Americanism of the Tories with some theoretical gambits and propaganda techniques of their own. Their most effective argument was simply to associate new-world democracy with new-world prosperity. As John Neal pointed out, the history of the world furnished no example of such rapid growth to empire.[68] Daniel Webster's words were dinned into Radical minds:

2 or 3 millions of people have been augmented to twelve; and the great forests of the West, prostrated beneath the arm of successful industry . . . We have a commerce that leaves no sea unexplored; navies which take no law from superior force; revenues adequate to all the exigencies of government, *almost without taxation*; and peace with all nations founded on equal rights and mutual respect . . . Mankind are not only better fed, and better clothed, but they are able also to *enjoy more leisure*; they possess more refinement, and more self-respect. A superior tone of education, manners and habits prevails. . . .[69]

The Benthamites praised the mechanical innovations of the Americans, their efficient canal systems, their steam-boats, their advanced husbandry, their progress in manufacturing, their housing, shipping, business and investment—almost everything, in fact, except their misguided tariff policy and Negro slavery.[70] The people were adventurous, with a spirit of resilience, initiative, and independence, although there were rough edges to their characters. In a period of great material development, the working-men and ordinary people enjoyed an unprecedented prosperity, illustrating the Benthamite maxim that truly popular governments took as their end 'the progressive improvement of the condition of the governed'.[71]

[67] Ibid. The above quotations are from this source.
[68] *WR*, Vol. 5, No. 9, Jan. 1826, p. 178 (The United States), by Neal. Information and evidence about authorship of articles in the periodical press is presented in an Appendix.
[69] Extracts of Webster's address of 1825 were extensively quoted in Neal's article, ibid. p. 176.
[70] See, e.g., *WR*, Vol. 2, Oct. 1824, pp. 554ff (Influence of America on the Mind); Vol. 2, July 1824, pp. 170ff (Travels in the U.S. and Canada); Vol. 17, No. 33, July 1832, pp. 168ff (Statistics and Political Institutions of the U.S.); Vol. 3, No. 6, Apr. 1825, pp. 448ff (On Emigration).
[71] For typical views of this nature in the 'thirties, see *London & Westminster Review* (hereafter *L & WR*), Jan. 1838, Art. VI (Miss Martineau's Western Travel), especially pp. 475ff.

Freedom of the press and a want of restrictive 'taxes upon knowledge' (such as the heavy stamp duty on newspapers in England) had encouraged a tremendous circulation of cheap newspapers, which constantly improved the literacy and reading habits of the people. Publishing was a flourishing business, and the standard writings of Europe had an extensive sale in cheap American reprints (although very often in contravention of European copyright laws). American education (continued the Benthamite brief) was virtually universal, tax-supported, cheap, and largely free from religious sectarianism. Perhaps most important from the utilitarian viewpoint, it provided a desirable training in political citizenship. Benthamites with a vital concern in schemes for national education in England placed the example of America alongside that of Prussia and France as a model in compulsory public education. They commended in particular the Massachusetts common school system, which incorporated their idea of educational control by local bodies elected on a democratic basis.

It was concluded that, by the American example,

. . . real representation, a free press, and complete religious liberty are shown . . . to be something more than the mere catchwords of demagogues, or the symbols of anarchy and demoralization. Their worth is demonstrated by practical results in the multiplied advantages of the many, and the argument is not to be destroyed by the railing of the interested few.[72]

The corollary to this argument was to divorce defects in the American condition from political causes. Good effects, in the Radical argument, were the result of American government; bad effects flowed from other causes (the Tories simply reversed the propositions). Although the Benthamites tried to minimize shortcomings, they were forced to contend against the highly publicized distaste of the sophisticated classes in England for the rawness of civilization in the new world. By such people American democracy was described at once as vulgar, venal, materialistic, mediocre, culturally sterile, and ridiculously over-valued by Europeans with political axes to grind. The Benthamites were anxious to prevent such allegations from prejudicing the case for the Reform Bill.

They attempted first to expose the deliberate distortions of the Tories as sheer polemic. James Mill, for example, devoted his considerable skill as a political in-fighter to attacking the *Quarterly*'s notorious Americophobic review of William Faux's travels; a task for which a complete

---

[72] *WR*, Vol. 2, Oct. 1824, p. 556. 'True Englishmen', wrote the *Review* in 1832, 'will rejoice at the steady progress of American prosperity and trace its source to the wisdom of its political institutions.' *WR*, Vol. 17, July 1832, p. 170.

article was set aside in the first number of the *Westminster*.[73] Mill accused the *Quarterly* of selecting the most unfavourable testimony of Faux,

. . . containing the details of individual instances of ferocity, violence, knavery, boasting and vulgarity, disappointment, failure, despondency, bad soils, bad climates, bad food, discomfort, dirt and barbarism—all on the debtor side of the account, without hinting at the existence of a single item on the creditor side.

The whole fabrication, he felt, was calculated to flatter the passions and biases of those with an instinctive hatred of responsible and economical government. The sneers at republican government were designed to persuade the reader 'that the evils, physical and moral, inseparable from every infant state of society, are altogether the result of American institutions'.[74]

In the same way, the Benthamites were later to discredit the diatribes of travellers like Mrs. Trollope as 'highly coloured caricatures'[75] which exaggerated the uncouthness and inconvenience of American life and refused to admit their economic and geographic causes. Settlers in remote areas, it was pointed out, could not expect an efficient magistracy and police force, or complete law and order. Frontier life was admittedly boisterous, although vital, and many social habits—such as spitting, profanity, and dram-drinking—were not calculated to flatter the fastidious tastes of a Fanny Kemble. The quality of newspapers was not universally high; religious enthusiasm sometimes degenerated into fanaticism;[76] and many other pioneering disadvantages existed. Most of these, predicted the Benthamites, would disappear with the advance of settlement, and the approach of markets.[77]

[73] *WR*, Vol. 1, No. 1, Jan. 1824, Art. XI (Periodical Literature 2—the *Quarterly Review*, No. LVIII). William Faux's book was entitled *Memorable Days in America*, etc. (London, 1823). The *Quarterly* article was by John Barrow and Gifford; the Tory side of the controversy is dealt with in Ch. 4.
[74] Ibid. *WR*, p. 251.
[75] See *WR*, Vol. 17, No. 33, July 1832, pp. 173ff.
[76] E. G. Wakefield described the 'phrenzy' of camp-meetings and frontier religion in *England and America* (New York, 1834), pp. 190–95. He ascribed this to the psychological effects of seclusion, caused by a colonial policy which dispersed land-holdings.
[77] Critics of democracy were alleged to suffer from confused notions of causality. Dram-drinking, for example, was the result of cheap whisky, said the Benthamites, not of universal suffrage. They liked to discover vices in Canada similar to those of the United States, for this seemed to prove that frontier conditions, not government, determined faults. Vulgarity in America was compared with vulgarity in England to make the same point. As a Viennese lady was said to have replied to an Englishman ridiculing American manners: 'Yes, you are perfectly right, they are odious; they are *des Anglais exagérés.*' (Quoted in *London Review*, Vol. 2, July 1835, p. 202.) The *London Review* is referred to hereafter as *LR*.

The truth was that hard-headed utilitarians were less shocked by the vulgarity of American civilization than were those of sensitive and aristocratic disposition. After all, the culture of their new industrialism, of Manchester and the provincial North, was also susceptible to sneers from the genteel. In further mitigation the utilitarians could point out that the more objective travellers in the new world, such as Adam Hodgson and James Stuart (both of liberal leanings), had been pleasantly surprised at the refinement of society in the large towns, especially of New England. The education of the better classes was less regular and classical than that of their counterparts in England, but their information was at least as general, 'although less scientific and profound.'[78] The Benthamites were on much stronger ground in praising the more enlightened character of the lower classes in the United States. Such people, according to Hodgson, were

. . . distinguished from the corresponding classes of my countrymen (the little farmers, innkeepers, shopkeepers, clerks, mechanics, servants and labourers) by greater acuteness and intelligence, more regular habits of reading, a wider range of ideas, and a greater freedom from prejudices, provincialism, and vulgarity.[79]

Their habits of social egalitarianism and independence of manner, according to Benthamites, caused offence only to that small aristocratic clique in England which esteemed privilege and depended upon the deference of the English lower classes to maintain itself in power. In social equality the aristocracy affected to detect the signs of mob-law and the rudeness of democracy, but in reality it recognized the threat to itself implicit in a too-powerful public opinion.[80] The Benthamites preferred the brash vigour, and occasional roughness, of the American popular character to 'that much more disgusting and contemptible real vulgarity resulting from the abject worship of rank and wealth that debases the lower orders . . . in our country'.[81]

Another national flaw of the Americans—their unrepentant materialism

[78] WR, Vol. 2, June 1824, p. 171; quoting from Hodgson, Letters from North America, etc. (London, 1924).
[79] Quoted, ibid. p. 172 (WR).
[80] See, e.g., WR, Vol. 18, No. 36, Apr. 1833, p. 318; review of James Stuart, Three Years in North America (Edinburgh, 1833). The article attacked the 'assumption of unearned superiority' which underlay privilege in England. Social segregation prevented detection of the inadequacies of this caste: 'If the House of Lords travelled in public conveyances' (as did Senators and Presidents in the U.S.) 'the peerage would be put in imminent jeopardy'. In America, station and social relations had reference only to ability—which is the only valid criterion by utilitarian standards.
[81] WR, Vol. 17, No. 33, July 1832, p. 174; quoted from W. G. Ouseley, Remarks on the Statistics and Political Institutions of the U.S. (London, 1832).

4

—was explained in terms of frontier conditions. The High Tories and thinkers such as Carlyle were alarmed at the overridingly commercial nature of transatlantic life, and used criticism to attack the doctrine of *laissez faire* in Britain and to cut at the rising industrial middle class (the saviours of English society in the crystal ball of utilitarianism). Carlyle spoke of the Americans' 'purse mentality', of their 'unquenchable, almost frightfully unresting spirit of endeavour, directed (woe is me!) to the making of money'.[82] To a sentimentalist like Thomas Moore the Yankees were a 'coarse, calculating, matter-of-fact people.' In France Stendhal expressed a cultivated disdain: 'I should be bored in America, amidst men, no doubt perfectly honourable and reasonable, but coarse, who think only of *dollars* . . . I cannot live with men incapable of delicate and subtle ideas, however virtuous they may be. I should prefer one hundred times over the elegant manners of a corrupt court.'[83] The Benthamites had little sympathy for such evaluations; they were emphatically men of the new age, disciples of the classical economists, more suspicious of traditionalism and the shallow humanitarianism of country gentlemen than of the commercial ethic. They were more inclined to praise the vigour, initiative, and activity of Americans, to commend their open economic society, a society of self-made men achieving success in a condition of minimal government, than to question the morality of such a society. The grosser disadvantages of economic individualism could be ascribed to the youthfulness of the nation. As Peregrine Bingham, one of the *Westminster's* brightest lights in the twenties, pointed out:

People who have scarcely existed as a nation so long as the ordinary life of man, must necessarily be for the most part engaged in the obtaining of subsistence: they have not had time to produce a very polished or very leisurely class; no class for whom the delicate gossamers of European aristocracy can entertain any great degree of sympathy.[84]

The Benthamites could at all times cushion attacks upon America's

---

[82] Carlye to Emerson, 3.2.1835, in C. E. Norton, ed., *Correspondence of Thomas Carlyle and Ralph Waldo Emerson 1834–1872* (London, 1883), I. 44.

[83] *Stendhal by Himself*, selected by Claude Roy (Paris, 1954), pp. 117–18; in *Editions du Seuil*. This passage is put in the mouth of Lucien Leuwen, the son of a banker who was a pillar of the régime of Louis Phillipe. However, the sentiments are entirely representative of Stendhal himself; see ibid, pp. 120, 124, 144.

[84] *WR*, Vol. I, No. I, Jan. 1824, p. 20 (Moore's Fables for the Holy Alliance), by Bingham. Moore's contempt for the Americans was attacked as an aristocratic sentiment. He saw their lack of drawing-room graces, but not their general amelioration. His love of liberty and hatred of oppression was too personal—he did not realize that the basis of oppression lay in prevailing *systems*. Had he done so he could not have failed to look kindly on America.

acquisitive society by pointing to the very impressive material advantages it had achieved. In time, they predicted, an admixture of culture would soften harshness; America's modern society would then display its virtues without accompanying vices.

The question of American culture, indeed, posed some ticklish problems for the apologists. For most Tories and many Whigs, for the apostles of a new liberalism, such as John Stuart Mill and Alexis de Tocqueville, it appeared (or was to appear) that democracy, in its extreme form, exercised a stultifying effect upon culture. This became a standard hypothesis in speculation after the mid-thirties. Up to that time, however, the Philosophic Radicals refused to entertain the proposition.

The *Westminster Review*, despite its Americophilia, was capable of severely criticizing the intellectual achievement of the Americans. In 1830 it commented:

The revolution did not emancipate intellect. . . . Their literature consists chiefly of abridgements and imitations. Their best writers are for the most part copyists, and not creators. They have many minds of great respectability and industry . . . but are unfortunately almost as devoid of the 'aristocracy of talent', and the 'despotism of genius', as they happily are of other aristocracies and other despotisms.[85]

Washington Irving and James Fenimore Cooper—America's leading literary figures at the time—were regarded as derivative. Sedgwick and Mitford were heralded in the 1830's as 'fresh national minds', but of the second order. Only Channing (in 1830) and Emerson (in 1840) were felt to exhibit originality of thought.[86] Most reviewers, like Emerson, were 'palpably taunted with the feeling that the American mind is at best an agglomeration of ingenious and laborious imitations'.[87] This condition was regarded, however, as simply the passing effect of a necessary transitional phase in the nation's development. Engrossed in building a nation, Americans had little time to devote to cultural activities, and therefore lacked a leisure class which might effect a cultural divorce from Europe.

[85] *WR*, Vol. 12, No. 24, Apr. 1830, pp. 475–6. See also *WR*, Oct. 1829, pp. 437ff; and *London Review*, July 1835, pp. 203ff.

[86] For the *Westminster* on culture and writers, see Vol. 2, Oct. 1824, Art. 4 (Irving's *Tales of a Traveller*); Vol. 17, July 1832, pp. 132ff (Irving's *Alhambra*); Vol. 12, Apr. 1830, Art. 14 (Dr. Channing's *Works*); Vol. 14, Apr. 1831, Art. 8 (Mitford's *Stories of American Life*). For later attitudes see *L & WR*, Oct. 1837, Art. 3 (Miss Sedgwick's *Works*), and Dec. 1838, Art. 5 (Yankeeana—*American Literature of Humour*). The Sedgwick was by Harriet Martineau. There is a notice of Mitford in *Examiner*, 15.7.1832; and an important article on Emerson by Monckton Milnes in *L & WR*, Vol. 33, Mar. 1840, Art. 6.

[87] Quoted, *L & WR*, Vol. 33, Mar. 1840, p. 349.

Independence in politics would eventually encourage literary emancipation. As the *Review* put it in 1852:

A noble national literature will, without fail, issue from a noble national life, which, amid the present isolation of her different races, she has not as yet realized, except in a very qualified sense. Give her [i.e. the U.S.] a century for ethnological amalgamation—give her another century for unitive development—and then![88]

During the period of James Mill's association with the *Westminster*, moreover, that journal showed a marked tendency to play down the importance of American literary and artistic deficiencies. Indeed artistic insensitivity was widely held to be a distinguishing quirk of utilitarianism —Bentham only reluctantly acquiesced in devoting part of the *Westminster* to what he called 'literary insignificances'. Benthamite reviewers frequently derided light literature and similar products of the imagination —American and British—as irrational and unproductive social sedatives. In this view the Americans at least did not waste so much energy upon empty sophistication. The United States, according to one reviewer, 'has succeeded so well in the useful, that we have no desire to see her exchange them for the fine arts.'[89] 'Polite' literature and *belles lettre* culture in England were regarded as a form of aristocratic lotus-eating; the province of the Somebodies, financed by the Nobodies, cultivating imagination at the expense of judgement and discouraging dangerous speculation. The labouring many in America knew better than to waste money in patronizing poetry and art for the benefit of an opulent and idle few. Again, polite society in England dismissed as a bore the discussion of vital topics and condemned as visionaries or jacobins those 'who shall dare to suppose it possible that any institutions can be better than the present, or shall seriously set out to ameliorate the condition of his species . . .'.[90] The Americans were happily free from this form of claustrophobic refinement.[91]

So far it is apparent that the Benthamites were successful in defending

[88] *WR*, Vol. 42, Apr. 1852, p. 359. Cf. the view of the *WR* in 1871 that American literature had been protected, for fifty years, in a "little paradise of European culture, refinement, and aristocratic delicatesse from the howling wilderness of Yankee democracy"; which the writer deplored as a sin against vitality (July 1871, in an article upon the poetry of Walt Whitman.)

[89] *WR*, Vol. 2, No. 4, Oct. 1824, p. 345.   [90] Ibid. pp. 337–8.

[91] Not all utilitarians took a doctrinaire view of literature, however. Even in the 1820's, but especially after J. S. Mill gained control of the *London and Westminster Review* in 1836, reviewers were often content to judge writers by the usual standards of literary criticism. On this point, and for a general discussion of the subject, see Louis Fraiberg, 'The *Westminster Review* and American Literature, 1824–1885', *American Literature*, XXIV (Nov. 1952), 310ff. See also G. L. Nesbitt, *Benthamite Reviewing—The First Twelve Years of the Westminster Review 1824–1836* (Columbia, 1934), Ch. V.

their legend about the Republic, in defending their political premises against those who were critical of republicans and republican culture; and they wielded an effective frontier theme to that end. However, they ran some risk, by doing so, of discrediting the great West as an emigrant's paradise. To their credit, they rarely pretended that the West was, physically, the land of milk and honey that emigration agents made it. It was, they said, far more attractive than the Tories allowed. Conditions there, although arduous, far surpassed those of the agricultural labourer who toiled for the landed gentry of England; and to such labourers 'it must be the height of bliss to sit down in the back settlements of North America.'[92] Town labourers and small landholders were also advised to avoid certain destitution at home for as certain a competence in the new world. But the *Westminster* by no means advocated wholesale emigration to the United States. Many classes and groups who were tolerably well off in England, and especially those who rejoiced in belonging to an enlightened class of society, might be ill-advised (it believed) in removing themselves to a different social and physical environment.[93] But the difficulties to be encountered were social and economic, unfortunately consequential to the facts of frontier existence. There was no question, at least for the liberal-minded, of any political self-abnegation involved in emigration. The emigrant might experience discomfort in the new world, but not at last the discomfort of old-world institutions. He encountered hardships, but not those of political insult and misgovernment. Indeed it could be maintained that emigration was 'a step which no one should venture to make, *unless he feels some enthusiasm for the progress of human improvement and considerable annoyance at the mischievous political institutions of the Old World*'.[94] The Benthamites, it transpired, were willing to take an impartial view of pioneering difficulties, but were careful to avoid any imputation of these hazards to the political system which had received Bentham's own imprimatur. To do so would have been to admit possible fallibility in their own doctrines at home and to deny a desirable generality to those doctrines.

4. *The Attack on Establishments*

The Benthamites were by no means usually, or even often, placed on the defensive by Tory critics. Benthamism was an essentially aggressive force

[92] *WR*, Vol. 1, No. 1, Jan. 1824, p. 104.
[93] The topic is discussed at length in *WR*, Vol. 3, No. 6, Apr. 1825, Art. 8 (On Emigration). At least as much emphasis was placed on the difficulties as upon the advantages of emigration.
[94] *WR*, Vol. 1, No. 1, Jan. 1824, p. 105 (their emphasis).

in pre-Victorian politics in England; its proselytes were dedicated refor-mers who challenged traditional philosophies, traditional usages, and existing class interests. They consolidated the idea that the middle class of the Machine Age was, and ought to be, an agent of change, and a very dangerous threat was thus posed to the landed and aristocratic interests. Not until that threat had been, in large measure, fulfilled, did utilitarianism cease to be a radical, almost a revolutionary, influence. By then the initia-tive had passed to Chartists and Socialists, who exhorted the working-men to dissociate themselves from middle-class reformers and to organize change in their own class interests. Benthamism then became a safe and orthodox, although still influential, philosophy.

Bentham's use of the American example to bludgeon the Establishment was entirely characteristic of utilitarianism in its radical phase; and his disciples enthusiastically followed the precedent. Like Bentham, they were deeply impressed by America's streamlined, non-corporate, non-aristo-cratic society, and they elaborated his ideas into a full-scale impeachment of the traditional and inegalitarian structure of English society and govern-ment. To them the United States represented a retrenchment policy exemplified. All institutions there were judged by the strict test of utility, and increased efficiency was the issue. Government administration was—unlike that of England—popular, efficient, and the cheapest in the world. James Mill in 1824 quoted statistics (which 'the *Quarterly Review* never will *dare* to give') to demonstrate that Britain's civil government cost nearly twenty times that of civil government in the United States: '. . . and yet America is, beyond all comparison, better governed than Great Britain and Ireland.'[95]

The Benthamites (like the liberals but unlike the Tories) heartily approved the severely restricted role of the state in the Union, which was the condition for economic government. Their approval derived primarily from *laissez faire* doctrine, from a typically middle-class dislike for aristocratic sinecures and paternalism, rather than from Bentham's later administrative ideas. As we have seen, in the *Constitutional Code* Bentham envisaged complex and powerful administrative departments whose activities would have wide social ramifications. He was set on granting all-pervasive powers to his essentially democratic Legislature. Again, as we have seen, he was quite often irritated by American checks upon

[95] *WR*, Vol. 1, No. 1, Jan. 1824, p. 262. John Neal in 1826 suggested that many Radicals exaggerated the cheapness of American government and put forward some pet schemes of his own for reducing its cost even further. He admitted, however, that 'contrasted with the abominable systems of costly misrule which prevail in Europe, the comparison is, no doubt, most advantageous to the United States'. *WR*, Vol. 5, No. 9, Jan. 1826, p. 179.

majority rule; and this might consistently have led to a wholehearted attack upon minimal and hedged-about government. (There was at least the possibility that such a government was hardly the best instrument for artificially contriving a harmony of interests in society.) There was no necessary connection, indeed much contradiction, between the economic and individualist ideas of utilitarianism, which became those of the Manchester School, and its political Radicalism. But Bentham's followers did not tackle the paradox, and the limited nature of Republic government continued to meet their favour. They praised Jeffersonian democracy and disliked Hamiltonian centralism; they were ever the champions of federal regionalism and of decentralization in politics and administration.[96] In all this their feelings were strongly influenced by traditional Whig sentiment (at odds finally with Bentham's Radicalism). It was so with Thomas Love Peacock, who, although an official of the East India Company—a hotbed of Benthamism—and a Westminster Reviewer, was more of a Whig than a Radical. In 1830 Peacock commended Jefferson's determination to have a general government 'strong to execute the national will, and impotent to coerce it'.[97] Like Jefferson and Whigs of all ages, Bentham's disciples feared despotism more than anarchy. They were willing to chance the prospect of popular excesses arising out of weak government, but were fixed in 'abhorrence of the inflictions of unrestrained power'.[98]

America's appeal for Benthamites was, indeed, largely in the curious liberal-cum-utilitarian nature of transatlantic politics. Remove power out of the hands of an hereditary clique and place it in those of the people, said the Benthamites, and public policy would be *at once* liberal and directed towards the greatest happiness. They pointed out that the Americans had not, like the oligarchs of England, ruinously indebted their country for the sake of imposing arbitrary governments upon their neighbours. Government was successfully maintained without the old appendages of despotism—without soldiery, police spies, nobility, and prelacy. American citizens, although sovereign, still saw fit to preserve property rights and the old Whig liberties of speech, press, and trial by jury. *Habeas corpus* could not be suspended in normal times, and all men had the right to petition and bear arms. These were enormous advantages in the eyes of Radicals who had suffered under the Six Acts and the Tory Reaction. As James Mill ironically pointed out, the English

[96] Perronet Thompson strongly commended decentralization in America in *WR*, Vol. 20, No. 39, Jan. 1834, Art. 13 (Prospects of the Coloured Races).
[97] *WR*, Vol. 13, No. 26, Oct. 1830, p. 319 (Randolph's Memoir of Jefferson).
[98] Ibid. See also *WR*, Vol. 3, No. 6, Apr. 1825, Art. 8 (On Emigration).

Tories had got up a new crime, that of unpatriotically emigrating to the new world. But who could rationally oppose the course of quitting England, 'where taxes, and gagging bills, and game laws, and unpaid magistrates, and aristocratical justice, and low wages, and the having nothing to do with the laws but obey them, constitute so many admirable grounds for the *amor patriae*. . . .'?[99] Liberal and utilitarian sentiments about American liberties were thus in practice indistinguishable. The utilitarians continued to reject natural rights as a basis for liberties, but found an alternative justification for them in terms of social amelioration.

America's open economic society had a magnetism of its own for Benthamites wedded to the ideas of Adam Smith and Ricardo. They welcomed the sweeping away of civil and religious establishments which cluttered natural economic processes. They approved the repudiation of the hereditary principle of primogeniture. This removed the foundation upon which might be built a privileged class of landlords, who extracted rents but were themselves unproductive. It was the idea of America as a vast continental free market which fired imaginations, however. There tithes and internal taxes upon trade had been abolished and commercial monopolies had been progressively undermined (a point underlined by Taney's decision in the Charles River Bridge case of 1837). No East India Company hamstrung external trade, and customary economic controls were virtually non-existent. America thus provided an excellent jumping-off point for an attack upon the corn-laws in England and strengthened the case for freeing trade from other legal controls. Only the Union's protectionist external tariff policy encountered criticism.

It was widely believed by radical Englishmen that the fluid society envisaged by the economists would be best served politically by a republican form of government. As has been suggested, however, the Benthamites were cautious about attacking the English monarchy. This would probably have alienated the support of moderates in the battle for the Reform Bill; but the threat of republicanism was kept hanging over the heads of recalcitrant Tories. Colonel Perronet Thompson, for example, frequently reiterated his belief that republican government was 'intrinsically the best calculated for the welfare of the governed'.[100] He conceded,

[99] *WR*, Vol. 2, No. 4, Oct. 1824, p. 484, by Mill. He described the *Quarterly*'s opposition to emigration as 'sentimental trash, applied to a mischievous purpose!' Another reviewer concluded that the United States was ideal for the emigrant 'anxious to secure . . . the largest portion of practicable liberty'. *WR*, Vol. 3, No. 6, Apr. 1825, p. 478.

[100] *WR*, Vol. 14, No. 28, Apr. 1831, pp. 453ff (Parliamentary Reform). The *Westminster* ridiculed American writers such as Washington Irving for preferring English institutions. An intellect must be weak, said the Review, that liked better 'the

however, that constitutional monarchy was capable of discharging the offices expected of it by the community, and argued that, so long as it secured good government, the people had no overwhelming desire to supplant it. He would, however, have none of the Tory prejudice against more popular forms of government:

The government which keeps up a bugbear opposition to republics in other countries, or sacrifices fair political advantages to such an apprehension, declares in language that cannot be mistaken, that it has something bad to protect at home. There is no warfare between republics and *just* monarchial governments; the interminable hostility is with the *unjust*.[101]

It was an effective argument designed to impress those of the political centre.

The formal separation of church and state in America was considered to be not the least significant of improvements upon the arrangements of the old world. Disestablishment, it was argued, had freed government from the influence of a privileged pressure group, and had established complete religious liberty in the community. Contrary to the assertions of the Tories—who, according to James Mill, discovered the cause of every evil in the want of an established church[102]—that condition was said to have encouraged the spirit of religion in America.

The *Westminster* frequently quoted church statistics to indicate the large number of American churches and clergymen and to illustrate the healthy attendances and popular enthusiasm for Christianity in the Union.[103] The standard of morality was deemed to be at least as high as, if not superior to, that of the best classes in England; and the legal enforcement of religious equality was held to have extinguished much of the sectarian ill-will that still existed in England. The *Westminster* reflected benevolently that

Without a splendidly endowed establishment—without a law against blasphemy —without a vice society—. . . without state prosecution for libel . . . religious observances obtain in the United States to an extent, and with a degree of rigour, of which Europe can furnish few examples.[104]

---

gee-gaws of a crown and sceptre, a star and ribbon, to the substantial comfort of millions; that can sympathize with the few in their plunder and oppression of the many'. Vol. 2, No. 4, Oct. 1824, pp. 340–1.

[101] Ibid. Apr. 1831, pp. 453–4.   [102] WR, Vol. 1, No. 1, Jan. 1824, p. 251.
[103] See WR, Vol. 2, Oct. 1824, p. 556. The writer commented: 'Such an un-exampled progress of religion, since America ceased to be within the diocese of the bishop of London, very well shows how advantageously tithes and test acts may be dispensed with'.
[104] WR, Vol. 1, No. 1, Jan. 1824, p. 115. See also WR, Vol. 10, pp. 61–3, and Vol. 18, pp. 326ff.

These arguments impressed the Dissenting wing of the utilitarians, and were freely used by them in their agitations for the removal of religious disabilities in England. W. J. Fox's unitarian journal, the *Monthly Repository*, commonly employed American parallels to this end, especially in the years immediately preceding 1832.[105]

5. *Parliamentary Reform*

The Benthamites were most doctrinaire in their appraisal of America's representative system; and they continued to be so as long as they were deeply committed to obtaining universal manhood suffrage, the ballot, annual elections, and equal electoral districts in Britain. According to Bentham's doctrine, these were the best instruments for ensuring the representation of majority interests and for preventing the use of corruption by aristocratic cliques intent on monopolizing power. It was therefore entirely necessary to demonstrate the purity of American politics.

Westminster reviewers were convinced that American electorates were too numerous to be bribed, and held that the ballot-box rendered bribery uncertain in any case. In 1824, upon the authority of Adam Hodgson, the *Westminster* ridiculed 'the absurd idea of *influence*' in republican elections.[106] In answer to Tory scepticism, voiced in the year of the Reform Bill, Godfrey Vigne's favourable testimony was widely publicized. He had said that in American elections 'individual wealth *has never yet been employed for any unconstitutional purpose.*'[107] There were, quite properly as the Benthamites argued, too many mechanical obstructions preventing corruption. 'Their whole political system', as the young diplomat and Radical William Gore Ouseley remarked, 'has been devised with a view to depriving wealth of all but its *legitimate* advantages.'[108] (This was of course the identical argument being urged in favour of Grey's Reform Bill.) The American millionaire would not gain entry into the assemblies

[105] See, e.g., *Monthly Repository*, Vol. 6, Jan. 1832, pp. 120ff; and also *L & WR*, Jan. 8138, Art. 6.
[106] *WR*, Vol. 2, July 1824, p. 178. Hogson, in his *Letters from North America* (London, 1824), praised the 'perfect practicability and usefulness of the broad representative system' in the Union.
[107] *WR*, Vol. 17, No. 33, July 1832, p. 172 (his emphasis); quoted from Vigne, *Six Months in America* (London, 1832).
[108] Ouseley, *Remarks on the Statistics and Political Institutions of the United States* (London, 1832), quoted ibid. p. 172. Ouseley had been Attaché to the British Legation, and was kindly disposed to the Americans. On his return to England, still a young man, he was impressed by the younger Philosophical Radicals and was enthusiastic in the cause of the Reform Bill. His book on the United States provided excellent propaganda for that measure. He was regarded with wry tolerance by Whigs and Tories as a wayward aristocrat.

by dint of wealth alone, but only by virtue of his talents and merit. Although aristocracies of a sort were growing up in the Tidewater cities they remained *social* not *political élites*.

Although the Benthamites as a group regarded the ballot more highly than even the extension of the franchise in England, and prosecuted a long and un-successful campaign to obtain it, they found themselves more often on the defensive than they liked when American precepts were referred to in this respect. This fact has received little scholarly attention. For example, George Grote, their most persistent advocate of the ballot, steered severely clear of the American example in his numerous parliamentary motions for the measure.[109] Opponents insistently raised objections that the ballot neither obtained secrecy in the various states in which it was employed, nor was highly esteemed by the Americans. Both sides were beset by ignorance of the real facts of the case, and relied a good deal upon assertion and counter-assertion. To illustrate, in 1831 Henry Warburton, a parliamentary ally of the Philosophical Radicals, voiced his uncertainties in a letter to Grote. Before Grote's election to the Commons, Warburton had been provisionally designated by the Benthamites to move the ballot in the House; he therefore requested information about its use in the classical democracies and in the new world.[110] Warburton wrote that Louis Maclane, the American Minister to England, 'declares himself an enemy to the system, and will be quoted as authority and voucher for its bad effects'. Warburton desired clarification on the issue whether or not, as had been alleged, Virginia had refused to adopt the ballot in Congressional elections. He pleaded for information of 'example and authority' upon these matters; and asked Grote to write upon the subject to Joseph Parkes, who 'has taken much pains in investigating the effects of the ballot in the United States'.[111]

James Mill wrote his classic defence of the ballot for the *Westminster* in 1830, and made it clear that he treated American arguments as prejudicial to a case best argued upon local and logical grounds.[112] Mill attempted to

[109] There is a useful summary of Grote's speeches in the Commons on the ballot in his *Minor Works*, edited by Alexander Bain (London, 1873), pp. 19–37.

[110] Warburton to Grote, 18.1.31, quoted in Harriet Grote, *The Personal Life of George Grote* (London, 1873), pp. 76–77.

[111] Further correspondence, if there was any, has not apparently survived, and Parkes has only a few, and not very original, things to say on the subject in one or two surviving pamphlets. See, e.g., J. K. Buckley, *Joseph Parkes of Birmingham* (London, 1926), p. 69.

[112] *WR*, Vol. 13, No. 25, July 1830, Art. I; e.g., 'We know well what secret voting is; and we know that it may be rendered a complete security against external influence, in voting for members of parliament. If the Americans did use it badly, that would be no argument against the thing itself' (pp. 25–26). He denied however that it was used ill in the United States.

confute those who said that 'the ballot did not answer expectation' in America, but he could only produce in its favour a French authority, Talleyrand. Mill suggested that the ballot must be esteemed, as it had never been discontinued in those states which had adopted it and was being continually extended to new states. He explained the failure of the system to obtain complete secrecy in terms of peculiar American circumstances. Because the people shared in the general wealth, and because there was a corresponding want of large fortunes, electors were economically independent, and therefore often disdained the security of the ballot for honest voting. In England, directly opposite conditions prevailed and independent voting could not be secured by any other means. This became the standard Benthamite defence on this point.

Mill neatly camouflaged any deficiencies in his own knowledge by aggressively attacking the ignorance of his opponents. No value, he declared, could be assigned to the views of ephemeral visitors to the United States, whom he suspected of making 'vague, hazarded declarations, respecting the interior and hidden working of the institutions of a foreign country.'[113] He believed that parliamentary testimony on the subject was even more uncertain and politically slanted, in view of the 'great circumstances of the case'.

American precedents continued to play a relatively minor role in the thinking of Philosophical Radicals upon the ballot.[114] However, after the group had enlisted to their cause H. S. Chapman, an able journalist and lawyer who had lived in Canada for eleven years and was familiar with American affairs,[115] they became much more positive in their affirmation

---

[113] Ibid. p. 23. 'Even individual testimony here', he said, 'is beyond measure less perfect than that which is delivered before the judge; both because it relates to matters of which it is infinitely more difficult to give correct testimony and because it is delivered in circumstances far less favourable to accuracy.' The last is clearly a reference to the propaganda use of American example in Reform England.

[114] For an illustration of this point, see Thomas Perronet Thompson, *Catechism on the Ballot* (London, 1862), which is a very full Benthamite defence against the detractors of the ballot, yet contains very few references to American experience. For the ballot in America, see also *WR*, Vol. 10, No. 19, Jan. 1829, p. 61; Vol. 17, No. 33, July 1832, p. 171; *Examiner*, 17.7.31, p. 457. In 1833 the *WR* cited Stuart's evidence in favour of the American ballot—'All voted by ballot, which is here considered the only way to obtain independent and unbiassed votes; and if so in this country, how much more in the British islands, where the aristocracy and higher orders are so infinitely more powerful, influential, and numerous.' Vol. 18, No. 36, Apr. 1833, quoted p. 333.

[115] Chapman (1803–81) emigrated to Canada in 1823 and established the first daily paper in that country in Montreal in 1833. On his return to England in 1834 he became associated with the Benthamites, and especially Roebuck and contributed to the *Westminster* and the *Encyclopaedia Britannica*. He took part in the campaign for municipal reform (1835) and in the handloom weavers' inquiry (1838). He practised

of faith in the American ballot. J. A. Roebuck's Benthamite *Pamphlets for the People* included a number of articles by Chapman with a Jacksonian flavour in June 1835, the time of Grote's second motion for the ballot. Opposing parliamentary comment to the contrary, he maintained that in America 'the Ballot-Box is deemed the safeguard of the Constitution; and so in fact it is.'[116] Unlike Mill, he asserted that there was indeed a rich class in America greedy for undue influence, but prevented from obtaining it because of secret voting. The wealthy, who were most influential in the large cities, termed themselves a 'natural aristocracy' and were prepared to resort to extensive bribery and corruption in order to gain for property its 'legitimate influence' (meaning 'sinister influence' wrote Chapman). Contemptuous of 'the mob', professed admirers of England's 'glorious constitution', the monied class had been represented politically by the Federalists and had recently endeavoured to obtain for itself economic hegemony by upholding such 'monster monopolies' as the Bank of the United States. In office (said Chapman) the Federalists had been illiberal, introducing a sedition bill and a standing army bill; while the monopolists had tried to preserve the Bank's sinister influence against the attack of President Jackson by using its funds in an attempt to 'fix' the Presidential election. The threat to democracy had, in each case, been frustrated by political safeguards against illegitimate influence. Chapman saw Jackson's re-election in 1832 as a triumph for democracy and an indication of the efficacy of the ballot as a check upon plutocracy. In a succeeding issue he challenged the 'fallacies' put forward by M.P.s such as Charles Russell, Lord Stanley, and James Barlow Hoy in the Commons debate upon the ballot.[117] English readers, he said, had obtained false impressions by reading the New York press, which was controlled by the monied interests. The ballot had in fact diminished tumult in the Tidewater cities, despite the efforts of the shop-owning class to aggravate disorder so as to discredit majority rule. Although many declared their

---

law after 1840 in New Zealand and Australia, was prominent in Australian politics, and ended as a judge of the Supreme Court of New Zealand. (*D.N.B.*)

[116] J. A. Roebuck, ed., *Pamphlets for the People;* article by Chapman, 'The American Ballot Box' (undated, 1835). The *Pamphlets* were a series of popular tracts published weekly by Roebuck from June 1835 to Feb. 1836 to circumvent the newspaper tax. They were sponsored by the *Society for the Diffusion of Political and Moral Knowledge*, established in 1833 by Joseph Hume, Grote, Warburton and Francis Place. The *Pamphlets* aimed at galvanizing the Radical M.P.s, and created much interest at the time. See R. E. Leader, ed., *Life and Letters of John Arthur Roebuck* (London, 1897).

[117] *Pamphlets for the People*, 'Fallacies of the House of Commons on the Ballot in America', by Chapman. This article was printed two weeks after Chapman's first article.

votes openly, wrote Chapman, secrecy was available for those who needed it, and was effective.

Orthodox Benthamites, then, still believed (and with some plausibility, as historians have shown) that Jacksonian democracy had ushered out the age of aristocratic corruption, rather than ushering in an age of democratic venality. They were equally complacent about the character of American representatives and the mechanics of representation. John Stuart Mill, however, did not share this complacency. In the thirties he broke with the strict utilitarians over the question of shackling representatives to their masters, the people; and the issue led to the writing of some of his major works. The American example was closely involved in the history of the schism.

The orthodox utilitarian analysis of American politics in this respect was coloured by the political ideas of James Mill. The elder Mill was not entirely dedicated to the proposition that representative democracy encouraged the election of the fittest men to office. The central problem, he believed, was rather that of providing sufficient checks to ensure an identity of interest between representatives and the community at large. Sanctions must be designed so as to enable the community to exercise power over the representative—to render it to his disadvantage to act in a selfish interest, and to his advantage to act in the general interest, which is the interest of the majority. Mill accepted the possibility that the people might not always clearly understand, or might mistake, their interest; but in general, he said, they were the best judges of their own interest. In any case, strict delegation—with momentary lapses of judgement on the part of the people—was a better system than continuous government by a few who favoured sinister interests. Mill had unbounded confidence in the ultimate supremacy of reason over the minds of the many. If all were educated and allowed access to all varieties of ideas, with complete freedom of discussion, democracy would succeed. The democratical part of society was not less wise or virtuous than the aristocratical. Mill included the more highly educated middle class in his democratical group, and was confident that the lower ranks would be guided by its example.[118] The *Westminster* reviewers, with these preconceived ideas in mind, looked to the United States to bear them out.

What Tocqueville and the younger Mill feared about delegation was that it might lead to a 'tyranny of the majority'. This, indeed, was precisely the accusation commonly levelled against American democracy by established opinion in Britain. Adam Hodgson, in his *Letters from North*

[118] See James Mill, *Essay on Government*, pp. 33–73; and J. S. Mill, *Autobiography* (London, 1924 ed.), pp. 89ff.

America, published in 1824, intimated some of Tocqueville's later criticisms when he attacked the docile subservience of American politicians before public opinion. Public men, he complained, were far too eager to obtain popularity. But the *Westminster*, defending James Mill's viewpoint, answered that this was no complaint at all. Hodgson had failed to reflect

that the members of a representative government are elected for no other purpose than to transact the business of the state in conformity with the popular will. Mr. Canning may disdain the sentiments of the people, without risking the loss of his place; but Mr. Crawford or Mr. Adams must bow to public opinion or abandon forever all hope of public favour.[119]

The reviewer was ready to admit the defects of representative government and delegation in the absence of enlightened public opinion, but could suggest no alternative that was not worse.[120] (And as long as the basic selfishness of all representatives remained an article of their faith, the Benthamites were perfectly consistent in advocating delegation rather than the younger Mill's theory of representation.) The evils of delegation they believed to be minimized in a society such as the American, where the natural condition of the people tended to be middle-class—'They are Englishmen who are well off; who never were conquered; who never had feudalism on their soil.'[121] The Americans tended to choose representatives whose calibre was not distinct from that of the majority of electors, but the popular standard was much higher in Europe because of more widespread education, material prosperity, and a more enlightened system of government. Captain Hall, the Tory traveller, had objected that representatives were mainly 'farmers, shopkeepers and country lawyers, . . . unaccustomed to abstract reasoning.'[122] The *Westminster* in 1829 replied that the people naturally chose representatives from its own midst, and suggested that, upon questions of most importance for the community, such persons best understood the popular interest, for it was also their own interest.

[119] *WR*, Vol. 2, July 1824, p. 178; cf. Perronet Thompson's exhortation to the new electors of 1832—'Chuse no man, that will not be your delegate, or resign when your opinions clash.' *WR*, Vol. 17, No. 33, July 1832, p. 259. (He also believed that M.P.s should be paid, as in the United States.)
[120] 'Under a representative government the national interests may be mistaken; under any other they will not only be mistaken but knowingly abused.'
[121] *WR*, Vol. 32, No. 1, Dec. 1838, p. 138.
[122] Quoted, *WR*, Vol. 11, No. 22, Oct. 1829, p. 443. It was a rare complaint of truly conservative thinkers that the people were not adept at abstract reasoning. Rationalism was often identified with a tendency to dangerous innovation, likely to break the 'cake of custom'. Most Tories, like Bagehot, preferred the stability of a working-class with a 'dull, animal attachment to the routine of sense-experience'.

For tactical reasons the Benthamites began, during the immediate campaign for the Reform Bill, to make wider claims respecting the merit of public men in the United States. The opponents of reform had been making great play with the idea that democracy had produced a race of political pygmies in the only country in which it had been tried. The Benthamites, relaxing for the occasion their less popular doctrine of delegation, sprang to the defence. In a strategically important article of July 1832 (probably penned in the crisis weeks of May and June), the *Westminster* attacked the assumption that large constituencies, voting on popular principles, returned unworthy representatives.[123] It used evidence which had been widely publicized in *The Times*, a temporary ally, in March, primarily with a view to supporting the campaign for obtaining a larger parliamentary representation for the London metropolis.[124] *The Times*, in an account of the recent New York elections, had noted the lack of disorder and corruption and the merit of the candidates put up. The typical candidate was not, as the Tories alleged, 'some greasy mechanic —some pot companion and worthy prototype of the illiterate and ignorant men who elected him'.

Indeed, with scarcely an exception, [said *The Times*] all the men elected by the larger bodies of constituents, are men distinguished for their talents, their services, or their standing in the estimation of the country.

It pointed to Van Buren, Clay, Webster, and Maclane in confirmation. It was suggested that the same situation would prevail if more popular elections were introduced into England, for human nature was much the same on both sides of the Atlantic. Men in the lower walks of life (it was argued) tended to elect their superiors to office, whilst representatives had every motive to elevate themselves in order to be advantageously considered by the electorate. The *Westminster* saw fit in 1832 to print these liberal, and slightly deviate, views without contradiction. It also permitted itself to compromise on the issue of the pledge which had already threatened to split the group.[125] Many Americans (it said) concurred in the theory, often uncongenial to Englishmen, that the representative should not be free to exercise untrammelled independence in his legislative capacity. On the other hand, that theory was disallowed by an equally large group, and certainly it obtained little currency in the affairs of the Senate. In general the situation was not unlike that prevailing in Britain.

[123] *WR*, Vol. 17, No. 33, July 1832, Art. XI (Statistics and Political Institutions of the U.S.), pp. 168–82. This was a review of Ouseley's book.
[124] *The Times*, 3.3.32.
[125] J. S. Mill's articles on the pledge at this time in *The Examiner* were unacceptable to many doctrinaire Benthamites. See *The Examiner*, 1.7.32 (p. 416); 15.7.32 (p. 450).

The electors chose those men who thought similarly to themselves on great national issues, but permitted them to exercise an unpledged opinion on all other topics not vital to the immediate interests of the electorate. In all cases the political views of the candidate were conned *before*, not after, election; while many public men (such as Clay) followed Burke in regarding themselves as advocates of national rather than territorial interests.

In 1838 the new journal of Philosophic Radicalism, John Stuart Mill's *London and Westminster Review*, indulged in open admiration of America's great men, its heroes being Webster, Clay, Livingston, Story, Marshall Madison, and Channing. It contended (in something of a last-ditch effort) against the prevailing English tendency to write down the American statesmen of Jackson's era. The new review maintained that most of them saw things in a truer light than 'our public functionaries'. It held in considerable contempt 'the small personages who are all this country will ever hold out to the gaze of the world as her statesmen while the people continue to look to the rich and titled for leaders, and not to themselves'— a reversion to earlier views. On Harriet Martineau's authority, the American Senate was considered to be 'a most imposing assemblage', composed of men of able and diverse character highly respected in the Union.[126] Even John Quincy Adams and John C. Calhoun, Ishmaels in the philosophy of Benthamism, were granted to be men of high calibre.

Many Benthamites were disposed to sacrifice the pledge if more frequent elections could be obtained. The Americans, they believed, had demonstrated that the people could exercise a sufficiently strict surveillance over public policy by means of the less doctrinaire device of annual and biennial elections. It was simply the employment of the threat of removal in a less objectionable form.[127] The critics complained that continual elections in the United States had quickened the turnover of politicians, thereby encouraging instability and sacrificing experience in affairs. The Benthamites placed far less value upon the concept of politics as a profession. Newcomers would soon learn the ways of the Legislature, 'and they will be less expert in jobbing and getting up little matters of private interest, if they are called to account once a year'.[128] Other advantages

[126] *L & WR*, Jan. 1838, p. 491. (Martineau's Western Travels), probably by W. E. Hickson. In 1824 the *WR* suggested that the orators of the new world languished in obscurity because of the siting of the capital in remote Washington. There was no high-quality newspaper in Washington to report the proceedings of Congress. Thus Tocqueville's problem of democratic mediocrity was interpreted as simply a problem in publicity. Vol. 2, No. 3, July 1824, p. 203.

[127] For a utilitarian defence of annual elections, see *WR*, Vol. 20, No. 39, Jan. 1834, Art. 16 (Short Parliaments).

[128] *WR*, Vol. 11, No. 22, Oct. 1829, p. 444.

rarely considered by theorists were seen in the American system. The *Westminster* observed that by means of frequent elections, coupled with a federal system duplicating institutions, thousands of representatives who were practically acquainted with the forms and principles of legislation were periodically returned to the bosom of the community and 'through the vivid medium of a free press, constitute, as it were, an auditory greatly superior to that of any other nation.'[129] The Benthamites rebutted a common objection made against frequent elections that they excited undue popular agitation. They pointed to the United States, where innumerable elections at all levels of government had in half a century' never produced insurrection, tumult, riot, or even inconvenient excitement.'[130]

The utilitarians made cogent use of American example to aid them in their struggle for another radical plank—law reform. It is well known that Bentham devoted his life to evolving a complete theory of law, and to campaigning for a systematization of English law in line with that theory. He was only converted gradually from a belief in benevolent despotism to political radicalism, and then primarily because he saw in parliamentary reform the only means by which root-and-branch legal reform could be achieved. Indeed the subordination of his political to his legal and administrative theories explains in part his failure to discern some of the more subterranean problems of democratic government, for he believed that in his legal-administrative ideas a democratic society would possess almost all the integrative policies it required. Bentham wanted a rational law, clear of customary obscurity; a law plainly and logically arranged, not the result of 'fortuitous or temporary necessity' or full of intricacies which served only the sinister interests of the legal profession. His code was based upon certain leading principles: for example, Beccaria's, that the scale of punishments should always correspond to the scale of crimes and combine greatest deterrent effect with least possible pain to the culprit; that judges should not interpret but only apply the law; that written law should supplant judge-made law; and so on—all being principles unearthed by applying the test of utility to jurisprudence.

---

[129] *WR*, Vol. 2, Oct. 1824, p. 555. The words are C. J. Ingersoll's from *A Discourse concerning the Influence of America on the Mind . . . etc.* [Philadelphia, 1823].

[130] *WR*, Vol. 20, No. 39, Jan. 1834, p. 212. See also *Pamphlets for the People*, article by R. Hammersley, 'Progress of Democracy' (undated, 1835). It is interesting to note the literal dependence of some *Westminster* reviewers on Bentham's written works on this topic; e.g., the writer of Art. 16, Jan. 1834, noted that 19 of 22 states had annual elections, but the Senate held biennial elections. The latter departure from annuality he explained in terms of the vast distances travelled by representatives to the seat of government, an objection which did not apply to Britain. The explanation is almost identical to that given by Bentham when treating the same point in his *Plan of Parliamentary Reform* (1817), *Works*, III. 562.

As we have seen, Bentham was first attracted to the United States as a virgin field for the application of his juridical ideas. In the years before 1815 he offered to draw up complete bodies of statute law for federal and state governments. He did so (as he wrote in unfortunately typical style to Madison) in order to replace 'that mass of foreign law, the yoke of which, in the *wordless*, as well as the boundless, and shapeless shape of *common*, alias *unwritten*, law remains still about your necks'.[131] This was one of his severest criticisms of the Americans, that they still retained an unwieldy common law derived from England and an unwholesome respect for Blackstone and his *Commentaries*, which revered judge-made law. Bentham believed, however, that the Americans had emancipated themselves to a certain extent from dependence upon English precedents, and hoped that they were on the way to constructing more rational codes of law. In this respect he expected a good deal from Edward Livingston, creator of the Lousiana Penal Code and an avowed disciple of his in jurisprudence. In general, Bentham held American jurists in higher regard than those of England. The United States, furthermore, had a written constitution, which in Bentham's eyes represented an advance over Britain's unwritten and irrational constitution (although he by no means approved of all the principles enshrined in American constitutional law).

In the 1820's and 1830's the utilitarian campaign for law reform got powerfully under way with Peel's reform of the penal law and the agitations of Henry Brougham and John Austin for revision of the criminal law and reorganization of the judiciary. Under these circumstances utilitarian publicists began to make a more organized reference to American jurisprudence to bolster their domestic campaign. In 1825—two years after Peel had restricted the number of capital offences, and at a time of active Radical agitation for further relaxation of the death penalty—the *Westminster* printed an article entirely devoted to Livingston's new penal code for Louisiana,[132] emphasizing the enlightened Benthamite principles on which it was based. The crude, the contradictory, the cruel had been replaced by a code 'uniform, consistent, mild, founded on principles which the science of jurisprudence has completely and beautifully developed'.[133] Sanguinary laws had been moderated and the death penalty

---

[131] *Works*, IV. 453 (Bentham to Madison, Oct. 1811). He told Madison that he was more hopeful of accomplishing his end in America than in England, for any effort to change existing arrangements at home was howled down with the cry, 'You want to republicanize us' (ibid.). For further reference ibid. 453–77; 502–4; and X. 462–3; for libel law in the U.S., V. 246; X. 512–13; for penitentiary system, IV. 212–48.

[132] *WR*, Vol. 3, No. 5, Jan. 1825, Art. IV (Penal Code for Louisiana).

[133] Ibid. p. 59. 'It is events like these', the *Review* added, 'that repay such men as Bentham and Romilly for the labour of a life.'

severely restricted. No established religion was enabled to retain its privileges and supremacy by penalty of law; freedom of the press was guaranteed; and the law itself was shorn of all mysticism and rendered readily understood by all. The will of the Legislature was established as the sole authority of the law, which excluded all offences against 'laws of morality, of nature, and of religion'. The article *in toto* was a devastating attack on the conservative mystique; but the Tories were coolly reminded that Louisiana's drastic changes had been accomplished without shaking the foundations of society—'social order has not been disturbed; neither the altar nor the hearth has been invaded'.

Bentham's disciple, the Birmingham Radical Joseph Parkes, kept American legal developments before the eyes of lawyers and reformers between 1825 and 1830. In those years Parkes was quite an important figure in the struggle for law reform. He wrote a *History of the Court of Chancery*, which aimed at improving the administration of justice in the English courts of equity (the *bête noire* of reformers, which provoked Bentham's scathing *Indications respecting Lord Eldon* in 1824). It was after consultation with Parkes, and Bentham, that Brougham launched his critical speech upon Chancery abuses in 1828, which ushered in an era of drastic reform. Parkes was interested in the same problems in America, and wrote a book upon the subject.[134] Bentham encouraged the project by lending Parkes some of his reference books. Parkes wrote to Bentham in 1830:

I return your American books with a little interest—in a copy of a volume of my own manufacture. It will be quickly succeeded by another—an account of United States Codification and Common Law. I can do no harm by putting the American example under the noses of our Governors. The Americans are suffering you will see under the effects of the Equity Legacy left them by the mother country.[135]

Parkes believed, according to the preface to this work, that

The laudable efforts of the British legislature and of the legal profession for the advancement of the science of jurisprudence and the amendment of municipal law will be promoted by the publication of information and the results of practical experience relating to legal reforms in other nations.[136]

He sent a copy to Francis Place, and remarked of real property law that 'the amendments we *propose* have been in action years in the U.S.'.[137]

[134] *The Statutes and Orders of the Court of Chancery and the Statute Law of real property of the State of New York, with a brief account of equity jurisdiction and the law of real property and registration in the United States of North America* (New York).
[135] Parkes to Bentham, B.M. Add MS. 33546, fol. 451. (Bentham Correspondence.)
[136] *Statutes and Orders*, etc., p. vii.
[137] B.M. Add. MS. 35, 148, fol. 77 (Place Papers). Buckley's biography of Parkes, *op. cit.*, gives the location of a number of very useful MSS. on law reform.

Parkes was able to give currency to his ideas in the *Jurist*, which was established to further the cause of law reform, and which he largely managed. At least five articles on American law and codification appeared in that journal.[138]

The *Westminster* produced three more full-scale articles on American law in the thirties, besides a plenitude of minor references.[139] The dominant note was one of praise for the relative simplicity and clarity achieved in American attempts at codification. Legal transactions—especially in conveyancing and property law—had been simplified and the technicalities of judicial procedure reduced to a minimum. Comment was made to serve more immediate purposes as well. In April 1832 an article on American law reform described the successful use made of local courts and registries and produced this as evidence in favour of Brougham's major projects of that year to set up a Land Register and Local Courts in England.[140] By reference to America's mild but successful penal laws, reviewers continued to support the Radical struggle for a more humane criminal code—for example, for reduction of the number of capital offences and for a tempering of the Mutiny Bill in 1832.[141] In October 1835 the *Westminster* publicized a report on American penitentiaries prepared by William Crawford. Crawford had been sent on a tour of inspection by Melbourne, who, as Home Secretary, had a view to amending the English prison system. Although critical of various defects in America's prison system, the Benthamites urged the adoption in Britain of such principles as more efficient and centralized organization of gaols, the appointment of 'superintending functionaries' responsible for prison control and conditions, the establishment of an effective inspection system, the adoption of more accurate crime statistics, and a more compassionate prison discipline.[142]

---

[138] Mar. 1827, Art. 2, pp. 22–41 (Progress of Jurisprudence in the U.S.); Jan. 1828, Art. 6, pp. 430–45 (American Law); May 1828, Art. 3 (Codification of the Laws of the U.S.); Apr. 1829, Art. 5 (Jurisprudence of Louisiana); Feb. 1833, Art. 6 (Houses of Refuge for Juvenile Offenders in the U.S. and France). There is also a short article in May 1828, Art. 7 (Attachment for Debt in America). Parkes wrote to Bentham about Art 3, May 1828, informing him that it would be headed with a long extract from Bentham's codification proposals to Madison made in 1811: '. . . you will be much interested to see the influence you have had on the *Nation* of calculating Yankees . . .' See Add. MS. 33,546, fol. 13; letter of 4.5.1828.

[139] See Vol. 16, No. 32, Oct. 1832, Art. 5 (American Law Reform); Vol. 17, No. 34, Oct. 1832, Art. 5 (American Penal Law); Vol. 23, No. 46, Oct. 1835, Art. 10 (review of Wm. Crawford, *Report . . . on the Penitentiaries of the United States, etc.*, Parlt. Paper, 1834).

[140] *WR*, Vol. 16, No. 32, Oct. 1832, pp. 361–2. Brougham's proposals were defeated in Parliament; Hansard, 3rd ser., XVIII, 1010; and XIX, 372.

[141] See especially *WR*, Vol. 17, No. 34, Oct. 1832, Art. 5.

[142] *WR*, Vol. 23, No. 46, Oct. 1835, Art. 10.

6. *The Decline of Bentham's Ideas*

At some time between 1829 and 1840 Bentham's ideas upon American democracy ceased to be regarded as original thinking in the circles of Philosophic Radicalism. Benthamites came to be more sceptical about the new world, to question the relevance of American comparisons to English situations. Transatlantic democracy was regarded as many-faceted, as a system with potentialities for evil as well as good.

This transition of opinion is partly explained by the fact that the older stereotype had outlived its political usefulness. Reality rather than myth better served the interests of a Benthamism about to merge into the philosophy of *laissez faire* and to draw away from political Radicalism and alliance with the working class. American precedents had been particularly useful, and of undoubted strategic importance, in the campaign for the Reform Bill. They were straws to break the camel-back of Tory resistance to even limited democracy in England. But after 1832 the Benthamites were placed in the classical dilemma of bourgeois reformers caught up in their own whirlwind of change. Like their counterparts in the French Revolution they were forced to say to the rash spirits, 'so far, but no further!' A conservative reaction followed the passing of the Bill, and the Benthamites flung the America example into the limbo of their forgotten political weapons. Republican America, with its (supposedly) unqualified democracy, even its disestablishment, had less appeal to those men who now opposed further extensions of the franchise, who were now willing to work within existing institutions for more reform. The attention of practical reformers was now, in any case, engrossed in the day-to-day prosecution of improvements through existing bodies and newly-created organizations (such as the committees of inquiry into municipal government and the poor law). As we shall see, the abolitionists and political economists among the Benthamites owed allegiance to their cause and subject independently of their belief in political Radicalism; and their criticisms of America intensified with the heightening of a transatlantic anti-slavery crusade and with the Anglo-American commercial crisis of 1837. Even the Dissenters, whose links with America remained strong, were faced in the late 1830's by an Anglican revival and began to be less hopeful of obtaining the American church system in Britain.

On the whole, the Benthamites could now afford to take a second, and more realistic, look at American politics, and they did so. Many continued to look benevolently upon the American experiment, but more especially in its social and economic aspect. They still drew upon American precepts to aid them in attaining specific planks in the Benthamite platform to which they were still loyal—the ballot, annual parliaments, national education, and a free press. But it was left to the Chartists and Ultra-Radicals to maintain a zealous and undiscriminating regard for complete democracy in the new world.

Pro-Americanism was also diluted in the 1830's as a result of a schism which developed between orthodox Benthamism and a deviate brand of utilitarianism espoused by the younger Mill. The debate revolved around the nature of representative government, and a questioning of Bentham's whole concept of Radical Reform took place. As was perhaps inevitable, assessments of transatlantic democracy became closely implicated in such an issue. John Stuart Mill accepted Tocqueville's analysis of American democracy rather than that of Bentham and the English Radicals; and he challenged some of the important premises of American politics. The combined intellectual authority of the younger Mill and Tocqueville finally prevailed, and Mill's appraisal, which pictured the Americans as a politically responsible middle class, became popular in informed opinion. John Mill's prestige was high, especially among the younger Philosophic Radicals. After the amalgamation of the *Westminster Review* with the *London Review*, edited by him, in April 1836, he had effective control of the sole Benthamite periodical, a control which he retained until the break-up of the parliamentary group in 1840, when the *London and Westminster* was sold to a non-Benthamite interest.[143] With one or two exceptions, discussions of America in Mill's periodical showed a marked divergence from the type of article featured earlier in the *Westminster*. They conformed more to current liberal standards, or resembled Mill's editorial attitude, as expressed for example in his 'State of Society in America'.[144]

The body of knowledge about the new world was being rapidly augmented in the 1830's and 1840's, and the 'New Radicalism' was receptive to more serious interpretations of American politics. With such appraisals the doctrinaire analysis of the 1820's could not compete, at least in speculative circles. Bentham's analysis had contained—and very successfully publicized—the large truths of free society in America. Tocqueville and Mill granted these truths, but regarded them as starting-points for further enquiry into the nature of democracy. The Benthamite use of the American example had made an impression in the twenties, when information about the new world was scantier and propagandist,

---

[143] See J. S. Mill, *Autobiography* (London, 1924ed.), p. 169; and C. M. D. Towers, 'John Stuart Mill and the *London and Westminster Review*', *Atlantic Monthly* (Jan. 1892), pp. 57–74.

[144] *London Review*, Vol. 2, No. 4, Jan. 1836, Art. 5. Mill's ideas upon the United States are dealt with in Ch. V.

when thinking about democracy was in an earlier phase. After 1832, however, the relevance of such arguments to the central problems of politics appeared much more tenuous.

The faithful Abdiels of orthodox Benthamism, the die-hards such as John Arthur Roebuck and George Grote, took the longest time to abandon their Americophilia. The response of such men to a Jacksonian America that was arousing scepticism in Britain is worthy of investigation.

Although Edward Gibbon Wakefield, the theorist of systematic colonization, was hardly the strictest of Benthamites, some (but not all) of his ideas upon the United States—contained in his *England and America* (New York, 1834)—were in the tradition of the twenties. His contribution was idiosyncratic, for his book was in reality a collection of essays centred around his personal theory of colonization, and deriving from an essentially economic rather than political view of causation in society. Nevertheless, one of its effects, especially in ascribing American disadvantages to economic causes rather than to democracy, was to support the analysis of orthodox Radicalism. Wakefield accepted as a statement of fact the criticism that American civilization was jejune, that Americans neglected the fine arts, science, philosophy, and the cultivation of learning. But he refused to derive a democratic cause for these effects:

Democracy, that is, political equality, which lays open to all alike every career of ambition, and makes usefulness the standard of merit, must surely be very favourable to the cultivation of learning; more especially, when accompanied, as it is in the United States, by universal ease, which bestows leisure upon all. The Americans are the only people in the world blessed with leisure and equality.[145]

He located the cause of degeneration in the widespread dispersal of land and population, a state of things ultimately ascribable to the cheap land policy of British colonial governments. Civilization was the product of a concentration of population: 'In the history of the world, there is no example of a society at once dispersed and highly civilized.'[146] Dispersal provided obstacles to social intercourse, to the interchange of ideas and the exercise of mental faculties. It also prevented the division of labour, and thence the creation of social complexity, which, as Adam Smith remarked, was the stimulus to intellectual enquiry and literary observation. This situation was aggravated, according to Wakefield, by the

[145] E. G. Wakefield, *England and America etc.* (New York, 1834), pp. 197ff. Not all Benthamites agreed that ease was universal in the U.S.; e.g., a reviewer in 1835 printed Shirreff's observation that there was an 'all work and no play' look about the country. *WR*, Vol. 23, No. 46, Oct. 1835, p. 321.
[146] Ibid. p. 193.

constant expansion of the North American frontier, which denuded the East—the potential centre of civilization—of population. Daily the population spread faster than it increased, whilst larger individual proportions of the land were being constantly alienated. Wakefield would have contended savagely against Turner, for he regarded unregulated expansion of settlement as an unmitigated evil in infant states. It retarded intellectual achievement, produced the uncouth traits of the backwoods, encouraged national conceit (characteristic of all colonies), and stimulated religious extremism. But these were the results of 'a faulty mode of colonization', of a fallacious land policy, not of the popular principle of politics.

J. A. Roebuck was perhaps the most doctrinaire defender of Bentham's ideas against the eroding influence of John Stuart Mill and Tocqueville. Together with his associates H. S. Chapman and Roberts Hammersley, Roebuck contended against such heresies in his *Pamphlets for the People*. He rightly fastened upon Mill's 1835 review of Tocqueville's *Democracy in America* for the *London Review* as a departure from orthodox utilitarianism. He strongly opposed the view expressed therein that delegation was a danger to democracy; in fact, according to Mill, 'the one and only danger to Democracy'. Mill had argued that, whilst the majority in a representative government ought to retain final sanctions over their representatives, good government demanded that the wisest and ablest should rule, with minimum popular interference. Roebuck poured scorn upon the prospect of a Platonic *élite* governing disinterestedly for the good of the majority. The problem of obtaining the best government was not to be solved, he believed, by persuading the people to give up their judgement implicitly to any set of men. Roebuck had all the suspicion of James Mill and Acton that power corrupts, that *any* governing minority was likely to make a bad use of its power. Representatives, no matter how wise, had strong interests to delude the people, to wield power for their own ends:

Wisdom [he wrote] is a good thing when directed by probity; you rob it of that worthy counsellor when you give it irresponsible power; and by inducing the People to have faith, you pursue the most efficient means to this mischievous end.[147]

Close and continuous supervision by the people over their representatives was thus a necessary condition against misgovernment. Roebuck admitted that such a government could be only as good as the national intelligence permitted. No democratic devices or machinery could make it better.

---

[147] J. A. Roebuck, 'Democracy in America', in *Pamphlets for the People* (undated, 1835), pp. 3–4.

Ever ardent in the cause of national education on American lines, he
therefore ended with the conclusion that democracy was best served by
education. His colleagues gave support to his claim by maintaining that
the United States exhibited the practical good effects of delegation
exercised by an enlightened public.[148]

John Stuart Mill, in 1835, was not unaware of the need for checks
upon minority government. He conceded to the Radicals that strict
delegation (e.g. in the form of pledges) might be imposed upon representatives in matters relating to *organic* changes in the constitution; for instance,
on questions of franchise, ballot, duration of parliament, codification of
the law, and primogeniture. Roebuck objected that these were not only
important constitutional, but also *social*, questions, involving the administration of justice and the whole transmission of property. Yet the people
—and not the experts—were, on Mill's admission, to judge of these
issues. Mill's argument simply illustrated the inconsistency of drawing a
line at all.

Roebuck alleged that Mill, whose views were in many ways original
and profound, had been misled by Tocqueville's too rapid generalization.
Like all Frenchmen, the latter considered France to be Europe, and
Europe the world. The dolorous history of France in the last forty years
had darkened Tocqueville's vision of democracy, yet it was not in fact a
history of democracy at all. Nor was it likely that the errors of France
would be shared by the people of England, who were educated to a
measure of self-government and were temperate in politics. Roebuck's
remarks were calculated to neutralize the disturbing accounts of French
and American democracy given by Mill and Tocqueville and to reassert
Bentham's ideas on the subject.

The *Westminster* sometimes during the thirties reiterated its sentiments
of the preceding decade. Colonel Perronet Thompson in 1833 gave
standard approval to James Stuart's liberal enthusiasm for American
republicanism.[149] In the following year the Review sided with Jackson and

[148] See, e.g., Hammersley in *Pamphlets for the People*, 'Progress of Democracy'
(undated, 1835). Democratic majorities, he wrote, could be restrained by public
opinion—'Witness the Anglo-Americans; witness the growing control of public
opinion even, recent as it is, in this country, over the House of Commons; see the
great good which these Anglo-Americans have obtained, and the growing good
which the Radicals are obtaining for the people here, solely by the direction of public
opinion' (p. 4).

[149] *WR*, Vol. 18, No. 36, Apr. 1833, Art. 4; review of James Stuart, *Three Years
in North America* (Edinburgh, 1833). The article commended the orderliness of elections, the efficiency of the ballot, the lack of corruption in politics; the egalitarianism
of the people, their prosperity, standard of education, freedom of religion and press.
It defended them against the charge of vulgarity, but savagely denounced slavery in
the South.

the Democrats in their wrangle with Nicholas Biddle and the Bank of the United States[150] (a theme taken up again, as we have seen, by Chapman in 1835). Whilst Roebuck campaigned in the House for a system of national education on the lines of the Massachusetts system, and Grote (assisted by the propaganda of Chapman and others) waged war there for the American ballot, the group's quarterly continued to publicize the evidence of travellers which gave support to their campaigns. The most important eye-witness accounts in this respect were Patrick Shireff's *Tour Through North America* (1835), Fanny Butler's *Journal* (1835), and Harriet Martineau's *Retrospect of Western Travel* (1838).[151] The case for another article of Radical faith—annual parliaments—was also strengthened by reference to America.[152] The *Westminster Review* also produced a useful, if brief, criticism of Thomas Hamilton's Tory account of *Men and Manners in America* in 1835.[153]

It was clear, even in the late 1830's, that a simple Benthamite admiration for American institutions still persisted, possibly because it was useful in bolstering the campaign for certain specifics in the programme of philosophic Radicalism. The review of Martineau, mentioned above, although sandwiched in time between the new interpretations of Mill (1835–6) and Monckton Milnes (1840) in the same periodical, contained most of the standard attitudes of the 1820's. The United States (it said) was a country in which the many were to the few as rulers to ruled:

in which the interests of the working classes govern, in which suffrage is universal, and the result is, not injury to themselves, nor discomfort to any class, nor faithlessness of man in man, nor any species of agrarian plunder, nor any widespread anarchy. Yet more. The districts of this country, in which universal suffrage prevails, have been the part in which prosperity has been developed with a vigour before unknown to man; and where there is no suffrage for the slave there is ruin hanging over the rich.[154]

Only unalloyed good had resulted from the sweeping away of customary restrictions and the establishment of political equality and self-government.

150 *WR*, Vol. 21, No. 42, Oct. 1834, Art. 1 (Jackson and the Bank of the U.S.).
151 *WR*, Vol. 23, No. 46, Oct. 1835, Art. 4; *LR*, Vol. 2, No. 3, Jul. 1835, Art. 7; *L & WR*, Jan. 1838, Art. 6.
152 *WR*, Vol. 20, No. 39, Jan. 1834, Art. 16 (Short Parliaments).
153 *WR*, Vol. 23, No. 46, Oct. 1835, pp. 332ff. Shirreff, it was claimed, had thrown 'merited ridicule' on Hamilton's book for assuming that there was an inherent principle of destruction in democracy. Hamilton had himself noted the existing safeguard in the fact that the majority were propertied and had a 'stake in the hedge'. Abolition of primogeniture had diffused property and ensured stability. Hamilton had imagined his demagogic 'workies' in New York, and Americans did not resent higher education as setting a few above the mass.
154 *L & WR*, Jan. 1838, p. 475. The article is possibly by W. E. Hickson.

America was in fact the only country which recognized the essential dignity of man:

it alone bade men give each other the right hand of fellowship as brothers, equal, except that the nobler spirits were to serve the humbler . . . In America alone is man, man. No wonder it is loved by religionists, fathers, and men . . . the blessings of a whole people are on the American institutions.[155]

Such eulogy was to be much more rarely heard in speculative circles in the future, although it survived as Ultra-Radical propaganda. There was already, after 1832, a noticeable decline of enthusiasm towards new-world democracy on the part of the *Westminster*; something of a reluctance to return more than occasionally to the panegyrics which characterized the twenties. This was manifest in a decrease in the number of review articles upon American affairs.[156] Important works upon the United States, such as Martineau's *Society in America* (1837), Hamilton's *Men and Manners* (1833), Marryat's *Diary in America* (1839), some of which questioned the main assumptions of the Benthamite analysis, received barely passing notice. Even Tocqueville's first volume of *Democracy in America* was left for Mill to handle in the *London Review*, at that time a rival journal. Many reasons may have lain behind a decline in output. What was unmistakable, however, was a falling-off in the standard of speculation about the new world after Reform. The utilitarians appeared to have lost their crusading spirit upon the subject, and, apart from individual articles by Mill and Milnes in the *London and Westminster*, standards remained depressingly low during the decade.[157]

It is perhaps as well at this stage to make the point that many of Bentham's disciples never shared as deeply his concern with American developments. American experience was never central to the formation of Benthamite opinion. The utilitarians worked on the deductive principle from several axioms and looked to foreign countries primarily to provide supporting evidence, to illustrate how things were better ordered elsewhere than in Britain. Thus France, and to some extent Prussia, played

[155] Ibid. pp. 476–7.

[156] In the period 1824–32 there were eighteen articles of central relevance to the United States. In the almost equivalent period 1833–40 there were thirteen articles of a similar kind.

[157] One possible explanation of the decline of standards upon American topics, as upon other topics, in the *Westminster* especially, may be the secession from that journal of the Mills and their followers in 1828, leaving control in the mediocre hands of Thompson and Bowring. One might deduce (in the absence of evidence on the subject) that the important articles of 1826–8 upon the U.S. were written by the associates of the younger Mill; that from 1828 to 1835 it was difficult for these to find a forum, and that after 1835 they either came to Mill's point of view, or stayed silent.

the same sort of role in their thoughts as did America, especially after the liberal revolutions of 1830. Some Benthamites, including such a crucially important reformer as Edwin Chadwick, were not interested in the United States at all. Bulwer Lytton, whose political views had considerable effect at the time through his book *England and the English* (Paris, 1834), was more interested by Continental, and particularly Prussian developments.[158] Charles Buller and William Molesworth (the so-called Radical Imperialists) were drawn to American affairs principally because of their interest in local self-government for Canada, and because of the delicate relations between Canada and the United States. Roebuck, Grote, James Mill, and Perronet Thompson were likewise drawn into debate upon the new world via their concern with such domestic questions as the ballot and representation, and wrote little independently upon the subject. In many ways the circumstances of the 1830's did not encourage such people to become involved.

Even those champions of strict utilitarianism who withstood the disillusion of the thirties finally lost their enthusiasm for American democracy. It took the Civil War to shake Roebuck's faith. The defender of Bentham against the doubts of Tocqueville in 1835, he concluded a gradual transition into Toryism by espousing in the 1860's a more pessimistic view of majority rule than the Frenchman. On the eve of the second Reform Bill he warned his friend William Ibbitt against the dangers of placing power in the hands of the ignorant:

I have great faith in my countrymen; [he wrote] but the experience of America frightens me . . . During my whole life I have looked to that country as about to solve the great problem of self-government, and now, in my old age, the hopes of my youth and manhood are destroyed, and I am left to reconstruct my political philosophy, and doubt and hesitation beset me on every point.[159]

He publicly embraced the cause of the South during hostilities, declaring openly (and with Palmerston's private approval) that the conduct of the North was 'insolent and overbearing', and suggesting that a divided America would benefit England. (It is almost certain that Roebuck was paid by the South for his anti-Northern campaign, and the cynic might adduce this as an urge towards a change of heart.) In his polemics he attributed the failure of American democracy to a mistaken policy of immigration, which permitted the entry into the North of the 'scum and

---

[158] Lytton's political thought is treated in G. K. Lewis, 'A Forgotten Classic of English Life and Government', *Canadian J. of Econ. & Pol. Sci.*, Vol. 19 (Aug. 1953), 377–91.

[159] Letter to Ibbitt, 26.4.64, in R. E. Leader, ed., *Life and Letters of J. A. Roebuck* (London, 1897), pp. 299–300.

refuse of Europe.' He thus came over to the popular view of Whigs and Tories, that the Anglo-Saxon race alone was capable of successfully managing a democratic form of government. He was also converted, in the end, to John Mill's theory of representation, which he had attacked in 1835; for he was forced to concede that a disintegration of the body politic in the United States had been helped by an 'almost universal withdrawal of rich and educated Americans from the business of politics' and their replacement by 'mere political adventurers'.[160] *Delegation*, it appeared, was no guarantee of political fitness or responsibility—nor had national education prevented a débâcle. The discovery pained Roebuck, and in one of his last addresses to his constituents at Sheffield (in 1869) his disillusion was apparent: 'Beware of trade unions', he wailed, 'beware of Ireland; beware of America.'[161]

George Grote, on the other hand, never completely lost his faith in democracy or republicanism—including transatlantic varieties—although his views were distinctly affected by the quiescence of the Victorian age and the trauma of the American Civil War. He did not write widely upon American topics, but we have his wife's testimony in 1837 that 'American politics had for many years occupied Grote's attention, and engaged his sympathy. He was a great admirer of the "Federalist", the pages of which, he always declared, revealed the highest qualities of philosophical statesmanship.'[162]

In the 1820's, as we have seen, his ideas upon America were radical. He argued that the participation of her people in public affairs illustrated the wisdom of universal suffrage and destroyed any argument that the ballot tended to stifle interest in politics.[163] He also contended at that time against a current dislike for the caucus as it was being used in America. He conceded that the leading members of the two great parties in the United States, meeting in committee, issued voting instructions to their

---

[160] Ibid. pp. 321-4.

[161] Ibid. p. 330. The *Spectator*, on Roebuck's death, described him as a 'political misanthrope', one whose radicalism 'was, indeed, more of a constitutional, political irritability than of a constitutional sympathy with popular policy . . . It was his mission to scold allies, rather than to assail foes.' His bitter attacks on the U.S. it regarded as perhaps 'due to the same feeling that there were a people of cousins, and that as a relative and friend of the family, he was bound to confess the disagreeable impressions made upon him.'

[162] Mrs. Grote, *The Personal Life of George Grote* (London, 1873), p. 123. The Grotes had a number of American friends, including the Stevensons (the American Minister to England and his wife). Grote's liking for the *Federalist* may have been inspired by Bentham, who consistently recommended it to his disciples (a curious choice, in view of the nature of some of the political thinking therein).

[163] Grote, *Statement on the Question of Parliamentary Reform etc.* (London, 1821), pp. 96-97.

partisans during elections, and agreed that these instructions were commonly acted upon, but denied that this violated any democratic forms. The American caucus, unlike English boroughmongers, was prevented by the provisions of secret voting from using bribery or intimidation to gain votes. Its only influence was therefore a moral influence—it could only 'instruct and persuade'. The ballot was not designed to extinguish such influence, for 'the ascendant of superior ability, the paternal guidance of a tried monitor, are inestimable blessings, when unperverted by any sinister interest, of which it would be unwise to bereave the community.'[164] The belief that all influence exerted by representatives must be moral influence, provided that a democratic identification of interests was mechanistically arrived at, was of course typical of doctrinaire Benthamism.

Grote continued to be a faithful proselyte of such views during the conservative reaction of the 1830's and 1840's. According to *The Times* in 1837, he personified the *movement* system, and was an 'incorrigible doctrinaire'. His advocacy of the ballot lost him electoral support after 1835 and earned him the reputation of being 'frontispiece of a revolutionary code.'[165] He attempted to apply utilitarian standards in the field of historical method and was alarmed by the 'sentimental backslidings' from orthodoxy of the younger Mill in his articles upon Coleridge and Bentham.[166]

Nevertheless, his views by 1869 had come closer to those of Mill and his old antagonist Mackintosh than to those of Bentham. Although still favouring the ballot, he no longer regarded it as a panacea for political ills. He believed that the widening of the English franchise in 1867 had already secured honest voting for all practical purposes; but he minimized this in view of the prevailing supremacy of *party*. The voter was now free to choose the representative he preferred, but his choice was virtually limited to candidates backed by the party machines (a system akin to the American caucus). Mackintosh in 1818 had declared that the caucus system in the United States was in reality an elaboration of the principle of party rather than a democratic device for expressing the popular will (and therefore a disciplinary influence against republican anarchy).[167] Grote's view in 1869 implied a sympathy with this interpretation, although he had repudiated it in 1821. Grote had, moreover, acquired a Victorian complacency about this situation. He thought that the actual composition of Parliament, despite or perhaps because of the party system, represented

[164] Ibid. p. 109. See also *WR*, Vol. 2, July 1824, p. 178.
[165] *The Times*, during the 1837 election, quoted in *Personal Life of Grote*, op cit.. p. 118.
[166] See L. Stephen, *English Utilitarians* (London, 1900), III. 336-8.
[167] *ER*, Vol. 31, No. 61, Dec. 1818, pp. 201-2.

with tolerable fidelity the British people; and he conceded (in opposition to Bentham's conception of the greatest number as a single interest group) that most social groups tended to have group or class opinions rather than any perception of general interests.[168]

Grote's faith in the Benthamite conception of democracy was, like Roebuck's, shaken by the Civil War. Like that of many other British liberals, his sympathy towards the North was alienated by what he regarded as 'the unreasonable and insane language of the Americans against England'.[169] The schism within the Union shattered the long-standing correlation of pure democracy with political stability. It seemed to reinforce the conservative claim that a free society was licentious and doomed to end in anarchy. This disillusionment was expressed in Grote's regretful words of 1869 (elicited in conversation about the United States):

I have outlived my faith in the efficiency of a republican government as a check upon the vulgar passions of the majority in a nation; and I recognise the fact that supreme power lodged in their hands may be exercised quite as mischievously as by a despotic ruler like the first Napoleon. The conduct of the Northern States, in the late conflict with the Southern States, has led me to this conclusion, though it costs me much to avow it, even to myself.[170]

Thus another old-fashioned utilitarian acquired a belated concern with the problem of the possible abuse of power in the democratic society.

The new ideas which challenged, and finally supplanted, the old were contained largely in British writings upon Tocqueville's *Democracy in America*, and especially in a number of articles by John Stuart Mill on American democracy. They will be dealt with separately in Chapter V. There were, however, other writings in Benthamite circles which gave indications of departure from the radical image of the pre-reform era. One intruding influence was that of the abolitionists, whose pessimistic, and often hysterical, accounts of the institution of slavery in the United States tempered the rose-water optimism of the democrats. Bentham had denounced American slavery, and none of the early *Westminster* writers could be found to defend it; but there was little abolitionist fervour

---

[168] *Personal Life of Grote*, op. cit. pp. 312–13.

[169] Ibid. p. 262; letter to G. C. Lewis, 29.12.62. Both Grote and Roebuck had a chauvenistic attitude to America; e.g. Grote commended England's 'perfect neutrality' and objected to the North blaming their misfortunes upon 'guiltless England'.

[170] Ibid. p. 314. Cf. his contemptuous dismissal of the theme of 'tyranny of the majority' in 1837; see *Speech in Favour of the Ballot in the Commons 8.3.37*, published in pamphlet form(Jevons Collection, L.S.E.), p. 89. His words above contrast strangely also with his utilitarian analysis of the causes of popular tumult in his *Statement etc.* (1821), p. 84.

expressed by Benthamite journals until the 1830's.[171] Colonel Perronet Thompson, whose influence in the *Westminster* was paramount after the secession of the Mills and their ablest associates in 1828, was the most fervent zealot in the anti-slavery cause in these years.[172] So savage were his denunciations that the whole democratic system in the United States was embroiled in his criticism, despite his completely orthodox Radical regard for that form of government. The southern slaveholders, he believed, had thrown discredit upon liberalism everywhere:

Take the worst of the bad governments of our Europe [he declared] and see what splendid virtue it is, in comparison with those nests of felons under the abused title of *republics* . . . There is neither tyrant nor barbarism but in America. Mrs. Trollope, and the rest of the musquito-fleet, just scratched America. But Mr. Stuart [whose book was in many ways a pamphlet against slaveholding] has squashed the character of the Southern States for the next two generations.[173]

The *Westminster* in 1836 reviewed E. S. Abdy's *Journal*, which contained a highly antagonistic account of slavery, and concluded that readers would have, after scanning it, 'a highly reduced opinion of American intellect and morals, and a strong sense of the insult put upon the Liberals of Europe by the affectation of fraternity with which they have been honoured'.[174] Harriet Martineau, recruited (somewhat reluctantly on the part of its editor, Mill) to the ranks of the *London and Westminster*, produced in 1838 a dark-hued account of the turbulence and emotionalism directed against the anti-slavery cause in the United States.[175] She passionately defended the American abolitionists, who were 'the spiritual potentates of our age', regarding them as true republicans endeavouring to purge the community of all oppressions of caste based upon colour. Violence and southern tyranny she interpreted in true Radical spirit as 'the immediate and visible off-spring of the old-world, feudal, European spirit which still lives in the institution assailed'.[176] Nevertheless, the picture

[171] John Neal's article in 1826, e.g., condemned slavery, and the mockery it made of 4th of July principles, but emphasized the difficulties of abolition; Jan. 1826, p. 183ff.
[172] See especially his review of Stuart in *WR*, Vol. 18, No. 36, Apr. 1833, Art. 4 (pp. 330–53), and his 'Prospects of the Coloured Races', Vol. 20, No. 39, Jan. 1834, Art. 13.
[173] *WR*, Vol. 18, No. 36, Apr. 1833, p. 352. The southerners had 'given the same kind of blow to every liberal in Europe, that the royalists of France received when their heroine of romance turned out with child'.
[174] *WR*, Vol. 24, No. 47, Jan. 1836, p. 245.
[175] *L & WR*, Vol. 32, No. 1, Dec. 1838, Art. 1 (Martyr Age of the U.S.). The article was later expanded and printed as *The Martyr Age of the U.S.* (New York, 1839, repr. Newcastle, 1840). Miss Martineau became subsequently implicated very heavily in the anti-slavery campaign.
[176] Ibid. pp. 58–9.

of passion, ignorance, and prejudice which she conjured up jarred strangely against the almost idyllic conceptions of pastoral and egalitarian democracy favoured in the earlier decade. Slavery increasingly appeared to be the most serious of cankers eating into the heart of democratic society. Although many Radical thinkers managed to accommodate enthusiasm for the American liberal experiment alongside intense anti-slavery sentiment, the issue was not infrequently a starting-point for a more searching enquiry into the dynamics of free societies—into their potentialities for ill as well as good.

America's failure in other respects to attain the utopia of Radicalism similarly encouraged re-thinking. Political economists of the utilitarian school were dismayed at the disastrous paper-money policy of the various national administrations in the United States, and at the extent of wild financial speculation and careless practices in banking and commerce.[177] The federal system was criticized as an obstacle to central control of currency, and the Americans were advised to link their note issues to a gold standard (advice which ignored the chronic shortage of specie). Some attempt was made to attribute these shortcomings to the undemocratic activities of America's monied aristocracy, represented by Biddle and the Bank of the United States; but the argument was not pushed by middle-class economists to the extent of an attack upon the role of the bourgeoisie in American society. (The time had not yet arrived when the British Left regarded American capitalism as an enemy, and by the time it did the utilitarians were no longer of the Left.) Nor did the economists permit their dislike of Biddle and Co. to blind them to the need in the United States of some measure of national monetary planning.

A deviant approach to the problems of democracy could be detected in some of the ideas of the systematic colonizers in the Benthamite ranks. The views of Wakefield in particular suggest a number of parallels to the attitudes of Tocqueville. Wakefield did not regard democracy as a millennium to be attained and virtually actualized upon the earth in the United States. Like Tocqueville, he regarded it as the inevitable end-product of the historical process, whose triumph must be accepted. He gave warning, however, that in the peculiar economic circumstances of England this triumph was attended by possible evils, which were to be avoided, *not* by the specific remedies derived by Mill and Tocqueville out of American experience, but by the application of sounder economic ideas, and especially by the adoption of his pet ideas upon colonization.[178]

[177] See, e.g., *WR*, Vol. 21, No. 42, Oct. 1834, Art. 1 (Jackson and the Bank of the United States).
[178] See E. G. Wakefield, *England and America—a Comparison of the Social and*

In his analysis Wakefield rejected some important theoretical premises employed in the standard Benthamite use of the American example. He thought it misleading to generalize about the operation of a popular system of government upon the basis of a universal interpretation of human behaviour, believing that, like all forms of government, democracy was affected by the particular economic and social conditions of particular states. If he was a determinist, he was much more an economic than a political determinist. He was ready to argue that, in order that democracy in England might achieve the success of democracy in America, certain socio-economic conditions in the two countries must be approximated. Most important, the condition of the English poor must be ameliorated, for until that class was at least as comfortable, satisfied, and wise as the working class in America, democracy in England was likely to be beset by vulgarity and tumult—a prospect which he delineated in some detail. He had not Grote's confidence that a poor and discontented labouring class, elevated suddenly to power, would refrain from appropriating the property of the rich and repudiating debts, although he believed such a course was opposed to their true interests. The working classes must be persuaded to accept a postponement of universal suffrage until they were better fitted to power, whilst all social effort must be diverted wholeheartedly to that end. Wakefield was convinced that all classes must accept the inevitability of democracy and must immediately, and sincerely, begin striving to render it safe and responsible. The alternative, given industrial conditions in Britain, was that of a violent popular challenge to the *status quo* in the near future.

Six years after the appearance of Wakefield's book a liberal Whig, Richard Monckton Milnes, made some much more critical observations upon the nature of democratic society in America, and his remarks attracted considerable attention when they appeared in the last number of Mill's *London and Westminster*.[179] His article came out in the same issue as Mill's essay on Coleridge, and both in their way exemplified the New Radicalism at odds with that of traditional Benthamism. Indeed, it is plausible to regard Milnes' review of Emerson as marking the *coup de grâce* to Bentham's hegemony in utilitarian thought about America.

Political State of Both Nations (New York, 1834), especially Note V, 'Political Prospects of the English', pp. 90–130. The book is not in fact a systematic comparison of the two countries and Wakefield objected to the sub-title added by the publisher. However, like Bentham, he believed that: 'Comparison is the easiest way to truth' (p. 2). Most of his factual material on the U.S. came from Stuart, *Three Years in North America* (Edinburgh, 1833), a popular work among liberals.

[179] *L & WR*, Vol. 33, No. 2, Mar. 1840, Art. 4 (Emerson's Works—American Philosophy).

Milnes—despite his celebrated amiability towards the Americans—suspected, with Tocqueville, that the likeliest vice of the American system was a moral oppression wielded by numbers. Reviewing Emerson's philosophical works (in the earliest printed appreciation of that writer in England), Milnes was drawn to the American's sorrowful consciousness of the want of originality in his country's literature and thought. The disappointment of liberals was great over this, for they had expected 'when all feudal straps and bondages were snapped asunder, that nature, too long the mother of dwarfs, should reimburse itself by a brood of Titans who should laugh and leap in the continent, and run up the mountains of the West with the errand of genius'.[180] Instead of which, the arts, poetry, and fiction were derivative, the national intellect was 'sluggard', and the new world was filled only with 'the exertions of mechanical skill'. (The words are Emerson's.) Milnes was dismayed by this development and insisted that the explanation was to be sought, *not* entirely in the pioneering condition of the people, but in the social effects of democracy. The constraint of public opinion, because it enjoyed legal confirmation in the political system, was more oppressive in the United States. This was simply the defect of the virtues of freedom of thought, liberal government, and social equality, but it posed a barrier to the free development of mental energy:

Public opinion, the sustainer and protector [he wrote] is also and often the depressor and destroyer . . . if she [the United States] has her Sinai-mounts and cities of refuge, she has too her Inquisitions and Star Chambers, no whit less rigourous in punishment, and thus no less effective for terror.[181]

He pointed to the existence of popular sanctions against the free discussion of the slavery issue in the United States—'and all this standing out in shameless self-contradiction to the most solemn national enunciations of universal liberty and equality'.[182] He also believed that the tyranny of opinion helped to perpetuate intellectual mediocrity, for all original speculation and discovery tended to be in opposition to the public opinion of its time: 'Genius has to create the very atmosphere in which it has to live. Its ideas, books, which energise the "brute, material universe" are by their very nature "unpopular".'[183] How many Galileos, in advance of

[180] Ibid. (quoted), p. 349.
[181] Ibid. p. 351.
[182] Ibid. p. 352.
[183] Milnes commented: 'It has often struck us that this dread of affronting general estimation, this superfluous estimation of the respect and regard of persons who are the mere indices of common opinion, is frequently the one disadvantageous point of contrast between well-informed Americans and good European society.' (Ibid. p. 352.)

opinion, had succumbed to the pervasive intimidations of democratic society in America? Admittedly, public opinion was becoming wiser and more tolerant with the progress of education, but every new truth would have its martyrs; and perhaps more so in the new republic than in the ancient. Milnes toyed with the idea that absolutist forms of government might provide a necessary security for some thinkers, which they would not obtain in a democracy, provided they were content to restrict their enquiry 'within the walls of fixed institutions'. German speculation had attained 'boundless heights' despite Germany's authoritarian governments. In any case free societies—and especially the American—were not prone to questioning their own variety of establishment. Despite their Revolutionary tradition, Americans were notoriously indisposed to political innovation, and preferred any usage of their own antiquity 'to the unproductive service of thought'.

In Milnes's view these unfortunate tendencies were aggravated by the ascendancy of materialistic values in the society—and here he allowed some credence to the orthodox view that pioneering circumstances had largely determined this cluster of attitudes. Deep philosophy was not to be expected as long as men were of necessity engaged in the pursuit of wealth— as long as money and gain were the 'sum and substance' of American life:

The task of reconciling the exercise of the daily duties of social existence with that of the higher faculties and the nobler aspirations is painfully difficult. . . . The work of the present moment there demands the entire man; he must be of the world or out of it; the sole tenure of respectability and regard among his fellow-men is his ability to do the thing that is before him; and this condition of itself operates as an exclusion from all search of truth for truth's sake; and, indeed, from all provinces of speculation whatever.[184]

Milnes was not completely satisfied with these explanations of American shortcomings, and sought for more general causes. In framing the questions he wanted answered, he revealed his sympathy with Tocqueville's, rather than Bentham's, mode of analysis:

Why [he asked] should America continue to authorise the assertion of the monarchists of the Old World, that there is something in the shape and character of those social institutions, which is inconsistent with the pursuit of nobler objects than lie in the street or the mart, or even the Hall of Congress! Why is industry there to be so sterile of intellectual elevation, and governed by laws 'à-la-mode et à la médiocrité'? Why is the man who is contented with the little that lies within his grasp, and prefers to limit his desires to his means, rather than extend his means even beyond his decent desires, an isolated phenomenon in the United States?

[184] Ibid. pp. 346–7.

Why is it disreputable to be poor, and retired, and thoughtful, and tranquil? Why is the whole country a home for genius of hand, and a desert for genius of head?[185]

Milnes suggested causes in the modern spirit of a commercial age and detected similarities between the English and American situations. His analysis showed affinities with Tory thinking. Both nations, he said, were infected by a modern concern for the 'dignity of labour'. As Carlyle put it, 'Tools and the man, that were now our epic.' Modern majesty consisted in work, in striving after commercial success, rather than in intellectual pursuits. In the final analysis, Milnes believed that these effects had a more complex causation than that of mere democratic ascendancy (a view similar to Mill's). He suggested, for example, that they might represent a reaction against the excessive introspection of the age.

This sort of searching enquiry into the deeper reaches of the American national character was a startling contrast to the often arid and doctrinaire discussions of the earlier Benthamites. It is possible that Milnes derived some of his ideas directly from Tocqueville, whom he met in London in 1835 and with whom he was to remain closely acquainted. He had almost certainly read the *Democracy in America* and Mill's review of it; and his ideas probably owed something to both, as well as to Emerson. What is certain is that, in a characteristic way, Milnes's ideas typified a current and growing liberal disposition to question American democracy. In doing so they marked the departure of liberal thinking from the categories of the utilitarian analysis.

[185] Ibid. p. 353. The works of Emerson reviewed by Milnes included his *Nature* (1836), *Orations* (1837, 1838), and *Address . . . before . . . Divinity College, Cambridge* (1838).

CHAPTER III

WHIGGERY AND AMERICA

. . . when the drivelling advocates of hierarchy and legitimacy vent their paltry sophistries with some shadow of plausibility in the history of the Old World, [freemen] can turn with decisive triumph to the unequivocal example of the New and demonstrate the unspeakable advantages of free government, by the unprecedented prosperity of America. (Francis Jeffrey, 1820)

There is an opinion that American democracy has outlived the virtues of its founders, and has become corrupt and acquisitive, envious, factious, and insensible to honour. (James Spedding, 1850)

As WE have seen, there has been a tendency among historians of the Anglo-American connection to suggest a fairly rigid dichotomy in English opinion about America before 1850.[1] On the one hand, it is suggested, there were the Radicals—the excluded classes of society— who, by tradition and in principle, favoured the United States and its institutions. Confronting them was the Establishment, opposed to innovation, and especially democratic innovation, embittered by memories of 1776 and 1812, and therefore thoroughly anti-American. The broad truth of this dichotomy is beyond doubt. But it involves a severe simplification. As shown in the last chapter, it is less than fair to the Benthamites, many of whom ceased to be apologists of American democracy after 1832, when their sensitivity about exclusion had been appeased. Less forgivably, it tends to ignore a force at least equal in strength to the Radicals or the High Tories, the whole weight of the centre, the whole weight of middle-of-the-way Whiggery. Whig impressions of America were of a different order to those of the Benthamites, but they also were affected by changing domestic circumstances in Britain. On the whole, Whig ideas are best viewed in the context of a distinctive Whig tradition, not as part of either Radical or Tory opinion.

Although Whig attitudes, as we shall see, were much more complex than a simple approbation or rejection, the Whigs certainly approved of

[1] See, e.g., Henry Pelling, *America and the British Left* (London, 1956), pp. 1–4; and Frank Thistlethwaite, *The Anglo-American Connection in the Early Nineteenth Century* (Philadelphia, 1959), Ch. 2, and his 'America and Two Nations of Englishmen', *Virginia Quarterly Review*, XXXI (Autumn 1955), 505–25. This chapter has appeared in an abridged form in the *Bulletin of the British Assoc. for American Studies*, No. 3, New Series (Dec. 1961), 4–17.

America—despite an American tradition to the opposite effect.[2] Whig
journalists praised unstintingly the achievement of an Anglo-Saxon people
carving out a great new Empire. According to Francis Jeffrey, the editor
of the great Whig journal the *Edinburgh Review*, the Americans were
'brave, enterprising, acute, industrious and patriotic'.[3] The Rev. Sydney
Smith, although perhaps better remembered for his criticisms, described
the Americans as 'a wise, a reflecting, and a virtuous people'.[4] William
Empson, another *Edinburgh Reviewer*, marvelled at America's mushroom
growth during the 1820's and predicted that here was being laid the
foundations of an Empire greater than that of the Caesars.[5] In 1842 the
political economist Nassau Senior wrote of the Republic that 'those now
living may see her possessing one hundred millions of people, irresistible
in her own hemisphere, and a match for all that could be opposed to her
in ours'.[6]

Like the utilitarians, the Whigs were impressed by the diffusion of
material prosperity in the United States. The Americans, said Sydney
Smith in 1824, 'quite put into the background everything which has been
done in the Old World for the improvement of the lower orders'.[7] 'We
must admit', wrote Senior eighteen years later, 'that the millions of
Anglo-Americans form a community enjoying more comfort and more
intelligence than any other equally numerous population.'[8] Would-be
emigrants were consistently advised by Whig journals to settle in North
America.

The majority of Whigs commended the stability of America's political
system, the lightness of her financial burdens, the freedom of her press,
her religious toleration, and her unparalleled system of education. They
were divided upon the subject of democratic institutions, but, as good
Whigs, sympathized with the broad characteristics of American liberalism.
They refused to defend the literary detractors of the Republic: William
Empson headed the *Edinburgh*'s attack on the Trollopes, Halls, and
Marryats who 'had come across the Atlantic to quiz the rustics through an

[2] See, for example, Robert Walsh, *Appeal from the Judgments of Great Britain
respecting the U.S.A., etc.* (Philadelphia, 1819), pp. 211–305; Henry Cabot Lodge,
One Hundred Years Peace (New York, 1913), pp. 43–63; E. D. Adams, 'The Point of
View of the British Traveller in America,' *Pol. Sc. Quart.*, XXIX (1914), 244–64.

[3] *ER*, No. 66, May 1820, p. 407.

[4] *ER*, No. 80, July 1824, p. 432. 'The example of America', he added, 'will in
many instances tend to open the eyes of Englishmen to their true interests.' Ibid. p. 427.

[5] *ER*, No. 110, July 1832, especially pp. 524–5; and an article of his in *ER*, June
1829, pp. 484ff. Ascriptions of authorship are given in an Appendix.

[6] *ER*, No. 151, Apr. 1842, p. 11 (France, America and Britain).

[7] *ER*, No. 80, July 1824, p. 432.

[8] *ER*, No. 151, Apr. 1842, p. 11.

opera lorgnette'.[9] Economists such as J. R. McCulloch emphasized the importance of the Atlantic economy.[10] Finally, in the sphere of tangled Anglo-America relations, the *Edinburgh* and other Whig journals tried to maintain, until the 1850's at least, a more balanced view than some other sections of the British press. The *Edinburgh* sided with the Americans upon the issue of impressment, the *casus belli* in 1812, and pleaded for a speedy settlement of the Maine and Oregon border disputes, which arose during the late thirties and early forties. On the latter issues the *Edinburgh* combined with the moderates in the party against the intransigent policies of Palmerston in office in 1840, and out of office in 1845.[11] Most Whigs deplored the prospect of a war, occasioned over negligible tracts of forest yet threatening the vast mutual interests and affinities of the two countries. This viewpoint reflected the opinion of the financial and commercial classes with whom Whiggism had long been in alliance. With the American annexation of Texas (in 1845), and the Mexican War (1846–7), attitudes became more jaundiced in England, but Whig opinion remained firmly opposed to war.

Regard for the United States was, however, tempered by reservations, for eulogy was by no means the long suit of the typical Whig. It was, indeed, the pragmatism of the Whig appraisal which distinguished it most readily from that of the Radicals. Whigs disliked many aspects of American life, and candidly stated their dislike without unduly considering transatlantic sensitivities. There was a widespread impression, as Jeffrey said, that no nation ought to desire such a 'constant cockering of praise'; and Sydney Smith echoed the sentiment: 'That Americans, who have done so much for themselves, and received so much from nature, should be flung into such convulsions by English Reviews and Magazines is really a sad specimen of Columbian juvenility.'[12]

[9] *ER*, No. 110, July 1832, p. 521 (America and her Detractors), by Empson. His biting review of Marryat's *Diary in America* in 1839 earned the comment from Jeffrey that it was 'something too savage, although . . . the castigation makes pleasant reading'. (Jeffrey to Macvey Napier, 20.10.1839, in *Selections from the Corresp. of . . . Macvey Napier*, ed. by his son (London, 1877).)

[10] See J. R. McCulloch, *A Descriptive and Statistical Account of the British Empire*, 3rd ed. (London, 1847), p. 532. Some of McCulloch's more important references to the United States were in the *Edinburgh*, e.g., No. 112, Jan. 1833, Art. 7 (Stuart on America).

[11] When Senior in 1845 argued that most of the American claims in Oregon ought to be ceded, he was strongly opposed by Palmerston, Russell, Clarendon, Macaulay, and other leading Whigs (now in Opposition); see *ER*, No. 165, July 1845, Art. 8 (The Oregon Question), by Senior; and *Selections from the Correspondence of the late Macvey Napier*, ed. by his son (London, 1879), pp. 500–1 (hereafter *Napier Corresp.*). For the Maine border issue, see *ER*, No. 144, July 1840, pp. 582–93.

[12] Smith in *ER*, No. 80, July 1824, p. 433; Jeffrey, *ER*, No. 66, May 1820, p. 430. One writer felt that the Americans 'reject everything as an insult which stops short of unqualified panegyric'. *ER*, Vol. 24, July 1835, p. 383.

The typical Whig found distasteful the 'swagger' of the American nation and the coarseness of manners. Unlike the Benthamites, he did not easily overlook the small achievement of Americans in literature and the arts. Censure of American culture was especially severe in these early years. Sydney Smith earned everlasting displeasure across the Atlantic by writing in 1820:

The Americans are a brave, industrious, and acute people; but they have hitherto given no indications of genius, and made no approaches to the heroic . . . they have done absolutely nothing for the Sciences, for the Arts, for Literature, or even for the statesman-like studies of Politics or Political Economy . . . Where are their Foxes, their Burkes, their Sheridans . . . where their Arkwrights, their Watts, their Davys?—their Robertsons, Blairs, Smiths, Stewarts, Paleys or Malthuses? . . . In the four quarters of the globe, who reads an American book? or goes to an American play? or looks at an American picture or statue? . . . what new constellations have been discovered by the telescopes of Americans? What have they done in the mathematics . . .?[13]

Nine years later, William Hazlitt complained that 'the genius of America is essentially mechanical and modern'.[14] The United States, it seemed, had neither the leisure nor the traditions to produce great literature: it was a practical nation engrossed in science and the necessary, rather than in meditation or the agreeable. By the 1840's, however, Whigs like Herman Merivale (Professor of Political Economy at Oxford) looked to the Tidewater cities as potential centres of culture, from which the boisterous West might ultimately be civilized.[15] By 1850 there were some indications that culture and enlightenment were spreading: Sydney Smith, it seemed, was being confounded by the Storys and Kents of the new world. As James Spedding, the literary Whig, put it:

There are readers who never crossed the Atlantic, who figure to themselves all America to be spitting on the carpet, all American religion to be that of a Smith and a Miller, and all American law to be that of a Lynch,—the truth being that Americans do spit more than is approved of in England; that Lynch is still an indispensable man in the backwoods; and that the Mormons have founded a State: but the truth being also, that the best society and manners are to be found in the States; that the gradations of law rise from Lynch, through Kent, up to Story,

[13] ER, No. 65, Jan. 1820, pp. 78–80 (Seybert's Statistical Annals of the U.S.), by Smith. Parts of this article were later reprinted widely in Smith's published essays.
[14] ER, Oct. 1829, p. 127 (American Literature). Hazlitt rated most highly Franklin, Crèvcoeur and Jonathan Edwards.
[15] ER, No. 167, Jan. 1846, p. 134; see also ER, No. 188, Oct. 1850, Art. 2, by James Spedding.

one of the first of modern jurists; and gradations of religion from the fanaticism of Smith up to the Christian theism of Channing. . . .[1]

The Whigs, who traditionally relied upon a modicum of Dissenting support, applauded the liberal aspects of the voluntary system in America, but they were very often repelled by the excessive 'enthusiasm' of American sects. They approved the freedom of the press from government taxation, but recoiled from the low standards, partisanship, and venality of the Union's cheap newspapers. The literary piracy of the Americans in matters of copyright also came under fire from reviewers with a bread-and-butter interest in the publishing trade. Whigs, finally, could never be prevailed upon to regard benevolently the South's 'peculiar institution' of slavery. Their cries for Negro emancipation, loudest in the mouth of Lord Brougham, swelled the chorus which provoked Calhoun and other Southerners into dogmatic defences of their way of life after 1830. America, indeed, was never a utopia to the Whigs; but, until the fifties, there was a very real feeling on their part that most faults were lesser matters. A ready explanation could usually be found for them, especially in the circumstances of the frontier.

1. *The Radical Phase*

It was not necessary that political conclusions should be drawn from the observations given above. James Spedding, one of the Whig intelligentsia, wrote of the Republic that 'it is altogether such a scene of political youth, strength, excitement, inexperience, opportunity, enterprise and hope as the world presents nowhere else between the poles';[2] but he did not therefore need to espouse, or reject, a democratic theory of politics. American experience was perceived to be so pertinent to British at this time, however, that observation frequently did lead to a political commitment of some kind. What is perhaps surprising is that the commitment of Whigs was often to a relatively radical idea.

This was especially true of the ten or twelve years preceding the Reform Bill, when facts about America were useful propaganda in the cause of change. Reform-minded Whigs had been urging some measure of Parliamentary purification since Grey's abortive move against patronage and corruption in 1793. By the 1820's many of the party were committed

[1] *ER*, No. 188, Oct. 1850, pp. 367–8 (Lyell's Second Visit to the United States), by Spedding. On spitting, Smith had this to say: 'We are terribly afraid that some Americans spit upon the floor . . . Now all claims to civilization are suspended till this secretion is otherwise disposed of. No English gentleman has spit upon the floor since the Heptarchy.' *ER*, No. 80, July 1824, p. 434.
[2] *ER*, No. 188, Oct. 1850, p. 371.

to some redistribution of representation in favour of the new and populous areas created by the Industrial Revolution. The pressure for reform came from the new industrial and trading interests born out of the changes in technology and the development of capitalism after 1760. Their cause was taken up effectively by the more forward-looking Whigs, who were conscious of the effeteness of Old Whiggery, and who found a platform in journals such as the youthful and relatively radical *Edinburgh Review*. Pressure was brought to bear against recalcitrant Whigs in Parliament, as well as against the Tories. By 1831 most of the Whig M.P.s had been won over and were campaigning for a franchise which admitted to the vote the bulk of the propertied middle class. Under such circumstances, the American example became popular. If universal suffrage worked in America—so ran the familiar argument—who could deny the feasibility of a £10 householder franchise in Britain? The Radicals were asking similar questions at this time, and these years saw the closest approximation between their language about the United States, and that of the Whigs. After the Tory Reaction both groups were influenced by an upsurge of liberal feeling which wished to transcend national boundaries. In these years the Greeks were struggling against their Turkish overlords, young Italian patriots strove for national independence, and Poland was in incipient revolution. Expatriates from Metternich's Europe thronged London and encouraged pan-liberalism. As the Unitarian orator W. J. Fox expressed it in 1824:

There is less of that narrow and selfish patriotism which used to exult in the slavish condition of other countries. It has given way to a nobler feeling—to sympathise with all who are struggling to be free. . . . The cause of liberty is one and indivisible. The sympathy of its friends is characteristic of the present age. The consolidation of their union may emancipate a future generation.[1]

The *Edinburgh Review* played a leading role in popularizing the United States before Reform; and for that reason the ideas of its contributors, who were numerous and constituted something of a microcosm of Whiggery, bulk large in the following pages. Founded by Francis Jeffrey, Henry Brougham, Francis Horner, and Sydney Smith in 1802 as an irreverent Whig journal, the *Edinburgh* was still ultra-liberal by Whig lights until the 1830's. Francis Jeffrey, as editor until 1829, had much to do with adding democratic overtones to Whig comment on American

[1] *WR*, Vol. 1, No. 1, Jan. 1824, p. 3. Fox wrote this first article in the first number of the *Westminster* in the nature of an advertisement and a statement of faith; and it is apparent why comparison with other liberal countries was a feature of following numbers.

affairs. In an article of 1820 he criticized 'scurrilous' Tory attacks upon American democracy:

There is a party in this country not friendly to political liberty, and decidedly hostile to all extension of popular rights . . . which thinks the peace and well-being of society in no danger from anything but popular encroachments, and holds the only safe or desirable government to be that of a pretty pure and unincumbered Monarchy, supported by a vast revenue and a powerful army, and obeyed by a people just enlightened enough to be orderly and industrious, but no way curious as to questions of right—and never presuming to judge of the conduct of their superiors.

Now it is quite true that *this Party* dislikes America, and is apt enough to decry and insult her. Its adherents never have forgiven the success of her war of independence . . . and, above all, the happiness and tranquillity which she enjoys under a republican form of government. Such a spectacle of democratical prosperity is unspeakably mortifying to their high monarchical principles, and is easily imagined to be dangerous to their security.[1]

Jeffrey declared the friendship of British liberals to America 'and to all that Americans most value in their character and institutions':

Freemen rejoice to see freedom spreading itself, with giant footsteps, over the fairest regions of the earth, and nations flourishing exactly in proportion as they are free . . . the very existence of such a country, under such a government, is a tower of strength, and a standard of encouragement, for all who may hereafter have to struggle for the restoration or the extension of their rights. It shows within what limits popular institutions are safe and practicable; and what a large infusion of democracy is consistent with the authority of government, and the good order of society.[2]

Such sentiments would have passed muster in a Radical dissertation: warm approval was given to American democracy; qualifications were muted (there was no clear indication within what *English* 'limits' popular institutions would be safe); and American principles were deemed to be universal —Jeffrey did not, like Mackintosh, emphasize 'propitious circumstances'. He asserted instead that the American experiment ought to be viewed as part of a world-wide contest between the principles of 'Reform and Liberty' and those of 'Established Abuse, Legitimacy, or Tyranny'. Jeffrey apparently suppressed for the occasion some of his private misgivings about the United States and democracy.[3] John Stuart Mill was

---

[1] *ER*, No. 66, May 1820, pp. 399–400.
[2] Ibid. pp. 400, 405.
[3] Before 1832 he had complained to his brother, and to his American friend Charles Wilkes, about party violence and vulgarity in the Union; and after 1832 he opposed further extensions of the suffrage in Britain. See Lord Cockburn, *The Life and Correspondence of Francis Jeffrey* (London, 1852), II. 49, 147, 183–5; and *Napier Corresp.*, letter from Jeffrey to Napier, 27.12.1837. Napier was editor of the *ER* from 1829 until 1847.

convinced that political tactics underlay the public expression of such opinions.[1] Jeffrey, he claimed, was using the Whig technique, which encouraged an exposition of democratic sentiments and loud praise of reform in general, but which in reality sought only to rally support for what would prove to be a bourgeois reform.

Jeffrey was ably supported by his son-in-law Empson, a Professor at Haileybury, a close friend of Macaulay and Malthus, and a later editor of the *Review*. Empson was no Radical—Henry Brougham once sneered at the 'Lansdowne House tone' of his writings.[2] He had read some American history, and was not inclined to idealize it, but had nevertheless a high regard for Republican government.[3] He rejected as nonsense the charge that the American system was repulsive to English feelings; this 'would almost justify the assertion that England will not tolerate the idea of any country prospering under a greater degree of liberty than what she herself enjoys'.[4]

It ought not surely to require any great philosophy or temper in a foreigner, however fresh about him he may carry his European sympathies, to bear in patient mind that he has got into a new world, where the religious and political atmosphere of a Republic, though at first a little sharp, may possibly be no less healthy than the artificial warmth of our old-established climate of Church and King. . . .[5]

Empson's assault upon Mrs. Trollope's 'libels' in 1832 was altogether in the Whig interest, for her book had been a threat to the successful use of American parallels in the clamour for the Bill:

Four and thirty chapters of American scandal are dished up with the immediate purpose of contrasting the graceful virtues of a boroughmonger with the profligate vulgarity of a ten pound franchise. . . . If she uncovers the nakedness of our Transatlantic children, it is out of pure alarm for the English Constitution. . . . The miseries of squatters, and the servant talk of Cincinatti, are the appropriate materials for establishing the advantages of a government by the few over a government by the many.[6]

The crushing refutation of her charges illustrated an equally obvious, but converse, political interest.

[1] *WR*, No. 2, Apr. 1824, p. 513.
[2] Brougham to Napier, 18.8.1837, in *Napier Corresp.*, p. 193.
[3] Of the Americans he wrote that: 'Their republican form of government, in its hardy attempt to solve out and out the old problem of ruling all by all, is necessarily the most striking object of hope and contemplation that modern politics have ventured to propose.' *ER*, June 1829, p. 474. See also ibid. p. 496.
[4] Ibid. p. 521.
[5] *ER*, No. 102, July 1830, p. 498. By 1839, however, he was much more cautious about the prospects of democracy—'. . . the periods are so short and the places so few, in which it has any probability of succeeding.' See *ER*, Oct. 1839, p. 133.
[6] *ER*, No. 110, July 1832, p. 496.

Although the Whig enthusiasm for American institutions waned after 1832, those institutions still had power to capture the imagination of individuals. Brougham in 1837 could describe the Declaration of Independence as the most important event in the history of mankind:

If tyrants are sometimes said to feel uneasy on the 30th of January, how much more fitted to inspire alarm are the recollections associated with the 4th of July, in which nothing like remorse can mingle on the people's part, and no consolation is afforded to their oppressors by the tendency of cruelty and injustice to mar the work they stain.[1]

Even Nassau Senior, a severe critic of the United States, admitted that 'with the exception of our own, we know of no great country whose institutions we prefer; and we doubt whether there is one of our readers who would not rather be an Anglo-American, than a Frenchman, a Spaniard, an Austrian, a Russian, or even a Prussian'.[2]

To liberals of a new school, America of the 1840's and 1850's was the land of progress in an age which was beginning to enshrine the values of progress. One such liberal Whig was Herman Merivale, Professor of Political Economy at Oxford from 1837 to 1842, a classical scholar, a man who was closely interested in emigration to North America and who became Under-Secretary for the Colonies from 1847 to 1859. In his *Lectures on Colonization* Merivale emphasized the value of the United States to Britain as an outlet for surplus British and Canadian labour.[3] Friendly relations must be maintained, he argued, or else there would be a population explosion in England, and revolution might be feared. But Merivale had more positive reasons for closely scrutinizing American politics. He believed that the advance of technology in the world was certain to encourage the spread of democratic government, because it accelerated unifying and centralizing political tendencies—tendencies which rendered free institutions workable. The United States, in his view, was living proof of the fact that, in an increasingly interdependent world, 'we must accustom ourselves to the contemplation of space and numbers as the greatest future elements of political greatness'.[4] Most Whigs recognized that the transition to this state of affairs involved dangers of dislocation and the creation of new vices in society. Transatlantic democracy, as James Spedding conceded, was 'vehement, turbulent, over-bearing, and

[1] *ER*, No. 131, Oct. 1837, p. 167 (Tucker's Life of Jefferson).
[2] *ER*, No. 151, Apr. 1842, p. 11 (France, America and Britain).
[3] Merivale, *Lectures on Colonization and Colonies* (London, 1841), I. 110-13. These were lectures delivered at Oxford, 1839-41.
[4] See Merivale's review of Chas. Lyell, *Travels in North America* (London, 1845), in *ER*, No. 167, Jan. 1846, p. 141. 'Steam', he added 'will render the action of the people on the government, in great emergencies, irresistible . . .' Ibid.

often overreaches itself'. As he added: 'It is however the toil and struggle of men engaged, with various fortune, in the battle of life.'[1] Spedding, best known as the editor of Bacon's works, was a staunch liberal who moved freely in Whig literary and intellectual circles; he had been a secretary on the Ashburton mission to the United States in 1842; and he thought that the American experiment in liberalism, tried in the best of circumstances, was a crucial one:

> The vigour of population corresponds there to the scale of nature. All the wants of civilized men are developed, and all the means of satisfying them are within reach; the war against the wilderness keeps all energies alive, feeding them with victory and hope; and all the experience of the Old World comes in to aid, to guide, to encourage, and to warn. If freedom be doomed to end in rebellion against God and anarchy among men, America will unteach the world an error of 2000 years. If, on the contrary, self-government be the secret of society, or the right way towards it, America is the land of promise, and the object of highest hope as well as of liberal curiosity.[2]

Spedding was impressed by the natural vivacity of American democracy and found in it the answer to those critics who prophesied the disintegration of the Union over slavery. His hopes resided with the northern states, which he expected to civilize the South as they were constantly civilizing the West.

Praise of democracy *per se* was, however, outside the true Whig tradition. The decade before 1832 saw the height of the flirtation with the American democratic idea. It seems plausible that the Whig publicists were sucked into the vortex of popular agitation for Reform, and assumed a position about transatlantic democracy more left of centre than they actually desired. It was certainly more left of centre than that of Old Whigs like Mackintosh, or aristocratic Whig M.P.s like the young Edward Stanley.[3] Yet even during the twenties the attitudes of Jeffrey, Empson, and their fellows could be distinguished from those of the Radicals.

[1] See Spedding's review of Chas. Lyell, *Second Visit to the United States, etc.* (London, 1849), in *ER*, No. 188, Oct. 1850, p. 367.

[2] Ibid. p. 341.

[3] Mackintosh favoured Reform as the lesser of evil alternatives. He urged on the Tories the need for concessions, pointing to the American Revolution as an example of what happened when the old guard refused to make them. See Speech in Commons on second reading of the Reform Bill, 4.7.1831, in *Miscellaneous Works of . . . Sir James Mackintosh*, ed. R. J. Mackintosh (Philadelphia, 1847), p. 590. But he never approved of representative democracy as such, once describing it as 'the most monstrous of all governments, because it is impossible at once to act and to controul, and, consequently, the sovereign power . . . must be left without any check whatsoever' (1797). See *Memoirs of the Life of . . . Mackintosh*, ed. R. J. Mackintosh (Boston, 1853), I. 92. For Stanley's views on the new world see his *Journal of a Tour in America: 1824-1825* (privately printed, London, 1930).

They were ready at times to sympathize with 'the pattern of that just equality'[1] in the condition of the Americans; but the tenor of their argument was never revolutionary. They at no stage advocated the transference of republican institutions to Britain,[2] or urged, indeed, any wholesale subversion of the established order. They repudiated any idea that political democracy could, of itself, encompass the salvation of mankind, and usually implied that only some, and those carefully selected, of the delicate growths of political usage in the Union would bear transplanting to the considerably different conditions of the old world. They refused, in short, to idealize the United States to the extent of the Radical eulogy. Although the party was under powerful pressure to extend the basis of power in the state, most Whigs retained a vested interest in an hierarchical society. They were emphatically not attempting to create a new America in England, but simply using comparison to achieve immediate and limited ends.

This being so, the Whig ardour for transatlantic panaceas faded noticeably after the Bill had been achieved and the middle-class millennium had been proclaimed. As the Chartist clamour rose for America's ballot and universal suffrage, liberal suspicion of these measures intensified; and when the reform issue was raised again in the 1850's, some of the Old Whigs became positively anti-American in their efforts to oppose change.

2. *Ebbing of the Tide*

William Hazlitt was a harbinger of later criticisms. American democracy, he declared in 1829, imposed a strait-jacket upon independent thought. Thus he accounted for the sterility of literature in the United States, His argument was similar to that used by Tocqueville four years later:

Where there is perfect tolerance—where there is neither Censorship of the Press nor Inquisition, the public takes upon themselves the task of *surveillance*, and exercises the functions of a literary police, like so many familiars of the *Holy Office*. In a monarchy or mixed government, there is an appeal open from the government to the people; there is a natural opposition, as it were, between prejudice, or authority, and reason: but when the community take the power into their own hands, and there is but one body of opinion, and one voice to express it, there can

---

[1] Empson, writing in *ER*, No. 110, July 1832, p. 521. 'The experiment they are trying', he continued, 'is . . . as reasonable in itself, as it is honourable to themselves, and deeply interesting to mankind.'

[2] A republic, said Empson, might be admirably suited to America, but 'in the present state of our general education, political morality, and starving population, we believe that a republic in England would not last twelve months' (ibid. p. 497). This view was typical: see Brougham in *ER*, No. 111, Oct. 1832, p. 257; and a review, No. 112, Jan. 1833, pp. 495–6.

7

be no *reaction* against it; and to remonstrate or resist, is not only a public outrage, but sounds like a personal insult to every individual in the community. . . . Hence the too frequent cowardice, jesuitism, and sterility, produced by this republican discipline and drilling. Opinions must march abreast. . . . Whoever outstrips, or takes a separate path to himself, is considered as usurping an unnatural superiority over the whole. He is treated not with respect or indulgence, but indignity.[1]

Even Jeffrey conceded that, of all sovereigns, the Sovereign People were most susceptible to the corruption of flattery: 'In America, everything depends on their suffrages, and their favour and support; and accordingly it would appear, that they are pampered with constant adulation, from the rival suitors for their favour—so that no one will venture to tell them of their faults, and moralists . . . dare not venture to whisper a syllable of their prejudice.'[2]

The consequence, as Emerson later observed, was to encourage the withdrawal of tender consciences from the social organization. The Whigs were firm believers in the need for property and education as essential qualifications for office, and they failed to notice the application of such tests in the Republic. Up to the Civil War they became progressively disillusioned about the stature of public men in the Union. It seemed that the Franklins, Washingtons, and Jeffersons—men of whom any nation might be proud—were being succeeded by demagogues and nonentities. Andrew Jackson made a poor impression in England, liberals fearing that he might suspend the Constitution and assume dictatorial powers; and names like Harrison and Taylor were unknown. Clay, Calhoun, and Webster were best known and respected; but why, it was asked, had none attained the Presidency? Men, as Chamfort said, became like the fiends of Milton: '. . . they must make themselves dwarfs, before they can enter the Pandemonium of political life in a republic.'[3]

Such doubts about democracy were muted in the *Edinburgh Review* during the 1830's, largely because Empson wrote most of the comment about the United States during that decade (as Smith and Jeffrey monopolized the subject during the 1820's). Even so, there were signs of unrest at the triumph of a thoroughgoing Jacksonian democracy apparently committed to more aggressive international and commercial policies. Many

---

[1] *ER*, Oct. 1829, p. 132 (American Literature), by Hazlitt.

[2] *ER*, No. 66, May 1820, p. 430.

[3] Quoted, *ER*, No. 194, Apr. 1852, p. 517. Is it not notorious, asked one reviewer, that 'the ablest, purest, and noblest of [America's] sons habitually retire from public life, or are snubbed or neglected if they enter it? and that their greatest statesmen are never chosen for the highest offices or honours of the State?' *ER*, No. 196, Oct. 1852, p. 464. On the other hand, it was often agreed that the United States needed little government anyway.

Whigs, furthermore, were bored with the indiscriminate praise of the Radicals, with whom political relations were now strained. McCulloch was irked into writing, in 1833, that

We are sick of the appeals so frequently made in this country, in political matters, to the example of America. Her experience is certainly not to be neglected, and it affords some valuable lessons by which we ought to profit. Still, however, her situation differs in so many respects from that of England, or any other European country, that nothing can be more absurd than to contend, that an institution may be safely adopted here, because it has been found to answer in America. . . .[1]

Laissez faire economists were able to spike a favourite argument of the Chartists by refusing to attribute working-class prosperity in the Union to democracy—such blessings, said one writer, depended not upon such 'indefinite notions' but 'upon the proportion between the supply of labour and the remunerating demand for it'.[2] The free traders located the cause in the absence of any internal barriers to trade, and only lamented that the federal government was not so enlightened in its external tariff policy. The delight of the Whig economists over American economic development was qualified, however, by their dismay over the unorthodox financial practices, and the welter of conflicting monetary policies, which were allowed to exist within the states. According to McCulloch, the *Edinburgh*'s economic expert, such practices had contributed directly to the wild speculation and inflation which caused the panic of 1837, and disrupted Anglo-American trade.[3] The 1837 crisis created a great stir in London, and resentment rode high against the American defaulters in the great merchant houses, some of which failed during the depression. If egalitarian democracy encouraged repudiation of debts, it was felt, then America was likely to lose many more of her erstwhile friends. Such sentiments were relayed to the Whigs, traditionally the party of the financial interests; and Sydney Smith coined the inevitable epigram. (Pennsylvania had suspended interest payments, so Smith proposed that the raiment of Pennsylvanian visitors to London should be shared among the state's creditors.) But American credit was basically sound, and resentment in commercial and Whig circles proved to be something of a storm in a teacup. Apart from this matter, many Whigs undoubtedly lacked interest in American affairs. Politics in the Union, they complained, were inextricably complex; parties were indistinguishable, their conflict was only for

[1] *ER*, No. 112, Jan. 1833, p. 481 (Stuart on America).
[2] *ER*, No. 124, July 1835, p. 385 (Mrs. Butler's Journal), possibly by Bulwer-Lytton.
[3] McCulloch on the 'Causes and Consequences of the Crisis in American Trade', *ER*, No. 122, July 1837, Art. 9.

place now that the momentous struggle between aristocracy and democracy had been settled in favour of the latter.[1]

During Macvey Napier's editorship, the *Edinburgh Review* became less
rebellious and more closely connected with the Whig leaders—such as
Russell, Lansdowne, and Monteagle, Macaulay and Cornwall Lewis. As
Bagehot quipped, a younger generation now regarded its appearance 'as a
grave constitutional event';[2] and with the change, its tone towards
America became more caustic. The credit, or blame, belonged mainly to
Nassau Senior, whose long and forceful articles set the tone for the decade.
Senior, the architect of the Poor Law Amendment Act of 1834, laboured
at the very centre of Whig politics, and was an energetic publicizer and a
brilliant party organizer. Although an associate of the Benthamites and a
pioneer in political economy, he came from a prosperous trading family
with Tory sympathies, and was strictly conservative in his approach to the
problem of popular government. The majority in every nation, he
believed '. . . consists of rude, uneducated masses;—ignorant, intolerant,
suspicious, unjust, and uncandid; without the sagacity, which discovers
what is right, or the intelligence which comprehends it when pointed out,
or the morality which requires it to be done.'[3] Such a sovereign body, he
argued, would get the government it deserved. Its representatives would
either reflect its vices or exploit them, while the wise and able would be
excluded from power. He ridiculed the suggestion (put forward in and
out of season by the Benthamites) that the American system at least ensured
the promotion of general interests, as opposed to those of a clique.
Individuals and factions had, throughout history, exploited the people for
selfish ends, and America was no exception to the rule. Circumstances
there were especially favourable for a trial of democracy ('their best men
are equal to ours; the mass of the population is superior to any European
population'), yet popular influence had been accompanied 'by popular
violence, by international litigiousness, by anti-commercial Tariffs, and

[1] See, for example, *ER*, No. 135, Apr. 1838, pp. 189-90 (Martineau's Retrospect
of Western Travel), written possibly by Bulwer-Lytton. English commentators
continued to be bemused by the complexities of the American scene. In 1856 one
writer complained that: 'The kaleidoscopic . . . play of principles and opinions
. . . bewilders the eye . . . In the whirl of "Know Nothings" and "Know Some-
things" . . . of "Hards" and "Softs", of "Fillmore Whigs", and "Old Line Whigs",
and "Fremont Whigs", and "Buchanan Whigs" and "National Democrats" . . .
and "Abolitionists", and "States Rights Men", one is utterly at a loss whither to look
for the representatives of tangible opinions . . .' *ER*, Oct. 1856, p. 563.

[2] Bagehot, *Literary Studies* (London, 1879), I. 1. Essay I, 'The First Edinburgh
Reviewers', gives an excellent account of the kind of Whiggism to be found in the
Edinburgh.

[3] Senior on 'Brougham's Political Philosophy' in *ER*, No. 163, Jan. 1845,
p. 29.

by Repudiation'.[1] Disillusioned by the actions of Americans in Texas and Oregon, appalled by accounts of slavery and political corruption, his faith shaken by their deviant approach to the sacred issues of political economy, Senior found little in the American example to confound his pessimistic analysis of democracy.

Senior insisted that many features of the American Constitution aggravated the natural faults of democracy—constitutional inflexibility, especially, hindering the adaptation of forms to new needs. He did not, like some other Whigs, place great faith in paper guarantees against demagoguery:

The American constitution was a compromise. Its framers gave to it only a qualified approbation. They believed it to be the best which, in the existing state of passions, prejudices, and interests, could be adopted and obeyed; and they looked forward to its working with an anxiety in which fear was predominant. It has on the whole been successful, but it is an unpleasant symptom that its success has not been progressive. During the period of nearly 60 years which has passed since it was constructed, almost every country in Europe has changed its form of government; in almost every country the new constitution has been altered from time to time as its defects became manifest, and has been improved almost from year to year. In the British Isles, where the apparent changes have been the least, the real changes and the real improvements, have been perhaps the greatest. But in the constitution of the U.S. few changes have been made; and most of these have been either unimportant or mischievous. . . .[2]

Senior was dismayed, too, by the convulsive spectacle afforded by Presidential elections: 'Every fourth year the whole Union is convulsed by the struggle which of the two great parties shall have the exclusive enjoyment of the honours, powers and emoluments of office. And the interval is spent in preparations for the contest, which distorts and misdirects the foreign and the domestic policy both of the Government and of the Opposition.'[3] He scathingly attacked the Presidential powers of patronage and the right of re-eligibility to office. The latter, he felt, provided the motive, the former the instrument, for a partisan interpretation of duty. To such corruptive influences he attributed 'the deterioration of the public, and, we fear we must add, the private character of America— the bluster, the vanity, the rapacity, the violence, and the fraud, which render her a disgrace to the Anglo-Saxon race'[4]—severe terms, indeed.

Even Radicals were affected by this mood of disenchantment. By

[1] Ibid. p. 30.
[2] ER, No. 167, Jan. 1846, p. 194 (European and American State Confederacies), by Senior.
[3] Ibid. p. 195.
[4] ER, No. 163, Jan. 1845, p. 35.

1846, according to *Blackwood's* (not an unbiased witness), America's prestige was fading 'as each successive post brings fresh evidence of her vices and her follies':

We can, indeed, recollect a time when the example of the model Republic was held up for admiration in the most respectable quarters, and was the trump-card at every gathering of Radical reformers. But now the scene is changed—now 'none so poor to do her reverence'. Even Chartist and Suffrage-men, Mr. Miall and the Northern Star, have at last

—— 'forgot to speak
That one familiar word'

. . . Mr. O'Connell himself can find no room in his capacious affections for men who repudiate their debts . . . and keep a sixth of their population in chains in the name of liberty![1]

Economic changes in England caused even the manufacturers and members of the Anti-Corn-Law League, hitherto very pro-American, to qualify their praises. As production and conditions improved in home manufacturing during the 1840's, the employers and industrialists began to resent the loss of valuable working-men to the United States. The Anti-Corn-Law League, for this reason, strenuously opposed Wakefieldian theories of systematic emigration. Prominent free traders such as Lord Kinnaird and Hamer Stansfeld, and prominent free trade journals such as *The Struggle*, urged artisans to stay in England and alleged that conditions in the United States were far more miserable than in England.[2]

Enthusiastic admiration for America's social and political system still came from Richard Cobden, the League's moving spirit. A letter to the Scottish educational reformer George Combe in 1848 shows that Cobden's approval was not merely for public consumption:

Look at our race in America—Was there ever in the history of the world a better government than that which plebian Englishmen have organised without crown, coronets or mitres in the New England states, and New York? . . . can such intelligence, civilization, and moral and material well-doing be elsewhere found?[3]

Yet even Cobden had his moments of disillusion. He disapproved of the tariff, of negro slavery, and of American indebtedness. He particularly

[1] *Blackwood's*, Vol. 59, Apr. 1846, pp. 440–1 (How they manage matters in 'The Model Republic'), by a Mr. Gardner.
[2] See *The Struggle*, Nos. 23, 25, 36 (1842). Illinois was singled out as especially inhospitable, in an effort to discourage Mormon emigration to that state. There is a discussion of the attitudes of the Manchester School to emigration in W. S. Shepperson, *British Emigration to North America* (Oxford, 1957), pp. 179–91.
[3] *B.M. Add. MS.* 43,653, Part 4, Cobden to Combe, 17.7.1848. The importance of the United States in Cobden's thinking is brought out in Thistlethwaite, op. cit., pp. 166–72; and in Lillibridge, op. cit., pp. 95–107.

feared, during the Age of Manifest Destiny, that the Republic might repudiate that isolationism which he cherished and embrace imperialism. Thinking on American policy in Texas and Mexico, he once wrote: 'I am more jealous of *their* falling into the marauding and conquering propensities of the old world than any thing besides.'[1] For this reason, he was incensed that military men such as Generals Scott and Cass should be spoken of as candidates for the Presidency in 1851.[2]

Cobden wrote often, too, of the opposition he encountered in his use of the American example. In 1852 he wrote to Sir Edward Watkin:

I have never missed an opportunity of trying to awaken the emulation and even the fears of my countrymen, by quoting the example of the United States. But the only result is, that I am pretty freely charged with seeking to establish a republican government here.[3]

It seems clear that Cobden had no such objective in mind, although he may at times have threatened his opponents with the prospect. His great preoccupation was with America as a gigantic free market, as a nation embracing pacifism, disestablishment, and enlightened social policies. He praised universal suffrage and the republican system, but only as they worked in America. These were not his panaceas for English problems. His faith was in Americans, in their attitude of mind towards other nations and the future, in their disregard for mere tradition and for other relics which were economically unjustifiable—his faith was certainly not in the democratic principle as such. He was much slower than Bright to accept the idea that further franchise reform was needed in England—indeed the two had frequent differences of opinion on the matter during the fifties. Cobden always held that universal suffrage was possible in Britain only in conjunction with universal education;[4] and he stressed to Bright that the middle classes, even the lower orders, were ineradicably conservative. As he wrote in his first pamphlet in 1835:

Democracy forms no element in the materials of English character. An Englishman is, from his mother's womb, an aristocrat. . . . The insatiable love of caste . . . pervades every degree from the highest to the lowest.[5]

Thus, until the fifties, there was not in practice such a wide gulf between

---

[1] Cobden to Henry Richard (of the pacifist *Star*), 23.3.1852, *B.M. Add. MS.* 43,658, Part 2.
[2] See Cobden to Sturge, 15.4.1851, in *B.M. Add. MS.* 43,722, Bundle 1, Part 6.
[3] Quoted in Watkin, *Alderman Cobden of Manchester, etc.* (London, 1891), pp. 166–7.
[4] See *Speeches on Questions of Public Policy by Richard Cobden*, ed. John Bright and J. E. Thorold Rogers (London, 1870), II. 551–2; and II. 522.
[5] Cobden, *England, Ireland and America* (London, 1835), p. 137.

the conclusions drawn by Cobden and the liberal Whigs from American experience—the Ultra-Radicals could not seek immediate consolation from either.

In the 1850's the pessimism of the Whig critics was reinforced by the apparently inexorable trend of events in the Union towards civil war. Indeed, there came to be occasioned something of a reinterpretation of American history. The contemporary slavery issue was read back into the past, and its history was regarded (as it had never been regarded at the time) as the primary theme of American development. American abolitionists directly fostered anti-slavery opinion in England. Nassau Senior, in preparing a leading article of 1855 on the negro question, was assisted by John Chandler Bancroft Davis, who was secretary of the American Legation to Britain from 1849 to 1852 and American correspondent of *The Times* from 1855–61. Another American, William Henry Hurlbert, a New York journalist, had an anti-slavery article published by the *Edinburgh Review* in 1856.[1] Both Davis and Hurlbert were from New York, and they imparted a strong Northern and abolitionist flavour to their writings, which were well received in liberal and humanitarian quarters. Nor was other evidence wanting to show that democrats could be corrupt and tyrannical, even in the Eldorado of the West. The Old Whigs were especially interested in making such criticisms, for the issue of Parliamentary Reform had been revived and they were resolutely opposed to any pervasive change in the basis of representation.[2] Through William Rathbone Greg this group more or less controlled the political policy of the *Edinburgh Review* during the first years of Henry Reeve's editorship; and a rancid Americophobia was the issue.

Greg, the son of a Manchester mill-owner, was a free trader who took up political writing in the fifties. He made quite a mark in this profession, was appointed commissioner to the Board of Trade in 1856, and later produced such anti-labour tracts as *Mistaken Aims and Attainable Ideals of the Working Classes* (1876). Greg described himself to Gladstone as 'decidedly Conservative in all that relates to the further infusion of the democratic element into our Constitution'. He was, he said, a Liberal by

[1] See the following: *ER*, No. 206, Apr. 1855, Art. I (Slavery in the U.S.), by Senior and Davis; *ER*, No. 212, Oct. 1856, Art. 10 (The Political Crisis in the U.S.), by Hurlbert; and *ER*, No. 220, Oct. 1858, p. 572 (The Slave Trade in 1858), anonymous. Evidence respecting the probable authorship of Davis and Hurlbert was obtained from the records of Longmans, Green and Co. (That Davis gave quite considerable help to Senior would seem to be shown by the fact that he received £20 for the article, while Senior received £32.)

[2] See, e.g., *ER*, No. 196, Oct. 1852, Art. 7 (Representative Reform); No. 200, Oct. 1853, Art. 9 (Parliamentary Purification); and No. 215, July 1857, Art. 4 (Representative Reform)—all by W. R. Greg.

early connection, but a thorough 'anti-democrat'.[1] Greg, in his leading articles for the *Edinburgh*, consistently rejected the typically American, and Radical, regard for the franchise as an inherent right of man in a free society. It ought to be conferred, he felt, only upon those who would use it to further desirable national ends. He doubted the capacity of any 'basement class' in society to act so responsibly: '. . . the highest culture will not be theirs; the deepest and knottiest problems of national life must remain insoluble by them.' To regard the will of the majority as sacred, to treat all men as if their virtue and competence were equal, was to invite government by demagogues (as in America) or ultimately by a despot (as in France). 'Is it not too unhappily notorious', Greg asked about America, 'that the tone of public morality has been gradually lowering since the days of Washington? that the standard of national policy is far less wise and worthy than it was?'[2]

Even friends of America, such as Spedding, were aware of the strength of anti-American feeling in Britain. 'There is an opinion', he wrote in 1850, 'that American democracy has outlived the virtues of its founders, and has become corrupt and acquisitive, envious, factious, and insensible to honour.'[3] Justice Story's *Life and Letters* was published in 1851, and his indictment of majority rule seemed to bear out the opinion.

Disparagement achieved its pinnacle in 1857, in an article of Greg's.[4] The Republic, he predicted, was about to pay the ultimate penalty for its institutions. The untutored majority, swollen by 'the promiscuous arrivals of Europe's surplus', had finally succeeded in sweeping away the bulwarks and precautions set up around the Constitution by the wise and noble founders of the Union. American administrations had consequently become subservient to popular caprice in their domestic and foreign policies. 'Most shameful outrages against person and property' were commonly perpetrated, and political corruption was rampant. 'Lobby interests', concerned to manage bills through Congress, were well supplied with 'the means of conciliating members', and the 'machine' had raised its ugly head in politics. Greg informed astounded Whigs that '. . . the whole machinery and management of elections seem to have fallen into the hands of a set of professional demagogues and agents, who

[1] Greg to Gladstone, in Gladstone Papers, B.M. Add. MS. 44,371; fol. 283. Greg was writing to the up-and-coming Gladstone for the first time, trying to convert him to a plan of Reform less radical than that proposed by Russell. Grey wanted the public to think less of Reform as a *lowering* of the franchise than as a remedy of abuses; he hoped his plan would suit the working class, although it would be 'anything but a step in the democratic direction'.
[2] ER, No. 196, Oct. 1852, p. 464; and pp. 455ff. for the preceding quotations.
[3] ER, No. 188, Oct. 1850, p. 367.
[4] ER, No. 215, July 1857, Art. 9 (Representative Reform).

make a regular business of the affair, and even go so far, in some cases, as to *contract for securing a majority*'. Finally, the independence of the Bench— the best security for individual freedom and even-handed justice—was being infringed by election of the judiciary, perhaps the most ominous sign of all.

Such language was in sharp contrast to that used by the *Edinburgh* in the 1820's and 1830's. Never before had the Whigs rejected, in such outright terms, the Radical orthodoxy about America:

Our Radicals [wrote Greg] used to hold up the example of the States, in season and out of season, for our admiration and imitation . . . our souls are vexed with few such paeans and exhortations now. Late events have shown more clearly than of yore whither the great Republic of the West is tending, and how serious are the dangers that wait upon the career of a pure and uncontrolled democracy . . . a few years ago the substantial, deep-seated, long-descended fabric of English liberty was in danger from the blind but honest enthusiasm of the sincere friends of popular institutions; *now*, if we succumb to that peril, we shall be wrecked with our eyes open. The tide has somewhat ebbed, and the rock is above water.[1]

3. *In Vindication of Whiggism*

To concentrate exclusively upon the pessimism of men such as Senior and Greg would be to distort the Whig image of America. Senior and Greg were obsessed by the weaknesses and excesses of republican democracy, and political interest accounted for some of their dismay. Before 1850 Whigs generally took a more balanced view: they showed, indeed, little inclination to view America as a commendation of Radicalism; but, as befitted apostles of minimal government, their vision ranged beyond political blemishes. They took due account of the fact that, in England, amongst the ordinary people and would-be emigrants of North America, the United States represented a land of economic opportunity and of civil liberties—there was little interest in the game of politics as it was played in the Union. As Merivale wrote:

What are slavery and repudiation, and all the black spots which European observation traces on the disk of that Western sun which lures them across the ocean? They [the emigrants] seek the land of promise; and in nine cases out of ten they find it a land of performance. . . . What has continental Europe to compare with this? What has even England, with all the ancient liberality of her institutions, cramped . . . by the necessity of maintaining existing orders of society in a struggling and restless position, and by the complex rights of property, which as necessarily arise in a space so densely crowded? Let us not deceive ourselves. The

[1] Ibid. pp. 263–4. The preceding extract is from p. 267 of the same article.

ultra-democratic career of America may be a warning to our statesmen. Her social and political deformities may be, and we rejoice that they are, fully appreciated by the educated classes of our community, and justly animadverted on by the ordinary guides of popular opinion. But, notwithstanding all this, America is still to the bulk of our population the land of requital and redress—the distant country in which oppressions cease, and poverty grows full-fed and bold, in which fortune opens her arms to the courageous, and the least adventurous looks forward to the achievement of independence and contentment before he dies.[1]

It was much more usual for Whigs who could sympathize with such feelings to applaud American successes, under American conditions, and to account for success in terms compatible with the political philosophy of Whiggism.

There was a difference of emphasis between Old and New Whigs in this matter. The Old Whigs, still oligarchs at heart, were intractably opposed to any political theory based upon *real* popular sovereignty. At times they were thus able to see more shrewdly the demerits of the American system, but they often permitted their distrust of the common man to distort their vision, to produce caricature. On the other hand, men such as Merivale and Spedding, who liked to consider themselves abreast of the times, were readier to acquiesce in Alexis de Tocqueville's thesis about the inevitability of democracy.[2] Attention could then be devoted to the questions—which was the most desirable form of democracy? How could it be best safeguarded against its natural weaknesses? How could it be rendered compatible with liberty? America, seen in this light, could be interpreted as a desirable evolutionary democracy enshrining basic Anglo-Saxon, middle-class values. Unlike other democracies (and especially unlike the French type) the United States respected freedom, authority, and law, and was as vigilant against popular excess as it was concerned for the enlightenment of the sovereign body. The Radicals, said the New Whigs, were mistaken in claiming that these highly desirable qualities had been achieved by some deterministic activity of the democratic principle. Success was due, rather, to the setting up of astute safeguards against the power of the sovereign people—to the doctrine of

---

[1] *ER*, No. 174, Oct. 1847, pp. 389–91 (Macgregor's American Commerce), by Merivale. For a short but lucid account of the *Edinburgh*'s balanced attitude to the United States, see Paul Mowbray Wheeler, *America Through British Eyes—A Study of the Attitude of the Edinburgh Review toward the U.S.A. from 1802 until 1861* (Rock Hill, South Carolina, 1935), especially pp. vii, 40. Unfortunately for my purpose, this little book is devoted mainly to literature and the arts.

[2] Merivale recognized that such ideas '. . . disturb old and favourite associations; they seem to reduce many cherished traditions, much painfully acquired knowledge, to obsolete lore; but these things are so, and we must accustom ourselves to regard them and their consequences without shrinking . . .' *ER*, No. 167, Jan. 1846, p. 142.

checks and balances endorsed by the Founding Fathers, to the constitutional division of power, the principle of judicial review of a fundamental
law unsusceptible to rapid change, to the status as higher law of a docu-
ment of human rights, and so on. Thus whilst the Radicals looked to the
Republic to vindicate democracy, the Whigs saw there a commendation
of Whiggism.

Another favourite endeavour was to explain American stability in
terms of the propitious circumstances of the nation—in terms of its
unparalleled natural resources; its small and scattered population of small
capitalists; the safety valve of the frontier; the weakness of America's
neighbours; the long-standing traditions of law and order inherited from
the British, and so on. The logic of this kind of argument was not always
faultless, but a cautious conclusion was invariably arrived at. Both
Mackintosh and Tocqueville emphasized America's natural advantages,
with which, as Tocqueville remarked, it was difficult to commit irrepar-
able mistakes. Sydney Smith feared that

. . . ancient women, whether in or out of breeches, will of course imagine that
we are the enemies of the institutions of our country, because we are the admirers
of the institutions of America. But [came the inevitable disclaimer] *circumstances
differ*. American institutions are too new, English institutions are ready made to
our hands. If we were to build the house afresh, we might perhaps avail ourselves
of the improvements of a new plan; but we have no sort of wish to pull down an
excellent house, strong, warm, and comfortable, because upon second trial, we
might be able to alter and amend it,—a principle which would perpetuate demoli-
tion and construction.[1]

Hardly Radical or revolutionary! W. R. Greg propounded a succinct
statement of the theme in 1852:

Those who point with triumph or who look with hope to the success of the
great popular experiment in America—who appeal to it as showing how safely
and how beneficially the concerns of a great country may be carried on under a
government chosen by universal suffrage—cannot, we think, be men whose
observation is very close or patient, or whose standard of requirement is very high.
We yield to none in a full and generous appreciation of the many excellencies and
the wonderful energies of our Transatlantic brethren. The United States may well
be proud of their Past, and sanguine as to their Future. But with them, it must be
remembered that the experiment has been tried under a combination of circumstances almost inconceivably auspicious. They were of Anglo-Saxon race; they

---

[1] *ER*, No. 80, July 1824, pp. 438–9. He added: 'America is so differently situated
from the old governments of Europe, that [it] affords no political precedents that are
exactly applicable to our old governments.' Ibid. p. 439.

were always free; for generations they had been inured and trained to self-govern-ment; they were descendants of the religious and self-controlled and self-denying Puritans; and they were pressed upon by none of those social or material difficulties which beset older and more populous countries. . . .[1]

McCulloch, Macaulay, and Senior substantially shared such views. Universal suffrage, they conceded, might suit an agricultural and semi-colonial United States, but would prove disastrous in over-populated, industrial, urban England.

The more intransigent deduction from the theme of America's 'pro-pitious' or 'peculiar' circumstances was that which refused to propose the American model as in any way relevant to a Europe with such different circumstances. (The argument has some interesting affinities with the view that history is *sui generis*.) Yet even those liberals who were willing to regard the United States as the fairest existing example of enlightened democracy, with lessons for all nations, saw there an excuse for only gradualist reform in England. They recognized that the American prece-dent (like that of 1688) was a revolutionary one. But they emphasized that the American Revolution had been managed by responsible and proper-tied men, without recourse either to ultra-democracy or to some authori-tarian salvation from débâcle. Few Whigs cherished the hope that England in the Age of Chartism afforded nearly such ideal conditions for root-and-branch changes in government. Jefferson himself, as Empson pointed out, had advocated the attainment of freedom by degrees and had given warning that '. . . ignorance and bigotry, like other insanities, are incapable of self-government'.[2] Trust in the people, the Whigs

[1] *ER*, No. 196, Oct. 1852, pp. 463–4. For other pronouncements upon the importance of the Puritan tradition in the evolution of 'wise and generous principles of civil and religious liberty', see the review of Bancroft's *History of the United States*, etc. in *ER*, No. 171, Jan. 1847, Art. 4, by Roebuck.

[2] 'Jefferson's Memoirs and Correspondence' in *ER*, No. 102, July 1830, p. 517. Jefferson, according to English Whigs, was a revolutionary who was always aware of the dangers of democratic revolution: most revolutionaries, he had once said, 'did not weigh the hazards of a transition from one form of government to another.' Empson saw clearly that 'Jefferson's own confidence, indeed, is in man only as he is found in America, and there only for a season.' (Ibid.) The Whigs embraced Jefferson as a most Whiggish democrat, an interesting departure from the American legend that grew up around him; and accountable in terms of different needs in different groups. See Empson again on Jefferson in *ER*, No. 112, Jan. 1833, p. 496; and Brougham on Jefferson in *ER*, No. 131, Oct. 1837, Art. 8. The Benthamites, during their Radical phase, depicted Jefferson as a democrat much more in the tradition of the Jeffersonian legend. They contrasted Jefferson—'undoubtedly the greatest public benefactor that has yet appeared in the nineteenth century'—with Hamilton, the 'Corrupter-General' of the United States, an advocate of 'despotic' government who was determined to betray the Constitution by Anglicizing it. See *WR*, Vol. 13, No. 26, Oct. 1830, Art. 3.

concluded, must await their maturity, and this depended upon the slow
piecing together in England of a religious and educational system comparable to that of the Americans.

James Spedding strongly defended such a viewpoint. He believed that
the seeds of civil liberty in the new world had sprung from 'that indomitable Protestantism which fled from the bondage of Europe to worship
God in the wilderness'. He insisted that the American church system, with
its atomistic tendencies, nourished the liberal spirit in politics:

The number and energy of the sects there bespeaks the life of religion among the
people; and popular religion is popular philosophy—the love and study of wisdom
—the cultivation of the spiritual part of man—the counter-poise and corrective
of mere animal existence; and the amity of so many zealous and independent sects
is an answer we think to the question—Can the majority be just when it is supreme?
Every sect is a small minority, among a multitude of rivals—yet the conscience of
every sect is respected both by the law and by society—and nobody appears
afraid of free inquiry and the light of knowledge.[1]

Spedding waxed even more eloquent about American education, which,
he thought, provided the fairest of trials for democracy. For the first time
in history, he said, the power of knowledge was being tried upon the
majority: '. . . here is a nation which takes measures beforehand against
the degradation of the people by making the ignorance, which is the
main source of it, impossible.'[2] Spedding, like many Whigs, had the
highest admiration for the Massachusetts schools system—he was so
impressed that he wrote: 'if America were sunk beneath the waves,
[Massachusetts] would remain the fairest picture on record of an ideal
commonwealth.'[3] George Combe, the friend of Horace Mann, who
virtually created the Massachusetts system of education, had as high a
regard for it; and he persuaded Napier to print a glowing account of the
transatlantic experiment in 1841. Combe, in the Edinburgh, strenuously
urged the creation in England of a similar national system of education;[4]
and the seeds planted in the 1840's ultimately bore fruit.

Finally, and perhaps inconsistently, British Whigs argued that particular
qualities in the common culture of England and America underlay their
political successes. Even Radicals might be tempted, in their off-guard

[1] ER, No. 188, Oct. 1850, pp. 359–60.
[2] Ibid. p. 358. In America, he felt, an earnest endeavour was being made to create
'a commonwealth of intelligent, industrious, just and humane men'.
[3] Ibid. p. 355.
[4] See his article in ER, No. 148, July 1841, Art. 6 (State of Massachusetts). For
Combe's correspondence with Napier about this article see B.M. Add. MS. 34,621,
fol. 564; and 34,623, fols. 373–7. For the subsequent history of American influence
upon educational reform in Britain, see Thistlethwaite, op. cit., Ch. 5.

moments, to agree that Americans and Englishmen were happily endowed with special aptitudes and excellencies in the art of politics. 'Loathing abstract thought, looking with suspicion or contempt on all endeavours after scientific accuracy in moral or political questions, empiric, tentative, often blundering, always unsystematic', both peoples were said to be sensible and cautious of fundamental change, imbued with a real sense of public spirit and habitual regard for established law.[1] Upon such virtues depended the success of their separate brands of liberal government, as compared with the disastrous failure of European experiments in similar forms (underlined in 1848). What was not acceptable to reformers in this plausible thesis was the inference drawn from it, that men, not systems, national character, not institutions, were the key elements in the political equation. It appeared as if the Americans, hitherto the heroes of the Left, were being clothed with the characteristics of the ruling class in Britain as an argument for pragmatic and undoctrinaire reform. Nevertheless, here was the beginning of a macroscopic rather than an insular view of British and American politics; the beginning of a greater toleration of possible democratic systems of government, provided that they benefited from the fruits of Anglo-American, rather than Continental, experience.

[1] *ER*, No. 188, Oct. 1850, p. 510 (Difficulties of Republican France), by Greg.

CHAPTER IV

THE CONSERVATIVE RESPONSE

IT BECAME a commonplace quite early in Anglo-American relations that the evaluation of American democracy by British conservatives was affected by their opposition to innovation in Britain. They disliked America, as their opponents clearly saw, largely because they feared democracy in Britain—a condition which challenged their class interests, but for which they had also a genuine theoretical repugnance. This fact has been acknowledged by scholars,[1] but, as we have seen, these scholars have so far been more concerned in investigating the attitudes of the Left towards America before 1850. The reforms achieved by Radicals and reformers, habitually using American propaganda to aid their crusades, ought not to be underestimated; but it is still true that the forces resisting the republican spirit in Britain won a substantial victory between the time of the Reform Bill and the Great Exhibition. Whilst Tories made their most successful stand against revolutionary change on traditional and local grounds, their opposition to subversive American precedent was concerted, and many of their antipathies to the United States were shared by a larger public (and have persisted into the twentieth century). It is the purpose of this chapter to examine closely this early conservative image of America.

1. *Motives*

It was during the post-Napoleonic period that the Tory press in Britain acquired an almost universal reputation for anti-Americanism, and Tories themselves in these years rarely denied that their cardinal attitudes were critical. Apart from the chasm between British conservatism in the style of Burke and the American mode of politics, which generated its own antipathies, the Tories still resented the events of 1776, the 1790's, and 1812. Too many Americans, they felt, had taken the part of French republicanism in its war against the mother country, thereby encouraging

---

[1] See, for example, G. D. Lillibridge, *Beacon of Freedom* (Pennsylvania, 1954), pp. xiv, 10, 18, 36ff.

the enemy abroad and traitors at home.[1] 1812 was another knife in the back, inflicted whilst England was engaged in a life-and-death struggle against Napoleonic despotism. In one way, therefore, the Tories were reacting against Anglophobia in America, which happened to be characteristic of the more democratic political groups there. For this reason they were more sympathetic towards the conservative elements in the Republic, which were more pro-British. They were also reacting against the Americophilia of their political opponents in Britain, a sentiment which was believed to be (especially during the Bonapartist wars) jacobinical in tendency.[2] In 1825 Edward Stanley (later the 14th Earl of Derby and leader of the Conservative party) sagely noted in his journal some of these cross-currents: 'It is one remarkable circumstance that during the act which separated them, and in all succeeding times, England and America have mutually been, each within the other, the themes of political animosity, and the watchword of political parties.'[3] He was aware that, in postwar Britain, circumstances and interest led the conservatives and radicals to embrace opposite, and extreme, views of the United States:

It suited the one [party], whose object it was to magnify the distresses of the country, in order to make more apparent the incapacity of the ministers, to paint in glowing and fanciful colours the independent Nation arising in the West, the prowess of her arms, the happiness of her people, the substantial basis upon which she rested, and to attribute all these and more imaginary merits to the freedom of her republican Institutions. It was convenient for the other party to institute comparisons, which should set America in the most unfavourable light, and in doing so, they did not hesitate to vilify her people, her government, and the whole theory and practice of her constitution.[4]

This vilification was at its most unscrupulous during the years of dislocation and repression following 1815, when it was feared that inflammatory propaganda about the new world would encourage popular insurgences at home. But, even during the 1820's and 1830's, when alarm had subsided, the Tories were continually harassed by Radicals, Benthamites, and Whigs because of their open prejudices against the Union. The bitterness

[1] See, for example, *Blackwood's Edinburgh Magazine* (hereafter *Blackwood's*): 'We hated the Americans nationally, because they were democratical, and sided with our enemies . . .' Vol. 18, Oct. 1825, p. 423.
[2] See the Tory pamphlet, *A Review of a Celebrated Speech on the Catholic Claims . . . in a letter . . . to the Rt. Hon. W. C. Plunkett* (London, 1820), esp. pp. 25–30. 'It is America, it is Paine, it is democracy, it is Jacobinism' from which the disorders of the age had sprung, according to the writer.
[3] Hon. Edward Stanley, *Journal of a Tour in America: 1824–1825* (privately printed, London, 1930), p. 1. Stanley, it should be noted, was at the time a Whig. This book is hereafter cited as Stanley, *Journal*.
[4] Ibid. pp. 5–6.

8

associated with these partisan clashes continued to colour Tory thinking about the new world for long afterwards, even when liberals and utilitarians had begun to water down their praises.

On a wider plane, conservatives felt themselves alienated from the American way of life at a number of points. Perhaps more thoroughly than any other group, they identified themselves with the national interest, and were obsessively concerned with questions of patriotism and national prestige. Their position was the diametric opposite of the internationalism and pacifism that characterized the thinking of humanitarians and Cobdenites. On every occasion when British and American interests clashed—and there were many such occasions between the incident at Pensacola in 1818 and the Nicaraguan controversy in 1850—an aggrieved Tory press rang with denunciations of America and American democracy.[1] Indeed, it might be argued that the Tory estimation of American foreign policy before 1850 played as important a part as any purely theoretical consideration in determining their response to the British democratic movement in these years.

Much friction owed its origin to the national myth, indulged in more wholeheartedly by members of the Establishment than by those outside it, that Britain had evolved over the centuries the world's highest civilization, whose destinies were presided over by an intensely cultured, but yet sturdy and reliable, ruling class. Members of this class not only recoiled from the *parvenu* civilization of America, but they resented as pretension the *gauche* and aggressive foreign and commercial policies of such a people. There was a general feeling among Tories that England, as befitted a mature nation used to European antipathy, had been long-suffering about (if at times even unaware of) anti-British sentiment in the United States. This was a corrective to the Radical and Whig emphasis upon the common characteristics of the two nations. England's role as a cosmopolitan world power was stressed, and a comparison made with the United States incestuously concerned with native political traditions because of its isolated and insular condition. The English, as writers like Captain Hall suggested, soon forgot their wars with America in their absorption in more momentous affairs. But the Americans were reared upon a tradition of antagonism towards the mother country. This charge touched the Radicals on the raw, for they had to encounter precisely this prejudice in their effort to build supra-national reform movements.

[1] This is true, despite the fact that Tory administrations probably enjoyed more amiable relations with the United States than did the Whigs when Palmerston was at the Foreign Office. On issues such as the Ashburton negotiations, and Oregon, opinion in the Whig camp was split by Palmerston's intransigence, a majority probably favouring more conciliatory policies.

To upper-class Englishmen, America had made no cultural contribution to Anglo-American relations, and had retrogressed in the theory and practice of politics. The Americans, unwilling to admit any colonial dependency upon British culture, and myopically proud of their political system, hotly resented these criticisms. Whilst ardently desiring British approval, they were hypersensitive to censure, even to misplaced panegyric,[1] and this made them appear more ridiculous to sophisticated eyes. They were suspected of being morbidly jealous of Britain's superior civilization. The necessary social contacts to alleviate friction were too rarely made during the convulsions which racked the world between 1776 and 1815; conversely, with the later improvement of transatlantic shipping facilities, there came an easing in the social relations of the two nations. Few cultivated Americans visited England before 1830, and even the *Quarterly Review* admitted in later years that America was singularly unfortunate in the type of British traveller who toured there before the mid-thirties. The common language and traditions shared by the two countries, as many observers noted, often served to aggravate irritation at the relatively less important deviations between their conditions.[2] Although economists and the trading community appreciated the special importance of Anglo-American economic links, many uncritical observers were preoccupied with the commercial rivalry between the two nations rather than with their interdependence. The tone of sentiment between England and the United States was, according to Stanley as early as 1824, 'not unlike that which subsists between a man of old family but reduced fortune, and a parvenu neighbour, who has raised himself in the world by bold adventure and successful industry'.[3] Gustave de Beaumont observed, eleven years later, that Britain was disquieted by America's economic prosperity[4] (although he may have noted in 1837 that London was more disquieted over a disruption to that prosperity).

It should be observed that a logical connection was not always drawn between the existence of republican institutions and the inferiority of American culture. George Canning, and other classical scholars, had a

[1] They were as much annoyed by the ignorance of friendly English Radicals as they had been by that of the French in the eighteenth century: 'They would have liked people to know their country and not its shadow, their life and not the dreams of the reformers who talked about it . . .', as Fäy wrote in his *Revolutionary Spirit in France and America at the end of the Eighteenth Century* (New York, 1927).
[2] See, for example, *Quarterly Review* (hereafter QR), Vol. 48, No. 96, Dec. 1832, pp. 513-21 (Mr. Ouseley on the U.S.A.), by William Jacob. Evidence for authorship is given in an Appendix.
[3] Stanley, *Journal*, p. 1.
[4] Gustave de Beaumont, *Marie* (Paris, 1835), quoted in QR, Vol. 53, No. 106, Apr. 1835, p. 306.

considerable respect for the civilization, and love of freedom, exhibited by the republics of ancient Greece and Rome, of Genoa and Florence. But, as Canning told the Commons during the war in 1813, one would vainly seek to trace such virtues 'in the hard features of transatlantic democracy'.[1] Again, as we shall see, conservative disapproval of the American way of life often sprang from a disapproval of commercial ethics rather than, or as well as, from rejection of republicanism.

Imbued with a pragmatic, rather than a doctrinaire or utopian, approach to political and international issues, the Tories were nettled by the behaviour of both the Americans and their Radical admirers. They believed, for example, that Britain had made a peace at Ghent in 1814 because she was engaged in a real war in Europe, not a side-show in North America; so that they were disconcerted to find the Americans writing that affair into their folklore as a resounding triumph, justifying a whole host of later pretensions. In their view, too, the language employed by Americans when treating of their institutions was panegyrical and unrealistic. Tory reviewers, as well as Whigs, were shrewdly aware of the circumstances in which the Union had been born and its constitution drawn up. They realized, after reading some of the published correspondence, that the Founding Fathers had hardly been inspired solely by utopian motives. They read, and recommended to their readers, the sobering accounts of democracy written by crusty American conservatives such as Fisher Ames; and they had a better than perfunctory knowledge of the strength of sectional animosity in the Union. It was for these reasons, as well as from political interest, that they challenged the mania for 'dissertation without documentation' shared by Americans and British reformers.

It would nevertheless be rash to suggest that the Tory view of the new world was therefore objective. The Whigs and the better-informed utilitarians had, on the whole, a more accurate view of the United States and a greater appreciation of its positive achievement. The Tory impression of American democracy was one of unrelieved gloom beside that of the liberals, and was without doubt a more obvious distortion of the facts to square with a political philosophy. The severity of criticism was sometimes justified as a corrective to the 'magniloquent pretensions' of the Republic and the 'sweeping assertions of her political admirers here in the old world'.[2] Yet the fact that judgement of America was thereby invited

---

[1] R. Therry, ed., *Speeches of the Rt. Hon. George Canning*, 3rd ed. (London, 1836), III. 391. The speech was given on 18.2.1813. Canning, who was embittered by the U.S.'s 'heartless and selfish' policy of war, added: '. . . I fear, that in the republic of America we look for the realization of our visions of republican virtue in vain.'

[2] The words are those of Francis Egerton, in *QR*, Vol. 58, No. 116, Apr. 1837, p. 522.

by the most exacting standards, was not sufficient excuse for judging by impossible standards. This at least was the feeling of Americans such as Fenimore Cooper, who continually encountered this variety of partisanship from the 'votaries of monarchy' in Europe:

I have often told our opponents that they pay us the highest possible compliment in their constant efforts to compare the results of our system with what is purely right in the abstract, instead of comparing it with the results of their own. . . . They do not affirm, but they always argue as if they thought we ought to be better than they.[1]

2. *From Waterloo to Reform*

Much of the enormous resentment felt by Americans against British upper-class opinion after 1815 can be directly traced to the attitude of the *Quarterly Review*, which was, and continued to be, the most important single organ of conservative opinion in the country. This journal had established its reputation for hostility towards America in a scathing attack upon Jared Ingersoll's *Inchiquin*[2] in 1815, and the reputation was consolidated between 1819 and 1823 in three articles which became notorious for their prejudice.[3] Established opinion during these years was alarmed by popular turbulence—it was a time of economic dislocation after the war, the age of the Spa Fields riot and Peterloo, of the Blanketeers and the Six Acts. The monarchy itself came into disrepute over the affair of Queen Caroline, and Europe was unsettled. Anglo-American relations, moreover, became embittered because of Jackson's execution of Arbuthnot and Ambrister in 1818. The intrusion of the United States into Spanish Florida was seen by the Tory press as deliberate expansionism, and alarm was expressed about American designs upon British North America and the West Indies.[4] It was not a time for the encouragement of democracy or republicanism.

Sir John Barrow wrote his critical review of Henry Fearon's *Sketches of America* against this background, in 1819. Barrow, who wrote the enormous number of 195 articles for the *Quarterly* between 1812 and 1841, was an amiable Tory of the old school, whose political philosophy was summed up in loyalty to King, Lords, and Commons. He had risen from lowly origins in Lancashire to the position of second Secretary of the

---

[1] J. F. Cooper, *Residence in France, etc.* (Paris, 1836), quoted in QR, Vol. 58, No. 116, Apr. 1837, p. 522.

[2] *Inchiquin, the Jesuit's Letters during a Late Residence in the U.S.A., etc.*

[3] QR, Vol. 21, No. 41, Jan. 1819, Art. 7 (Fearon's Sketches of America); Vol. 27, No. 53, Apr. 1822, Art. 3 (Views, Visits, and Tours in North America); and Vol. 29, No. 58, July 1823, Art. 3 (Faux, Memorable Days in America).

[4] See, for example, QR, Vol. 21, No. 41, Jan. 1819, p. 19, by William Jacob.

Admiralty (1807–45); he owed some of his success to the patronage of the aristocracy—of Sir George Staunton, Lord Macartney, and Henry Dundas —and he never repudiated that debt in his writings.[1] The tone he employed towards America was exactly calculated to raise the ire of the Radicals, and James Mill devoted an article in the *Westminster* to demolishing Barrow's arguments and exposing his prejudices.[2] By the use of a cutting wit, probably sharpened by his sarcastic editor Gifford, and the selection of graphic details from the travel literature, Barrow essayed a task of disenchantment. The Americans were described as a slovenly people, addicted to spitting, brawling, drinking, and boasting. They were said to be relatively uneducated, bumptious, self-seeking and materialist. Their cities were drab and brutalizing; the West was even more barbaric. Slavery was a cancer gnawing at the vitals of a supposedly free society. Religion was nominally widespread, but was not deeply rooted in the affections of the people. More poverty existed than was admitted by British friends. Conditions in the backwoods were arduous; and dis-appointed emigrants, led astray by roseate visions, pined for the security and order of England's village system. American politics, again contrary to the assertions of English democrats, were full of place-seeking and corruption, vilification, and abject subservience to an ignorant majority. Cheap government, the object of Bentham's praise, was in fact a vice, for it encouraged venality; whilst freedom of expression and opinion were myths unless one's views and behaviour accorded with those of the multitude. The Americans were, in Fearon's words, 'not a social or generous people; not a people of enlarged ideas . . . not a people who understand liberty from investigation and from principle; not a people who comprehend the meaning of the words "honour" and "generosity" . . .'[3]

These charges, selected (as James Mill showed) exclusively from un-favourable testimony,[4] provided a startling contrast to the uncritical

[1] Barrow had accompanied Macartney on his China mission, as an administrator. He served under Dundas at the Admiralty during the Pitt administration of 1804, and acquired a high reputation for his work in reorganizing the civil administration of the navy during the Napoleonic wars. He was created a baronet in 1835 by William IV, under whom (as Duke of Clarence) he had served at the Admiralty. He was a founder member of the Royal Geographical Society; and was very well known for his encouragement of Polar exploration and his popular writings upon travel, mari-time affairs, and biography. Most of his *Quarterly* articles were upon these subjects.

[2] *WR*, Vol. 2, No. 4, Oct. 1824, Art. 9.

[3] See *QR*, Vol. 21, No. 41, Jan. 1819, Art. 7. The quotation from Fearon is cited on p. 163. Fearon, incidentally, was a writer who commanded the respect of such a deep-thinking Whig as Sir James Mackintosh.

[4] See *WR*, Vol. 2, No. 4, Oct. 1824, pp. 486–7. Mill alleged a political motive for this passion against the U.S., viz. 'the hatred of the Quarterly Reviewers to a people

admiration of the Left and galvanized Radicals into new and more effective defences of their favourite Republic. Meanwhile the *Quarterly* lost no opportunity to ridicule the enthusiasm of their opponents, and to suggest unpatriotic motives underlying it. William Gifford especially appreciated the threat offered to the English ruling classes by the 'friends of America'. In 1818 he attempted editorially to neutralize the effective propaganda of one such man, Morris Birbeck, the English Quaker who had organized an immigrant settlement in Illinois. Birbeck's widely circulated *Notes on a Journey in America* (1818) and *Letters from Illinois* (1818) painted an attractive picture of political life in the new world. Gifford quickly projected a slashing review of the *Notes*, writing to John Murray, the publisher, in a revealing letter:

I am very glad that you have sent Birbeck. He appears to me the most dangerous man that ever yet wrote from America, and is likely to do us much mischief. Our friend [Barrow, who had written a draft review] has missed his character; and I have nearly re-written the Article.[1]

Four years later a similar fate was meted out to Richard Flower's *Letters from Illinois* (1822), an account of the Birbeck enterprise by a member of one of the original families.[2]

In Henry Fearon the *Quarterly* found an easier target than the incorrigibly optimistic Americophiles, the Birbecks and the Flowers. Fearon, commissioned by a group of dissatisfied business men in England to canvass their prospects as emigrants in the American East and West, began his tour prejudiced in favour of the United States. He was, according to Barrow, 'a democratic fieffé', who combined 'a sovereign contempt for the civil and religious institutions of England' with a 'blind and sottish admiration of those of America'. 'With the gullibility common to the party', wrote Barrow, 'he appears to have swallowed all the rancorous abuse of this country, and all the outrageous panegyrics on America, which he found in Cobbett, and Wooler, and Sherwin. . . .'[3] Fortunately

---

which had set a dangerous example of throwing off the yoke of aristocracy', and Francis Jeffrey concurred. Mill was broadminded enough to see, however, that Radical propaganda was often exaggerated. Fanny Wright, he conceded, was 'not perhaps sufficiently discriminating'.

[1] Gifford to Murray, 4th Aug. 1818, in Murray MSS., London; cited in H. Shine *et al., The Quarterly Review under Gifford, etc.* (Univ. of N. Carolina, 1949), p. 61. See also S. Smiles, *A Publisher and his Friends—Memoirs and Corresp. of John Murray* (London, 1891), II. 50.

[2] *QR*, Vol. 27, No. 53, Apr. 1822, Art. 3 (Views, Visits and Tours in North America).

[3] *QR*, Vol. 21, No. 41, Jan. 1819, p. 126.

for the Tory cause, Fearon was forced into an agonizing reappraisal of his
attitudes by contact with actual conditions in the Union, and he turned in
a discouraging report to his sponsors. Barrow exploited to the full all
evidence of Fearon's disillusionment, and ended by commending him for
his change of heart: '. . . his sincerity overpowered his prejudices, and he
perpetually bewails the ungrateful truths which the monitions of conscience will not allow him to suppress.' Admirers who did not recant
continued to be roughly handled. William Tell Harris, an emigration
agent of Radical tendencies, was dismissed as a 'poor driveller', and
Fanny Wright's account of American society was rebuked as 'ridiculous
panegyric'.[1] The *Quarterly* had, by 1824, become quite querulous about
those 'wretched hirelings', who as travellers 'supply the radical press with
the means of mischief'.[2]

Tory feeling veered between an hidalgo contempt for the speciousness
of the Radical vision of America and fear about the possible effects of
such propaganda in Britain:

We can smile [wrote one writer] at the bloated vanity which proclaims a Solon
and Lycurgus to be mere simpletons in legislation compared with a Jefferson;
and Hannibal a bungler by the side of a General Jackson . . . that the American
government is the perfection of all human institutions . . . that a spirit of universal
benevolence pervades all classes of society—that poverty is unknown, oppression
unfelt, and dishonesty unpractised—but when we are told 'that the people of the
United States are far superior to the English in all intellectual endowments . . .
that they have not, like us, *disgraced* themselves with an established church, supported by penal laws, the work of statecraft and priestcraft united'—in short, that
'relief from all the evils which the old governments of Europe have inflicted upon
the poor and industrious is only to be found in America',—it becomes a duty to
rise up and expose the fallacies, in order to check the ruinous consequences which
they are but too well calculated to entail upon those credulous people who are
liable to be deluded by them.[3]

This duty was taken up in perhaps the most notorious exposé of
America's seamier side—a review of William Faux's *Memorable Days in
America* by Barrow and Gifford, which appeared in 1823[4] and provoked
indignant replies from Edward Everett and the Mills and even a rebuke

[1] See the reviews of W. T. Harris, *Remarks made during a tour through the U.S.*
(1821); [Frances Wright], *Views of Society and Manners in America, etc.* (1821); in
QR, Vol. 27, No. 53, Apr. 1822, Art. 3. This article also contains an account of the
disappointment experienced by emigrants who had joined Birbeck's group.
[2] Ibid. p. 73.
[3] Ibid. p. 73. (The extracts quoted are from Fanny Wright's book.)
[4] QR, Vol. 29, No. 58, July 1823, Art. 3.

from *Blackwood's*.[1] With the aid of Gifford's incisive sarcasm,[2] attention was drawn to the lawlessness of the frontier with its 'Rowdies' and 'Regulators'; to the coarseness of national manners; to the want of culture and a cultured class; to the crude horse-trading character and restless ambition of even the respectable classes; to the malevolence of party strife; and the religious fanaticism of the backwoods. The article succeeded in demonstrating that the Americans were no race of innocents who universally respected a higher law and enjoyed unmolested the fruits of a splendid constitution. Democracy, rather, appeared to have encouraged a degradation of civilization, which was the only real test of a state.

On the whole it was unfortunate for the Tory cause in the 1820's that the task of exposing America's faults, and justifying the British system as an alternative, should have fallen into the hands of Barrow, Gifford, and like spirits. Their taste for the splenetic and their inability to transcend a narrow Toryism or the social outlook of their set prevented them putting a case which might have converted moderate Whigs or intellectual Radicals. Despite their vindictiveness, they had many significant things to say about America. But in recoiling too far to the right they failed to profit from the weaknesses of the Ultra-Radical position, and succeeded only in attracting retaliation from Americans and able men like the Mills and the Edinburgh Reviewers. William Jacob and Robert Southey were conservatives with a more balanced view of the Republic, and *Blackwood's*, in its first flush of reaction against orthodox Toryism, asserted its benevolence towards the Yankees.[3] These voices were drowned, however, by the furore created by the *Quarterly* and its critics.

[1] For the criticisms by the Mills, see *WR*, Vol. 1, No. 1, Jan. 1824, Art. XI. According to *Blackwood's* (Vol. 15, p. 84), the article was done 'like all the *Quarterly*'s papers on such books, with infinite labour and skill', but was too grave about America's defects. In a relatively liberal number, this essay was 'the solitary effervescence of the old bigot gall of the *Quarterly*'. Everett's remarks were in the *North American Review*.

[2] Barrow, who wrote the substance of the article, submitted it to Murray with this remark: 'It is well peppered, and if Gifford will add some of his double-refined salt, I have no doubt we shall work up a well-seasoned devil for Jonathon to digest over his whisky.' 11.8.23, quoted in Smiles, op. cit., II. 157.

[3] *Blackwood's* claimed to be the first British periodical to do justice to American poets, such as Brown and Irving. See Vol. XI, June 1822, pp. 684–8. It nevertheless believed that most American literature was imitative of Byron, Pope, and Addison; and it did not hold with 'buttering' the Americans as did the liberal press: 'John Bull looks upon the Yankees, and is looked upon by them, with an ambiguous sort of feeling, that can by no means be called *love*. "Tarnation Tories" as we are, we look with all the vanity of self-importance down upon our quondam sons; and it is well to tell them this flatly with English frankness, as to dissemble for a time, and then let it burst forth—a black flood of long-retained spleen . . . The Yankees appear to us a testy and quarrelsome race and we like them the better for it; they show young blood and swagger becoming a nation in its teens.' Ibid. pp. 684–5. See also Vol. 16, Dec. 1824, pp. 640–1.

In some ways the spleen of Gifford and his associates was the last-ditch stand of an Eldonian-type Toryism against the *fait accompli* of American republicanism. Liberal Toryism had, since Ghent, been much more ready to treat with the Americans. Practical statesmen such as Liverpool, Castlereagh, and Huskisson had, since 1814, become more inclined to repudiate the older and antagonistic mercantilist view of America, which sought to crush economic and political competition. They endeavoured rather to encourage free commercial relations between the two nations. As Lord Liverpool, the leader of the party, told the House of Lords in 1820:

Of all the powers on earth, America is the one whose increasing population and immense territory furnish the best prospects for British produce and manufactures. Every man, therefore, who wishes prosperity to England, must wish prosperity to America.[1]

This did not imply approval of America's political system or culture; but it did imply that it was more important to preserve peace, in order to retain the American market, than to wage a war against abstract principles. Thus a conflict over Pensacola was avoided in 1819, despite an angry Tory press and an aggressive landed gentry. The 1820's saw a further infiltration of liberal economic doctrines into Tory ranks, as well as the restoration of economic and political stability in England. Under these circumstances, and under pressure from able opponents using American example to encourage reform, some reappraisal of the United States was in order.

Robert Southey, the Poet Laureate, and William Jacob, the *Quarterly*'s sole economic expert, had already discovered in the condition of the new world valuable arguments for applying the brake to unrestrained democracy. They noted the conservative nature of many political forms in the Union; they emphasized the difference between conditions there and in Britain; and they found a slogan with appeal both to Tories and the labouring poor in the denunciation of 'rampant commercialism' in the United States.[2] Observers like Stanley, who stood on the threshold between Whiggery and Conservatism, took also a more tolerant stand than the reviewers. After his tour of 1825, Stanley wrote:

America and England must have many points of common attraction, perhaps some of collision: in some points they may and will be rivals; in habits, manners, and ways of thinking they are so different, that it is perhaps as well not to expect between

[1] Hansard, 2nd ser., I. 575 (16.5.1820)
[2] These themes are dealt with below, pp. 254ff. William Jacob (1762–1851) was Tory M.P. for Sussex (1808–12), and was an active pamphleteer in favour of the corn laws until about 1828. He then became comptroller of corn returns for the Board of Trade until he retired in 1842 (*D.N.B.*).

them much of mutual . . . attachment: but if I left the United States without much admiration for the *attractive* qualities of their citizens, I left them also with feelings which I would fain hope are gaining ground in England, of respect for much of solid and sterling merit, and with a full persuasion of the firmness of the foundation on which their politcal structure is built. . . .[1]

It was symptomatic of a desire to appear more objective that *Blackwood's* in 1824 acquired as its expert on America John Neal, the ubiquitous man of letters from Portland, U.S.A. Neal, during his three years in Britain, wrote over two dozen articles in periodicals of all leanings, besides sitting at the feet of Bentham and finally becoming a proselyte of utilitarianism. It was his express purpose, as he admits in his *Recollections*, to strike a blow in defence of his country by infiltrating the organs of opposition opinion in Britain and creating 'American departments' furnished by himself in each. He was annoyed by the tone of comment that prevailed before his arrival: 'American affairs were dealt with in short, insolent paragraphs, full of misapprehension, or of downright misrepresentation, as if they were dealing with Feejee Islanders, or Timbuctoos. . . .'[2] Neal's personal crusade to effect a change in this situation was remarkably successful, and he managed to diffuse vast amounts of information about American politics, life, and literature[3] into the journals. Although he was able to impose his own polemical views to a marked degree in these matters, he was not, in the Tory reviews, permitted to praise democracy outright as he did in liberal and Benthamite publications, and was under an obligation to acknowledge the outstanding faults of his countrymen. It is necessary to remember also that Neal was at the time a supporter of the more conservative elements in American politics. He favoured John Quincy Adams as Presidential candidate in the election of 1824, portraying Andrew Jackson to the

---

[1] Stanley, *Journal*, p. 336.

[2] J. Neal, *Wandering Recollections of a Somewhat Busy Life* (Boston, 1869), pp. 251–2. Neal failed to get regular comment into the newspapers, which were not interested in American affairs (p. 248); but he got papers into *Blackwood's* ('the cleverest, the sauciest, and the most unprincipled of all our calumniators'), into Colburn's *New Monthly*, the *Monthly*, the *London Magazine*, the *New European*, James Silk Buckingham's *Oriental Herald*, and the *Westminster*. He in fact wrote articles simultaneously for the *Westminster* and *Blackwood's* in 1825, skilfully adapting his political emphases for each. It was an indication of British opinion at the time that Dr. Alex. Walker, editor of the *New European* and a Scot (a race 'more . . . obstreperously loyal, than any native-born Englishman'), rejected some of Neal's work because it was (in Walker's words) 'too partial to the U.S. to be well-received, even by liberal Britons'. (Quoted, p. 253.)

[3] Neal wrote a notable series upon 'American Writers' for *Blackwood's* which began in Sept. 1824 and ran until Feb. 1825. It gave thumb-nail sketches of America's leading statesmen and politicians, besides men of literature. His favourable verdict upon Jefferson, and others, contradicted Tory tradition. (See, e.g., Jan. 1825, p. 68.)

English as a dangerous man and a possible dictator.[1] He endorsed the view that those states were best regulated which had the highest franchise qualifications,[2] and complained about corruption in national politics.[3] On the whole, Neal's influence upon Tory thought proved to be transitory; and as *Blackwood's* became involved in the campaigns against Catholic Emancipation and the Reform Bill, its bitterness against America began to exceed even that of the *Quarterly*.

A change in editorship of the latter journal resulted in some abatement of savagery towards the United States. John Gibson Lockhart, Walter Scott's son-in-law, took over from Gifford,[4] and although he was contemptuous of American culture, Lockhart's interests were primarily literary, not political, and his Toryism was moderate. Before 1831, when John Wilson Croker assumed responsibility for the *Quarterly*'s political policy, political articles were written by John Miller of Lincoln's Inn and John Fullarton, neither of whom displayed any great interest in the new world. These circumstances go a good way in explaining why the conservative press did not fully exploit American parallels in the case against Reform. American affairs in the *Quarterly*, the most widely read of Tory journals, were retained in the hands of Barrow, Jacob, and Southey, none of whom could match Croker as cut-and-thrust controversialists.

Barrow's articles, bereft of Gifford's acid, became noticeably more amiable. Barrow, who kept up conscientiously with the growing travel literature and statistics upon America, was a down-to-earth observer, and he became increasingly impressed by material achievement in the Union.[5] He extended high praise to the ingenious improvements effected in communications, to New England's remarkable canals and the Mississippi's steam-boat system. He followed the course of national consolidation so successfully carried out since the War of 1812, noting the irresistible extension of population, territory, and commerce; and his imagination was touched. 'The United States . . .' he wrote in 1828, 'may be considered a prodigy, to which we should in vain seek for any parallel in the history of nations—as infant in years, a giant in size and strength, and in intellect an adult.'[6] On the other hand, he was irritated by America's

[1] See, e.g., *Blackwood's*, Vol. 15, May 1824, p. 512. If Jackson was elected, Neal predicted, there would be 'a thorough revolution in the present system of things . . . his influence would assemble all the rash and adventurous material of the nation about him.'

[2] *Blackwood's*, Vol. 16, Dec. 1824, p. 645.

[3] *Blackwood's*, Vol. 18, Sept. 1825, p. 365 (North American Politics).

[4] Gifford's place was taken by John Taylor Coleridge in Dec. 1824, but he relinquished it to Lockhart in Dec. 1825. Lockhart remained editor until 1853.

[5] See, for example, *QR*, Vol. 37, No. 73, Jan. 1828, Art. 8 (United States).

[6] Ibid. p. 262.

foreign policy,[1] and was still doubtful whether a Republic of such gigantic extent could remain united. Such a state was 'an anomaly in the history of governments', its mere existence 'contrary to all elder experience'.[2] Like most Tories, and many Whigs, Barrow believed that democracy could exist only in a thinly-peopled country of limited extent. He suspected that under the pressure of population and diversifying sectional interests it would succumb to other forms. Should a poor class be created, should a 'love of distinction and power' seize the nation, then the stage would be set for a military or despotic government. Like John Neal, he was prepared to cast General Jackson in the mould of classical tyrant. He pictured him as supported by a boisterous electorate, as a man 'of ungovernable temper, a ferocious courage and a contempt for the constitution and laws'.[3]

Such criticisms were bound to proliferate in the years between 1828 and 1832. Feelings in the Tory party had already been stirred by the clash between Canning and President Adams over the Monroe Doctrine and Latin America. Advanced thinkers on economic questions, such as Liverpool and Huskisson, looked to the wants of an expanding industrial economy beginning to lean towards free trade. They were consequently irked by the Union's protective tariff of 1824, and by the interminable wrangling with the Adams administration over the complicated question of America's access to the West Indian carrying trade.[4] Not until the 1830's, moreover, were suspicions relieved that Jackson was not to be trusted as a head of state. The outstanding need, however, was to refute

[1] Upset by American policy regarding maritime rights and the Maine border, he complained that Americans 'are generally prepared to start so many points of controversy, to put forward so many unfounded claims . . . their self-interest is so predominating a feature and pursued with so much urgency and perseverance, without the least regard for mutual concession and mutual accommodation, that the word *reciprocity* would seem to be banished from their diplomatic code' (p. 262, ibid.).

[2] Ibid. p. 264.

[3] Ibid. p. 292. This estimate of Jackson is in fact taken by Barrow from F. Fitzgerald de Roos, *Personal Narrative of Travels in the U.S. and Canada in 1826, etc.* (1827). *Blackwood's*, on the eve of the 1828 election, was also concerned about Jackson becoming President and deplored the fact that part of the London press 'has been puffing this uncivilized, uncouth being as "the friend of all that is liberal and enlightened"'. Vol. 24, Nov. 1828, p. 634.

[4] See F. Lee Benns, *The American Struggle for the British West Indian Carrying Trade, 1815–1830* (Indiana, 1930), pp. 105–22. The issue sharpened when the so-called Reciprocity Act was passed by Parliament in 1825. It contemplated the restriction of American trade with the W. Indies unless American navigation laws governing British shipping in American ports were relaxed. The Union's intransigence in refusing freer access to British ships had led Liverpool to fear that the American marine was determined to supplant the British over the globe—see C. D. Yonge, *Life and Administration of the 2nd Earl of Liverpool* (London, 1868), II. 301. Huskisson, too, harshly criticized the American restrictions—see House of Commons debate, 1825, Hansard, 2nd ser., XII. 1107.

the case of Radicals and Whigs who were using the American precedent to encourage Parliamentary Reform.

Unluckily for the Establishment, most writers upon the United States had been, up until this time, of Radical or liberal leanings—the Cobbetts, Birbecks, Wrights, and Fearons. From 1829 until 1840 Tory travellers came into their own. Captain Basil Hall's *Travels* appeared in 1829, Frances Trollope's *Domestic Manners of the Americans* in 1832, and both were exploited to preach the gospel of no reform in England.[1] Robert Southey's *Colloquies on the Progress and Prospects of Society* (1829), which challenged some of the prevailing values of the new industrial society and was one of the more important conservative works of the period, included a long and critical section on new world democracy. Thomas Hamilton's *Men and Manners in America,* easily the ablest Tory interpretation of America to date, came out in 1833, just too late to affect the campaign for the Bill. In 1832 the *Quarterly* also took the opportunity of dismissing the strongly pro-American work of William Gore Ouseley, the young ex-Attaché to the British Legation at Washington, whose book on the United States was being widely used as propaganda by the Benthamites.[2] Some American works which contained criticism of transatlantic society were also unearthed. One was Timothy Flint's *Recollections,*[3] which suggested that frontiersmen were indifferent to religion. The case against the Americanization of British life was conducted with fierceness in Parliament;[4] it was continued in S. L. Giffard's daily *Standard,* in Theodore Hook's Ultra-Tory weekly *John Bull,* and in pamphlets by unswerving Old Tories such as Henry Drummond.[5] After the fight against the Bill had been lost, conservatives could select

[1] Hall's ideas are examined below, pp. 225ff. Mrs. Trollope's book was warmly reviewed by Hall in the *Quarterly* (Vol. 47, No. 93, Mar. 1832, Art. 2). Although this article provoked numerous replies from defenders of America, it was in fact very poor propaganda; it was in the worst tradition of antipathy to the U.S. and contained little comment of political significance. Hall later admitted, after reading Tocqueville, that his earlier views had been misguided. William Maginn also reviewed Trollope for *Fraser's Magazine* (Vol. 5, Apr. 1832, pp. 336–50), but his treatment was literary and satirical rather than political.

[2] See review of Ouseley, *Remarks on the Statistics and Political Institutions of the U.S., etc.* (London, 1832), in QR, Vol. 48, No. 96, Dec. 1832, Art. 9, by Jacob. For the *Westminster* on the book, see Ch. II.

[3] *Recollections of the Last Ten Years . . . in the Valley of the Mississippi* (Boston, 1831), reviewed by Lockhart in QR, Vol. 48, No. 95, Oct. 1832, Art. 7.

[4] See, for example, *Lillibridge,* pp. 37–38. Lord Wynford and Sir George Rose, who had been on a government mission to the U.S., led the opposition against the American example during the Reform debates.

[5] See, for example, his 'Reform not a new Constitution', 1831, contained in Lord Lovaine, ed., *Speeches in Parlt. and some Misc. Pamphlets of . . . Henry Drummond* (London, 1860), II. 79–118 (and also 344–5).

from the writings of Henry Tudor, Captain Marryat, and a number of liberal, but still critical observers, including Alexis de Tocqueville. Upon this basis was built up a formidable indictment of democracy.

3. *The Case against Democracy*

I

The plausibility of political doctrines is always dependent upon accompanying historical circumstances. For this reason the assault mounted by the Establishment against America was received in England with different responses at different times. Attitudes were related to a number of variables, including the accretion of further knowledge about the new world and modification of the political situation at home. During the early years of William IV's reign, circumstances frowned upon the conservatives. They opposed the doctrines of political equality then current in Radical circles by reasserting a theory of inequality, and by justifying, in Burkeian terms, a system of deference, of protective rights and obligations. The argument was made stronger by ascribing the vices of American society to an unnatural political system, which ignored hierarchies established by God and encouraged men to abandon their duties towards each other. In the political circumstances of 1832, however, few groups were prepared to listen to this talk. The Left was imbued with visions of rational systematization, and a sweeping away of customary restrictions. The Benthamites had effectively discredited as cant the narrow ideas of reactionary Toryism, and the Whigs were intent on widening the basis of power in the state. Visions of an idyllic new world were still dominant, and the propaganda-value of American precedents had been, if anything, strengthened by the prejudice of Tory reviewers.

After reform had been achieved, however, a different situation came to prevail. Reform, as we know, had come about essentially because a political readjustment of power was required to accord with economic and social change. Those groups wanting access to political power—especially the new middle-class manufacturing, capitalist interests—had been willing to use democratic propaganda to gain that end. But, after 1832, they had little further use for that propaganda, including little further use for the *political* model of America. In many cases they retained a favourable impression of the United States, which represented a desirable social and economic model to aid them in the still considerable task of rationalizing outdated aspects of the English system. But they had no desire, as new members of the Establishment, to encourage revolutionary political ideas. They gradually abandoned any fulsome praise of

universal suffrage in America, for they were united in opposing the entry
into English politics of an underprivileged working class. They hardly
shared the patrician contempt for American culture which Tories displayed, for that contempt was as easily directed against 'Manchester
culture', which had many affinities with the American. But they did
become much more willing to listen to Tory criticisms of demagoguery
in the Union.

In these same years, men's knowledge of North America was broadened
and deepened. During the thirties British news coverage of American
affairs was extended, and a spate of new travel literature provided the
source for more thoughtful interpretations of Western society. In 1835
alone six important works were published or reprinted: C. J. Latrobe's
Rambler in North America, an able Tory interpretation; a liberal and
antislavery account by E. S. Abdy;[1] two volumes on the American
churches by the visiting Congregationalists Andrew Reed and James
Matheson;[2] Francis Lieber's *Stranger in America*; Gustave de Beaumont's
social novel *Marie*; and, the most influential of all, Henry Reeve's
translation of Part I of Alexis de Tocqueville's *Democracy in America*.[3]
Michel Chevalier's *Lettres sur l'Amérique du Nord* were available in French
from 1836, and in an American translation from 1839. These writers
set a new standard in objective interpretation of an augmented store of
facts. Most, although they wrote as friendly counsellors for the United
States, were dispassionate in approach, and their comments about the
political process there were often distinctly critical. The overall effect of
their writings upon British opinion was to trim the exaggerations of
both Left and Right, but, as was inevitable, this proved more traumatic
to the reformers and idealists, whose utopian vision of the new world
was closely bound up with their political beliefs. The conservatives, on
the whole, benefited from the resultant beginnings of liberal and utilitarian disillusion about transatlantic democracy. Their star had already
begun to rise under Peel's guidance; the alarms associated with Reform
had temporarily subsided; and Anglo-American relations were comparatively placid until the end of Jackson's presidency. Tory comment
thus became less hysterical, and its strictures on the Republic, borrowed
wholesale from the new literature, became more effective.

But established opinion by no means concurred in the aim of philosophers such as Tocqueville, who studied American democracy expressly

---

[1] *Journal of a Residence and Tour in the United States, etc.*
[2] *Narrative of a Visit to the American Churches, by a Deputation from the Congregational Union of England and Wales* (London, 1835).
[3] 2 vols (London, 1835). See below, Ch. V.

in order to discover the form of popular government best suited to European needs. As Tocqueville complained, the opponents of universal suffrage in England used his criticisms in an alien spirit to discredit democratic foes and to justify aristocratic government. The old partisanship was simply writ new in the light of new circumstances. One justification given for this was the need to preserve society from precipitate change, which comparative politics encouraged. There were still Ultra-Tories like Henry Ewbank, M.P., who in 1835 anticipated an imminent democratic revolution in Britain and lamented that 'the old supports of government seem, unhappily, only to exist in recollection'.[1] The temper of the age remained inimical to conservative thought. Doctrines of *laissez faire* and Owenite socialism jostled uneasily for place. Established usages and institutions continued to be subject to challenge and rational enquiry; and Chartism and popular disorders of the later 1830's represented a mass recoil from the new industrialism. Both past and present were the subject of abuse. According to conservatives, an addiction to theory, rather than to history or experience, lay behind the apparent compulsion to destructive change which gripped Britain; and it was their complaint that theory was too often fortified by a fraudulent appeal to fact. America, as Ewbank said, was a case in point:

. . . it is the fashion of the day to consider the Americans as outstripping us in the race of liberty, and every Leveller rounds his paragraph by an appeal to the United States of America, of which he knows little more than that they have no King nor Church Establishment.[2]

Lord Mahon, the Tory historian, warned the Radicals to beware of emulating the French example of Lafayette and his visionary followers, who had been so disastrously infatuated in 1789 by vague American ideals of republican equality. The infatuation in both cases, he implied, was undiscriminating, and not based upon an historical appreciation of separate national conditions.[3] Citation of America's faults was justified, therefore, as a means of shocking radical thinkers back to their senses.

America in the age of Jackson provided much evidence for the disenchanters. A levelling egalitarian spirit seemed to be pervading politics,

---

[1] See his introduction to Fisher Ames, *The Influences of Democracy on Liberty, Property, and the Happiness of Society, etc.* (London, 1835), p. 18.

[2] Ibid. p. 2.

[3] Lafayette and others, he argued, did not consider the historical differences between France and America. The U.S. lacked 'hereditary attachments which give stability to institutions', and possessed in the back-settlements 'a constant and easy outlet for that superabundance of population and of activity which, in old countries, seeks a vent upwards by pressing against the government and richer classes'. See *QR*, Vol. 49, No. 97, Apr. 1833, p. 167 (Russell on the French Revolution), by Mahon.

and unease was felt, by British liberals as well as by Tories, that a new group—the propertyless masses organized by professional party men—was attaining power since Jackson's accession to office. Alarming accounts of the riotous scenes which occurred at the White House on the occasion of Old Hickory's inauguration appeared in the Tory journals; and a distinct impression was abroad that the Union was about to take the classical republican path into decline. The Tories played upon the widespread English dislike of rotation in office to engender suspicion of the new régime, which quickly achieved notoriety for attempting to implement that principle in the American administration. Sectionalism also appeared to have increased since Jackson's accession. The nullification debate, ending in South Carolina's threat to secede from the Union over Clay's tariff bill of 1832, seemed a portent of disunity. '. . . in how short a term', wrote Ewbank, 'has Democracy uprooted one, as I vainly fancied, of the fairest flowers of Republicanism—an ardent attachment to the integrity of the Constitution!'[1] Jackson's wrangle with Nicholas Biddle and the Bank of the United States also attracted attention.[2] To many observers this episode seemed proof of the authoritarian tendencies of American democracy. Francis Egerton, a Tory of the Canning school, thought that 'this singular contest has exhibited to the world the spectacle of the chief of a republic, raised to popularity and its consequent power by military exploit, shaking at will the social fabric of a great people by acts as arbitrary as those of the Czars or Sultans'.[3] He deplored Jackson's attempt to subvert one of the firmest financial institutions in the Union, and attributed to the President a motive of personal antipathy towards Biddle. Egerton was inclined to sympathize with the monied interests: 'To us on this side of the Atlantic, the apprehension of danger from a nascent aristocracy of wealth, which has so strongly influenced the President, appears visionary.' America's voluntary system in religion also came under fire in these years from Anglicans—such as J. J. Blunt and Henry Hart Milman for the *Quarterly*—who were perturbed by a threatened dissociation of church from state in England.[4] Visiting Americans now sensed a strong antipathy towards America, and Yankee notions, in English society: 'It is extraordinary', the writer N. P. Willis

¹ *Influences of Democracy*, op. cit., p. 8.

² Biddle in fact came to England after the panic of 1837 in an effort to obtain credit from the Bank of England for the Bank of Pennsylvania (under which name the Bank of the U.S. was trading). See B. R. Crick and M. Alman, ed., *Guide to MSS. Relating to America in Gt. Britain and Ireland* (Oxford, 1961), p. 123.

³ *QR*, vol. 58, No. 116, Apr. 1837, p. 500 (Chevalier and Cooper on Europe and America), by Egerton. He derived his facts and much of his thinking from Chevalier's *Lettres sur l'Amérique du Nord* (Paris, 1836).

⁴ See below, pp. 281ff.

confided to his diary in 1835, 'how universal this feeling seems to be against America. A half-hour *incog.* in any mixed company in England, I should think, would satisfy the most rose-coloured doubter on the subject.'[1]

II

Let us now examine in the above context some of the more systematic ideas of individual British conservatives about the American example.

One of the most powerful and closely argued cases against universal suffrage, and for the retention of property qualifications, was put forward by Thomas Hamilton in his *Men and Manners in America*, written after a tour in 1830–1. Hamilton, the brother of Sir William Hamilton, the Scots philosopher, was a member of the *Blackwood's* circle in Edinburgh, which included John Wilson, Lockhart, William Maginn, and Robert Pierce Gillies.[2] His book, when published in 1833 was quickly taken up as an anti-democratic treatise by 'Maga', and William Blackwood, as publisher, had it reprinted in 1834 and 1843.[3]

A soldier and a gentleman, Hamilton recoiled from the boisterousness of American life. During his tour, although he mixed widely in society, he preferred the company of cultured Americans such as Edward Livingston, Albert Gallatin, George Ticknor, and the circle of the *North American Review*. He especially cherished memories of his residence with the Bostonian aristocracy. He admired the polished and intellectual Alexander Hamilton, whilst accepting the blackest views current of Jefferson ('continually puling about liberty, equality, and the degrading curse of slavery'). During his stay he was subject to periodical bouts of nervous depression, which may have sharpened the vituperousness of some of his comments. Vaguely Whiggish in outlook before his visit, he returned

---

[1] N. P. Willis, *Pencillings by the Way* (New York, 1835), quoted in QR, Vol. 54, No. 108, Sept. 1835, p. 455. See also J. Fenimore Cooper, *England, with Sketches of Society in the Metropolis*, 3 vols. (London, 1837), which is at times a chorus on this theme. 'It is not easy', he wrote, 'for an American to imagine the extent of the prejudice which exists against his country in England, without close and long observation.' (Quoted in QR, Vol. 59, No. 118, Oct. 1837, p. 333.)

[2] Hamilton became known to the group through his brother, and through his novel *Cyril Thornton*, which was based upon his military experiences in the Peninsular campaign. He contributed verse and prose to *Blackwood's* under the pen-name 'Ensign O'Doherty' (later assumed by Maginn). See Elsie Swann, *Christopher North—John Wilson* (London, 1934), pp. 95, 107; and Sir George Douglas, *The Blackwood Group* (London, 1897), pp. 151–8.

[3] The *North American Review*, which objected to many of Hamilton's criticisms, described his book as 'the ablest and best written work upon this country which has appeared from the pen of a British traveller'. Quoted in *Men and Manners in America*, 3rd ed. (Edinburgh and London, 1843), p. xxv (note).

more of a Tory[1] and a convinced opponent of Reform. Indeed his book, he declared, was written because

I found the institutions and experience of the United States deliberately quoted in the reformed Parliament, as affording safe precedent for British legislation, and learned that the drivellers who uttered such nonsense, instead of countering merited derision, were listened to with patience and approbation, by men as ignorant as themselves.[2]

Hamilton believed that the American system of representation was based upon a fallacy—that men were equal in capacity and morality, and that they should therefore share equally in the framing of laws. He appreciated that no responsible American really believed the first proposition, and implied that their acceptance of democratic theory was therefore hypocritical. His sympathy was with those Federalists who had been willing to follow the logic of natural inequalities and to impose barriers in the path of the multitude. In his view, a necessary connection existed between property and morality in any social system. Indeed, that connection was probably closer in North America than in the old world:

. . . the man must either be idle or profligate, or more probably both, who does not in a country where labour is highly rewarded, obtain a [property] qualification of some sort. He is evidently unworthy of the right of suffrage, and by every wise legislature will be debarred from its exercise. In densely peopled countries the test of property in reference to moral qualities is fallible—perhaps too fallible to be relied on with much confidence. In the United States it is unerring. . . .[3]

Nevertheless, the American system was able to ignore, with impunity for the present, the need for a special representation of property interests, simply because property, in the form of land, was readily available to all, and all had thereby a 'stake in the hedge'. This, however, only delayed the day of ultimate ruin. He looked to the time when the vast resources of the West would be exhausted, and when the masses would be congregated in large industrial cities plagued by economic strife. Then, he

[1] *Men and Manners*, pp. xiii, xix, xxxiv. See, for example, a letter to Lady Hamilton of 24.1.31: 'The view I take of the American constitution is *most unfavourable*. I shall come home more of a Tory than I went out. In writing of the Americans—should I ever do so—I see I shall be hampered terribly by my sense of their kindness . . . The most educated class of Americans are very good; the less so detestable and disgusting. Then their habits—tobacco-chewing, and eternal spitting! They must be cut up' (p. xiii).

[2] Ibid. p. xxxiii. In a letter to Dugald Bannatyne, his uncle, he added: 'I wish every Radical in England could be condemned to spend a year in America; and if he is not in less than that time, utterly cured, he may be set down as hopeless' (p. xix).

[3] Quoted in *Blackwood's* review of the book, Vol. 34, Sept. 1833, p. 294 (America, No. 1).

reasoned, social pressures would become intensified and class antagonisms sharpened. In short, American conditions would be similar to those of Britain—and then would be the greatest danger of popular revolution and national disruption. Then the weakness of extreme democratic forms would be exposed, for they provided no permanent entrenchment for those classes and institutions in society likely to oppose a barrier to the fury of the mob. Political power would lie in the wrong hands—in the irresponsible hands of the suffering classes of society—and civil order could hardly survive. If Britain followed the advice of her Radicals and repeated the republican experiment of the United States, sweeping away established institutions and privileged classes, her descent into anarchy would be short and sharp. This was because all the conditions for dis-integration were already present.

Hamilton's misgivings about America were not all expressed in prognostications. He was uneasy about the present existence in New York of 'Worky Parliaments', working-men's organizations stimulated to growth by industrial hardship and clamouring, *inter alia*, for absolute equality and universality in education. It was the beginning, he suspected, of a sinister proletarian movement which aimed at undermining all intelligence and refinement. He thought it ominous that some of the extremists in the movement were already crying for a division of property. (He did not note that craft unionism was failing because of an unprole-tarian restlessness and ambition for status.) He objected to the 'fatal ascendance of a single class' in national politics, and to the elimination of the best men through the instrument of 'a vulgar but irresistable body of electors'.[1] In his opinion, the progressive and enlightened elements of society were, because of democracy, constantly assimilated to the level of the masses, to the detriment of culture, taste, and intellect.[2] He thought America's popular press scurrilous, and affirmed the Tory principle of a restricted press for Britain as the only means by which journalistic licence could be trammelled according to the standards of enlightened opinion and good taste. Hamilton deplored the effects of the voluntary system, which produced religious extravagance and sectarian

---

[1] Quoted, *Blackwood's*, ibid. p. 299.

[2] Hamilton allowed some credit in low standards to the all-consuming obsession with the frontier; but *Blackwood's*, reviewing Hamilton, was almost deterministic in describing the 'degrading equalizing tendency of democracy' as the main cause. Ibid. p. 296. Hamilton, writing to Bannatyne, declared that the 'despotism of a mob' is 'most unfavourable to the *development of mind*. Men here are judged by a *lower standard* than in England; and this standard, both in regard to knowledge and manners, is becoming lower every generation. The crop of young men now coming forward is decidedly more vulgar and more ignorant than the preceding . . .' *Men and Manners*, p. xviii.

strife. He emphasized the paradox of a slave-system endorsed by demo-crats. He critized the paucity of really good higher education[1] and predicted little prospect of the United States ever becoming a 'mental benefactor to the world'. Hamilton's experiences in the new world therefore only served to consolidate his faith in the English system of government. Such a system, he said, encouraged an assimilation of the lower orders to the higher, because the latter enjoyed both power and independence; and the result was a cumulative increase of information and intelligence. Thus Britain could expect a continuing improvement, America only a progressive deterioration, in its enlightened citizenry.

Hamilton's arguments particularly impressed Archibald Alison, the Tory historian, who was also the vigorous and opinionated leader-writer for Blackwoods in the 1830's and 1840's.[2] In reviewing *Men and Manners*, Alison fastened upon Hamilton's analysis in an attempt to refute al-together the Left's use of national comparisons to facilitate change in Britain. Rousseau had been right, said Alison, when he predicted that the American war would usher in an era of revolutions. Since then a whole series of contests had been provoked, not by monarchical rivalries, but by 'the impatient spirit and interminable expectations of the people'.[3] Rebellion had been set in motion by the contagion of American example: 'More powerful than the eloquence of Mirabeau or the sword of Napoleon, the democratic government of America has struck far and wide into the minds of the European people . . .'[4] It was therefore of 'incalculable importance' that America should be presented to the British public in its 'true colours', for the revolutionists of the age were making dangerous capital out of misguided eulogy.

---

[1] For example, he noted the lack of good libraries: '. . . at present an American might study every book within the limits of the Union and still be regarded in many parts of Europe—especially in Germany—as a man comparatively ignorant.' Quoted *Blackwood's*, Vol. 34, Sept. 1833, p. 297.

[2] Alison, author of a voluminous *History of Europe*, was a distinguished Scots lawyer. He wrote the main political comment in *Blackwood's* between 1832 and 1836, and continued to contribute until 1851. His defences of Toryism were noted for their confidence and reliance upon history. His *History* was effective but prejudiced, designed, as Disraeli said, to prove that Providence was on the side of the Tories. His antipathy to majority rule may have owed something to the fact that, as sheriff of Lanarkshire, he took a leading part in suppressing the serious Scottish riots and strikes of the 1830's and early 40's. He wrote relatively little upon America, but what he wrote was of strategic importance—the most important being his reviews of Hamilton in 1833 and of Tocqueville's *Democracy in America* for *Blackwood's* in 1836 and 1847. For Alison's account of the expectations of revolution held by Tories in 1832–3, see his *Some Account of My Life and Writings: an Autobiography*, ed. by his daughter-in-law, Lady Alison, 2 vols. (Edinburgh, 1883), I. 325–6.

[3] *Blackwood's*, Vol. 34, Sept. 1833, p. 285 (by Alison).

[4] Ibid. p. 285.

The first duty of conservatives, according to Alison, was to dispel the illusion that prosperity in America was related to the existence of political equality and to indicate to the unstudied masses that democratical principles were inapplicable to the aged dynasties of Europe. Such people were too easily misled by the splendid vision of material success in the Republic:

The facts of a nation existing without a monarch or nobles, or public debt, rarely engaged in war, steadily advancing in opulence; without pauperism in many of its provinces, without a standing army in any; with an immense commerce, and a boundless territory; with a population doubling every thirty years, and public wealth tripling in the same time, are amply sufficient to account for the powerful interest which they have excited in the Eastern World. . . .[1]

The special circumstances of the new world, however, explained this achievement. They included the vast resources of the continent, and the absence of a dense population, of a public debt, and of any relics of feudalism. Success was due, not to any political system, but to the dispensations of God and the historical accident of Anglo-Saxon settlement. Without a British heritage of law and order, without the sturdy characteristics of the Anglo-Saxons, the United States, alleged Alison, would long since have succumbed to the pernicious influence of democracy. Here was a view which was the exact contrary to that of the Benthamites, in that it attributed all bad effects to the nature of American government and all good effects to 'other causes'. Both sides were clearly more determined to fit the facts of America into their existing political prejudices than to verify hypotheses about politics from the rich mine of material in existence there.

Alison was endeavouring to deny that comparison could legitimately be made between new and old worlds. Institutions which worked in the unique circumstances of America were wholly unsuited to old nations, 'grown grey in a certain political career, overflowing with inhabitants, overwhelmed with debt, with vast property accumulated in a few hands, no unoccupied land to divide and millions dependent upon the wages of labour'.[2] Hamilton had shown what would happen should democracy be transplanted to such conditions. The whole mania for generalization from one set of national conditions to another was dangerous, in Alison's opinion. The French Revolution had occurred out of a passion for imitating the political models of Britain and America. The Parisian revolt of 1830, still fresh in mind, had touched off similar uprisings elsewhere. Never, he asserted, had one country's institutions been successfully

---

[1] Ibid. p. 286.   [2] Ibid.

transferred to another; even the English constitution was unamenable to transfer, as the failure of Sicilian and Portuguese attempts at imitation had proved. It was unthinkable, therefore, that the ancient fabric of the British constitution should yield to the shock of an irrelevant transatlantic example. This variant upon the theme of 'propitious circumstances' was a good argument to present to upper-class English opinion. Similar considerations had impressed deeper thinkers than Alison, including Sir James Mackintosh among the Whigs and John Stuart Mill among the intellectual Radicals.

Because they loomed so large in Tory opinion from 1832, John Wilson Croker's ideas about America are important. Croker was commissioned by Murray in 1831 to write the main political articles for the *Quarterly Review*, and he retained virtually sole control of its political policy until 1854, enjoying close relations with the Tory hierarchy for most of those years. Unlike his predecessors Miller and Fullarton, Croker wrote a stream of articles upon American affairs and strove energetically to oppose Radical propaganda about that country. He was said, whilst earlier at the Admiralty, to have prepared political agitation for the British New Orleans campaign against the United States. Yet he was never Americophobe, despite his intractable opposition to democratic theory. In many ways he was saved from exaggeration by his sense of history. He read a number of documents upon the American Revolution and thereafter always refused to regard that event as in any way analogous to the French Revolution. It was, in his view, not a thoroughgoing revolution at all. 'A distant metropolis, an unknown aristocracy, and an unseen sovereign' had been repudiated, but 'the stations of men, the rights of property, the territorial divisions, the form and force of the law suffered little change'.[1] The political changes made in 1787 had been accepted without trouble, for they were not very abrupt. They had not been engineered by men of Jacobin or Chartist ilk; in many ways they simply confirmed the essentially republican character of colonial society.[2] Instinctive enmity to Church and King, and other traditions of the Great Rebellion, had been preserved in a society dominated by dissenters. Even physical conditions, he saw, favoured social equality and political democracy. This was a thoughtful analysis, not provoked merely by propagandist motives. Croker preferred to look upon the Revolution

---

[1] *QR*, Vol. 53, No. 106, Apr. 1835, p. 555 (Essays of Fisher Ames).

[2] See *QR*, Vol. 68, No. 136, Sept. 1841, p. 476 (Letters of Mrs. Adams). He wrote: 'Much, therefore, as we may regret the grand original mistakes in the system of colonial polity, and blame the conduct, at once rash and weak of the British ministers, which drove the provinces to revolt, it is clear that their independence could not in the natural course of things have been long postponed' (p. 476).

not as an ideological decision in favour of democracy—as did both the Radicals and the Ultra-Tories—but as a secession from imperial rule in order to confirm a way of life natural to the American environment.

By taking this attitude, Croker was able to draw the conservative inference that governments ought only to be changed in accordance with the habits and history of their people, and never radically. Like Alison, he employed effectively the argument of 'propitious circumstances'. America was of vast size and did not have any turbulent metropolis like Paris or London, where *sans-culotte* uprisings could occur. The nation, he wrote in 1835, 'accords room for the emigration and self-removal of the discontented and turbulent; it renders difficult, if not impossible, the assembling democratic crowds in such numbers and such places as could affect the general security'.[1] He was impressed by the federal system of government and by other features of an ingenious constitution that provided effective impediments against rash change and popular paroxysms.

Croker was an advocate, for hard-headed reasons, of conciliatory relations with the United States. He agreed, in public, with the liberal-Tory view that Anglo-American interests were complementary. In 1841, at a low point in Atlantic affairs, he wrote of the two nations:

In truth, we know of no material and substantial interest in which they are *opposed* —nay, in which they are separated: their origin, their laws, and their language are the same; their business, their prosperity, are identified: New York is but a suburb of Liverpool, or, if you will, Liverpool of New York: the failure of the Pennsylvania bank ruined more fortunes in England than in America; the manufacturers of Manchester share more wealth with Carolina than with Middlesex. We are not merely brothers and cousins—the ties of consanguinity, we know, are not always the bond of friendship—but we are *partners—joint tenants*, as it were, of the commerce of the world. . . .[2]

Such sentiments were worthy of the Manchester School. They were not, however, the whole of Croker's view. Indeed, shortly before preparing the above passage, he had stated in a letter to Lockhart his opinion that democratic France 'was and is, and will and *must* be, world without end—our natural enemy, and therefore the natural ally of our other natural enemy, America'.[3] There was no necessary inconsistency

[1] QR, Vol. 53, No. 106, Apr. 1835, pp. 555–6. He also placed emphasis on the fact that the labouring class in America was a landed one. See QR, Vol. 46, No. 92, Jan. 1832, p. 584.

[2] QR, Vol. 69, No. 137, Dec. 1841, p. 271 (Letters of John Adams).

[3] Croker to Lockhart, 8.10.1840, in the Murray Collection, London. The passage is quoted in M. F. Brightfield, *John Wilson Croker* (California, 1940), p. 392. Brightfield has a useful discussion of Croker's views on America on pp. 389–94.

here, however. His unfavourable views of America sprang from a particular idea of history and of the role of conservatism in Britain, which had little to do with any notion of economic interdependence between Atlantic states.

Croker's mind never adapted itself to the changes of 1832. Uneasy about the disturbing new doctrines which challenged old orders and settled things, he continued to look nostalgically to the time when the formula of Kings, Lords, and Commons was accepted, but when in reality the monarch and aristocracy retained control through influence. As he admitted in 1851 to his friend and fellow-conservative Guizot, 'for parade we kept up the *forms*, rather more than the principle, of Kings, Lords, and Commons'.[1] The mistake had been made in 1832 of granting real power to the 'democratical estate', and the way opened for 'that many-mouthed Cerberus' to swallow all. The efforts of Peel and Disraeli, in their profoundly different ways, to re-shape the Conservative party in a new image dictated by this *fait accompli* never received Croker's wholehearted approval, although he gave Peel every practical assistance to revitalize the party. The main extraneous influence upon Croker's political thought was that of recent French history, which he had studied closely. He believed that France, with its cyclic revolutions and despotisms, was the prototype to which all countries embracing representative government tended; and he managed to fit most English and American history after 1830 into this hypothesis. Looking back in 1851, he viewed Peel, and Whigs like Lord John Russell, as apostates who had bowed before an increasingly tyrannical public opinion and allowed restraining influences and the remnants of older authority to be weathered away. In America, in the same way, an even faster development towards complete democracy had taken place. Croker constantly drew attention to this depressing fact.

When Croker first began to write regularly for the *Quarterly*, he was of the opinion that a tremulous equilibrium existed in the new world between democratic tendencies on one hand and the conservative influence of physical conditions and constitutional checks on the other. Already he feared that majority rule bred authoritarianism in politics and in all spheres of opinion; and he predicted further encroachments upon liberty as population increased and the frontier receded.[2] Like Mackintosh and Hamilton, he prophesied an attack upon property when democracy became industrial and institutions were exposed to trial from

[1] Croker to Guizot, 14th July, 1851; quoted in *Brightfield*, pp. 400-1.
[2] See *QR*, Vol. 46, No. 92, Jan. 1832, pp. 583-5; and Vol. 53, No. 106, Apr. 1835, p. 556.

'the pauperism of great towns or the vicissitudes of demand and supply'.[1] In these doubts, as he shrewdly noted, 'we only concur with the wisest and most patriotic of the statesmen of America—of the authors of the experiment—of the very founders of the constitution!'[2] Croker, like Lockhart, was contemptuous of American culture and appalled by the rawness and vulgarity everywhere apparent. He dwelt upon these blemishes, as when he reviewed Dickens's *American Notes* in 1843, because he attributed them to political institutions: '. . . the fruits, in short, of a *despot-democracy*, which we believe to be essentially hostile to the advancement of civilization, the refinement of manners, the purity of morals, the growth of the human mind, and the consequent extension of human happiness'.[3] This belief was confirmed for him by American actions in Maine, Texas, and Oregon after 1837, and by the growing sectional bitterness generated by slavery in the 40's. Croker, however, had no pat solution to American problems. A chronic defender of the *status quo* in Britain, he also feared that change in the United States might disrupt Anglo-American relations, or cause more evils than it abolished.[4] He was committed to the opinion that American society, being essentially republican, was naturally suited to democracy. Nevertheless, on occasions he made what must have seemed to serious students of America a curiously barren suggestion, that only a return to monarchy or a quasi-aristocracy could resolve the Union's legion difficulties. This represented the groping attempt of one not familiar with the dimensions of the task to rescue the nation from the grasp of abstract principles. By some means he wanted the Americans to evolve a system of restraints and obligations in society comparable to that of unreformed England.

Neither Samuel Taylor Coleridge nor Benjamin Disraeli, the two most eloquent voices of conservatism in the nineteenth century, wrote very much upon transatlantic affairs or seemed much influenced by them; and this is a fair indication of the limitations of American example as a stimulus to thought. Both, however, when they did consider the new world, repudiated any effete insular view of it, and this attitude gradually became more common in the Tory press. Coleridge had written before his death in 1834:

The possible destiny of the United States of America—as a nation of a hundred millions of freemen—stretching from the Atlantic to the Pacific, living under the

---

[1] Ibid. p. 583 (Jan. 1832).
[2] QR, Vol. 69, No. 137, Dec. 1841, p. 270 (Letters of John Adams).
[3] QR, Vol. 71, No. 142, Mar. 1843, p. 522.
[4] He stated in 1841 that he had not the 'slightest desire' that the American system should fail—'On the contrary, we think it of great importance to the future welfare

laws of Alfred, and speaking the language of Shakespeare and Milton—is an august conception. Why should we not wish to see it realized? America would then be England viewed through a solar microscope—Great Britain in a state of glorious magnification! How deeply to be lamented is the spirit of hostility and sneering which some popular books of travels have shown in treating of the Americans![1]

Lockhart took this admonition to heart, and the *Quarterly* publicly apologized in 1835 for its earlier spleen against the United States.[2] In practice this meant that propaganda against democracy, during the placid years of the mid-thirties, took the form of granting American successes, then explaining them away, rather than of just abusing the Americans. Coleridge's emphasis upon the racial contribution of the Anglo-Saxons to American culture was admirably plausible as an explanation of success which had, however, no association with democracy.

Disraeli in the 1820's had speculated in a South American mining venture (which lost him £7,000) and prepared an English edition of a *Life of Paul Jones*. He wrote a short section upon America in his *Vindication of the English Constitution*, published in 1835; and, on the occasion of the Commons debate upon the Webster-Ashburton treaty (which he strongly defended), he surprised his colleagues by his knowledge of the intricate Maine border dispute. This virtually summed up his interest in the new world before 1845. He took a liberal and never a depreciatory view of the Americans. Their splendid success he believed to be a product, quite apart from geography, of their long-standing love of liberty, which had enabled a republican system to be founded on a stable basis of habit and opinion:

He is a short-sighted politician who dates the Constitution of the United States from 1780. It was established by the Pilgrim Fathers a century and a half before, and influenced a people practised from their cradles in the duties of self-government. The Pilgrim Fathers brought to their land of promise the laws of England, and a republican religion; and blended together, these formed the old colonial constitution of Anglo-America. The transition from such a government to the polity

---

(Continued from p. 121)
of mankind that it should succeed.' *QR*, Vol. 69, No. 137, Dec. 1841, p. 270. These may have been empty words, but they are consistent with his appreciation of Atlantic links.

[1] *Specimens of the Table Talk of S. T. Coleridge* (London, 1835), quoted in *QR*, Vol. 53, No. 105, Feb. 1835, p. 95.

[2] *QR*, Vol. 54, No. 108, Sept. 1835, p. 408 (Tours in America by Latrobe, Abdy, etc.). Regret was confessed at the tone employed towards the Americans in reviews of Mrs. Trollope and Basil Hall. 'Let us hear no more then—at least, let us hear nothing in harsh, contemptuous, or arrogant language—about the petty circumstances which may happen to strike an English eye, accustomed to the highly-cultivated features of society in the upper walks of life in England, as offensively characteristic of the people of America. . . .' (p. 408.)

of Washington was certainly not greater in degree than the difference between Great Britain of 1829 and our country at this hour. Anglo-Americans did not struggle for liberty: they struggled for independence; and the freedom and the free institutions they had long enjoyed secured for them the great object of their severe exertions. He who looks upon the citizens of the United States as a new people commits a moral, if not a historical, anachronism.[1]

The conclusion that Disraeli drew from the American condition thus accorded with a basic premise of his conservatism:

. . . that political institutions, founded on abstract rights and principles, are mere nullities; that the only certain and legitimate foundation of liberty is law; that if there be no privity between the old legal Constitution of a country and the new legislature, the latter must fall; and that a free government on a great scale of national representation is the very gradual work of time, and especially of preparatory institutions.[2]

This justification, used freely for denying any substantial extension of the franchise until the 1860's, caused little joy to the Radicals.

Free traders, for their part, found more gratification in the views of Francis Egerton. Egerton, the younger son of the Marquis of Stafford, served in Tory administrations as a Lord of the Treasury in 1827, as Under-Secretary for the Colonies in 1828, and as Secretary for War in 1830. A liberal Tory, a follower of Canning and Huskisson (besides becoming in 1822 the son-in-law of Charles Greville), Egerton was an Anglican, but also a believer in free trade, and a supporter of London University. He was therefore more inclined than many conservatives to take the modern industrialist-whig view of America. He was much influenced by Michel Chevalier's stimulating and sympathetic account of the United States in the *Letters from North America*, which he read in French in 1836. Egerton, in the *Quarterly*, advocated a more tolerant consideration of that country's political affairs: 'There is an innate principle of vigour in the condition of America which may enable her long to endure without flinching the shocks which universal suffrage generates.'[3]

---

[1] Benjamin Disraeli, *Vindication of the English Constitution*, etc. (London, 1835), reprinted in William Hutcheson, ed., *Whigs and Whiggism: Political Writings of Benjamin Disraeli* (London, 1913), Ch. X, p. 144.

[2] Ibid. p. 145. Disraeli, at the time of the struggle for the 1867 reform, used the 'propitious circumstances' argument to oppose democratic institutions in Britain. If they were adopted, Britain 'from being a first-rate Kingdom, would become a third-rate Republic'. Quoted in Pelling, op. cit., p. 12.

[3] *QR*, Vol. 58, No. 116, Apr. 1837, p. 501 (Chevalier and Cooper on Europe and America). He added: 'It is only when in actual conflict with those who, neglecting differences of condition and relations of space, would advocate the rash substitution of American institutions for our own, that we are willing to prefer topics of doubt and animadversion to those of eulogy' (p. 519).

Good sense, he pointed out, triumphed more often than not in American politics (an observation which could hardly have been made in a Tory journal five years earlier, or five years later). Egerton risked the censure of Tory nationalists by wondering whether American institutions were not best suited 'for the performance of that mighty mission of territorial occupation and civilization to which she is evidently destined'.[1] Being a free-trader, Egerton saw the Union as a 'vast scene of speculative enterprise' in which ideas circulated with commerce. He compared it to a giant gaming-table where fortunes were to be won or lost, but the game was balanced in favour of the player. He held no brief for democracy in new or old worlds, but he was fascinated by the economic scope of a non-corporate society which offered unlimited individual opportunities. Others in the group which supported Peel's new Toryism undoubtedly felt the same.

III

So far it seems apparent that between 1832 and 1837 attitudes towards America became more liberal. However, by employing certain general propaganda techniques, especially the theory of 'propitious circumstances', conservatives managed to be more tolerant without making any concessions to democratic doctrine.[2] Instead of being abusive, they put forward eminently reasonable objections to Jacksonian democracy and made plausible predictions that an industrial America could not afford to bear the cross of universal suffrage. The Tories emphasized the influence of tradition and continuity in American history and politics—neglected by British democrats—and made deductions unfavourable to radical change in Britain.

It now remains to look more closely at the way in which the Tories countered Radical propaganda upon specific issues of democratic theory—to examine, for example, how they assessed public men in the Union, how they estimated corruption, the effect of the ballot, and so on. Conservatives themselves gave very great weight to these empirical considerations. To them the American Revolution had produced no great or novel principles by which it could alternatively be judged. The leading ideas of the Founding Fathers, of Jefferson and the Jacksonians, had been debated by the Greeks, had enjoyed a lively existence in English

[1] Ibid. p. 501.
[2] I do not mean to suggest that such techniques were not, or could not be, legitimate thinking. In the hands of Mackintosh, John Mill, Disraeli, and other serious thinkers, they were undoubtedly so; but, in many instances, they were more obviously a device to protect the premises of the writer than a genuine attempt to get at the truth.

political thought of the seventeenth century, and had flourished in the natural rights schools of eighteenth-century Europe. Long before it was enshrined in the American Constitution, English Tories had to encounter the subversive proposition, put forward by men like Algernon Sidney and John Locke, that mankind enjoyed inalienable rights and liberties proceeding from nature. They had to encounter too the common corollaries of this view, that all lawful government rested upon consent and that the law was above all rulers. Radically democratic theories had been aired by the Levellers during the Civil War. James Harrington, Milton, and Sidney had openly espoused republican principles. Countless royalist and Tory pamphleteers had tried to repudiate these doctrines by reaffirming the royal prerogative, by ridiculing the contract theory of politics and the natural rights dogma, and by demonstrating the meaninglessness of the idea of popular sovereignty.

The essence of the conservative case against the principles professedly underlying the American constitution was expressed most succinctly in the works of Burke. Hume and Burke together had shown that the belief in natural rights was untenable, and by so doing they enabled later critics to assert that the United States was bound ideologically to a mere dogma. The conservatives were interested in making this point because they believed that a British Radicalism tied to a doctrine of immutable individual rights would be politically dangerous, as French jacobinism had been. They hoped that natural rights theories would be displaced, not by Bentham's utilitarianism or by Hegel's idealism, but by Burke's conservatism. In Burke there could be found justification of a British political system which had no room for sweeping innovations based on an American comparison, or indeed upon comparison at all. He, unlike the Americans, took a pragmatic, and never a doctrinal, view of individual liberties, even whilst he was defending those of the rebellious colonists. He revered tradition and a British constitution based on a balance between Crown, Lords, and Commons. His idea that society was a very complex structure based upon history and custom, not upon reason, precluded political systematization of the type envisaged by idealists and intellectual Radicals. (Indeed, it was in many ways the idea of Americans as systematizers that frightened the Tories most during the first half of the nineteenth century.) Burke's view of the constitution as a balance between the great vested interests of the nation, and his theory of virtual representation, were also incompatible with universal suffrage on American lines. He rejected egalitarian theories in favour of an hierarchial view of society, and he always stressed the need to conserve customary relations and obligations. His powerful and complex conservative philosophy was a reply to the Radicals of the past and a warning against the dangerous new Messianism of the French Revolution; but it also supplied nineteenth-century Tories with a theoretical answer to the American example.

Because, on the whole, the political philosophy underlying the American system appeared to conservatives to be derivative, the significance of America was seen to be as a case-study in the translation of theory into practice, as a test of principles rather than as a fruitful new source of theory. The discussion of its results was therefore often more valuable when it turned upon specific problems. Abstract rejections of American political theory were too often, as Hazlitt said, 'saying ditto to Mr. Burke'. Conservatives usually conceived it as their task rather to demonstrate, from actual conditions in the United States, that Burke had been right and the democratic theorists of the ages wrong.

One of the most popular test cases concerned the calibre of the American representative. It was Basil Hall among Tories who provided concrete support for the suspicion that 'tall poppies' were few and far between in the United States and were becoming rarer than ever in the Jacksonian era. Before the publication of his *Travels* (1829), opinion had been divided on America's public men. John Neal, in *Blackwood's*, had given fulsome praise to Franklin, Jefferson, Hamilton, Marshall, the Adamses, and, among lesser men, to Edward Everett, Henry Clay, and Jared Sparks. But Tories in the past had distrusted Madison and Monroe. Many strongly disapproved of Jefferson, the democrat and Francophile; and they were until the 1830's unanimous in their dislike of Jackson, the slayer of Arbuthnot and friend (they thought) of the plebeians. (Jackson, however, was successfully to establish cordial relations with the heads of the Tory party during the middle years of his presidency.) Basil Hall attacked the calibre of the average representative elected democratically in state and federal assemblies. He objected that they were no better than the mass of voters who elected them, in capacity or morality. They were inexpert in matters of government, which was carried on by a 'few abler and more intriguing heads', and were often venal. American debates were, he claimed, emptily rhetorical, jejune, partisan and time-wasting—even at the highest level. He blamed frequent elections, which quickened the turn-over of politicians, for preventing the creation of an experienced cadre of men. They also rendered representatives even more grossly servile to an untutored electorate.[1]

These points were hammered home after 1829, for the Benthamites

[1] Hall's ideas are succinctly condensed in the *Quarterly*'s review of his book; Vol. 41, No. 82, Nov. 1829, Art. 6, by Barrow.

were weakest on the issue of representation. Both Whigs and Tories believed that government depended upon sound administration by good and able men. The utilitarians placed more emphasis upon making the representatives responsible to the electors; and, as we have seen, their doctrine of delegation was something of a political liability in the early thirties.[1] They attempted to regain the initiative by asserting that their system of universal suffrage might produce able men who were *also* responsible to the electorate. The Tories denied them the best of both worlds, however. They agreed wholeheartedly that American representatives were bound to the people, but insisted that this was achieved only at the sacrifice of ability or honour in public men. Egalitarian dogmas bred jealousy of superior talents, a disapproval of distinction or difference. As a result, the American of ability was debarred from politics, *unless* he prostrated himself before the god of public opinion. As Thomas Hamilton wrote to his uncle from Washington in 1831:

No man can even enter public life without first truckling to the mob, and too often paltering with his conscience. He must profess—often falsely profess—to entertain all the prejudices of the ignorant men by whom he is elected. He goes to Congress with a halter round his neck. Let him dare to differ from them by one hair's breadth, and he is kicked out, and his hopes blighted for ever.[2]

It is difficult to underestimate the importance attached to this type of criticism by all sorts of thinkers in Britain, from moderate Benthamites rightwards, to whom the idea of 'truckling to the mob' was abhorrent. Evidence was simply needed to confirm that the allegation had some basis of truth for American prestige to slump sharply. The 1830's provided this evidence. Even Andrew Reed, a Dissenter and a liberal, was disappointed by the mediocrity of politicians in the America of 1835.[3] Men of initiative, he pointed out, went into business, or some more lucrative profession than politics, which tempted only the needy. He feared that Americans might awake one day, after a crisis, 'to find their free country, and all its fine prospects, in the hands of a few ambitious and illprincipled demagogues'. Tories kept repeating the prophecy until 1861. Sir Robert Peel used Tocqueville's strictures upon the subject in some of his public speeches of the late thirties;[4] whilst reviewers picked out from the memoirs of distinguished diplomats such as Sir Augustus Foster proof that the political influence of the well-born was being systematically

[1] See above, pp. 60ff.
[2] Hamilton to Bannatyne, 15.2.31, quoted in *Men and Manners*, p. xvii.
[3] Reed and Matheson, *passim*.
[4] See, for example, *A Correct Report of Sir Robert Peel's Speeches at Glasgow, Jan. 1837* (London, 1837), pp. 80–84.

undermined.[1] The Tory press pointed to the American adventure in Texas, to the activities of demagogues in Maine and Oregon, to the election of small-minded expansionists such as Polk, to verify the truths stated by Hamilton and Tocqueville.

Concern for the quality of politicians was part of a broader theme— Tocqueville's celebrated 'tyranny of the majority'. The opinion was abroad long before Alexander Beresford-Hope expressed it in 1862, that a 'miserable, levelling democracy' was rapidly landing the United States 'in a perfectly Assyrian despotism'.[2] Even before Tocqueville made his authoritative analysis, there had been disquiet in England about the persecution of the Federalists and their ideas, about the scrutiny to which a man's beliefs and behaviour were subjected before he was deemed suitable for any office.[3] In 1831, Richard Chenevix, the Quarterly's Irish expert on France, described American democracy as quasi-despotic, 'because it consults the wishes of one class, to the exclusion of all the rest'.[4]

To the British conservative there was something sinister about the unanimity of support given by Americans to the political system drawn up in 1787. He suspected that the majority was using its powers of oppression to maintain a status quo favourable to itself. (He had not the Whig confidence that love of liberty preserved the Union, or the utilitarian belief that selfish interest was producing happiness for all.) There was virtually no opposition to the fundamental attributes of the prevailing system, as Croker pointed out, because none was likely to be tolerated:

In few countries . . . is there really less freedom of thought or action for any individual, who may be disinclined to swim with the stream, than there is in the

[1] Foster, envoy at Washington until 1812, believed, for example, that the attack upon the B.U.S. was one aspect of such a campaign. He stressed the democratic jealousy, especially in the West, of the educated and wealthy: Democrats 'see an Aristocrat in a well-dressed banker, who, used to order, naturally dislikes their rowing, noisy, bullying ways; and, reckless of the consequences, they pursue the institution with an inveteracy unworthy of the chiefs of the party'. Upon this jealousy he also blamed the widespread practice of removing state capitals from sea-board cities to pioneering towns of the interior. See Sir A. J. Foster, Notes on the United States. Excerpts from these memoirs, then unpublished, appeared in the QR, Vol. 68, No. 135, June 1841, Art. 2, by Lockhart. The quotation above is from p. 52 of this article.
[2] A. J. Beresford-Hope, England, the North and the South, etc. (London, 1862), pp. 9–10. This politician's books on the civil war, anti-north and anti-democratic, are excellent examples of upper-class Americophobia.
[3] See, for example, QR, Vol. 37, No. 73, Jan. 1828, p. 291, by Barrow.
[4] QR, Vol. 43, No. 85, May 1830, p. 224 (Political Condition and Prospects of France).

United States. . . . A single despot may often be a sufficiently stern master; but against a tyranny of ten millions who can hope to stand up?[1]

Hamilton also recoiled from a system that imposed democratic orthodoxies upon public men.[2] Although, as he observed, the British Parliament was reputed to be a corrupt organ of old-world decadence, it contained a much greater variety of allegiances (ranging from high Toryism to 'lightly veiled republicanism') than any American assembly.

Gustave de Beaumont's novel *Marie*, published in 1835 and received with favour by the Tory press, was a further indictment of tyrannical public opinion, this time as it sanctioned the oppression of the negroes.[3] Beaumont, whose ideas were profoundly influenced by those of his close friend and travelling companion, Tocqueville, suggested that, where the masses ruled everything, the individual became a small cog in large movements. He could oppose the values and prejudices of the majority only at the risk of ostracism or annihilation. Civilization itself was affected by a form of claustrophobia, because mediocrity—the standard of the many—was enforced as a leading principle in culture and politics. 'Middling understandings reject great minds, just as weak eyes abhor the broad light of day.'[4] National self-adulation went unchallenged; and, ultimately, in an homogeneous society, the unsocial values of the market would become universal. Beaumont, like Tocqueville, was ready to accept these vices as the price of self-government—but the aristocrats in Britain were not. As Lockhart commented, it was impossible to expect Englishmen to undergo such travail, simply in order to obtain ' "Le Peuple Homme d'affaires"—i.e. the Joseph Hume nation'.[5]

Keen dislike of 'Yankee despotism' produced a veritable wail of anguish during the deterioration of Anglo-American relations after 1837. The international situation strengthened the hand of the Tory nationalists. It cut short the disposition of more liberal brothers, such as Egerton, to savour vicariously the sense of American enterprise and mission, which appealed so much to English economists and manufacturers. America preoccupied with her Manifest Destiny was obviously

---

[1] *QR*, Vol. 46, No. 92, Jan. 1832, p. 585.

[2] 'Every man in Congress', he wrote to Bannatyne in 1831, '*must* and *does* profess himself a *democrat*, though he may be at heart a monarchist.' *Men and Manners*, p. xvii.

[3] See *QR*, Vol. 53, No. 106, Apr. 1835, p. 295 (M. Beaumont on the Americans). Beaumont pointed out the dependence of (especially Southern) magistrates and functionaries upon the people: 'The popular sovereignty is irresistible . . . its least hints are commands; it does not *mend* its indocile agents, it *breaks* them' (quoted, p. 295). *Marie* was written from the impressions received of America on his celebrated tour with Tocqueville.

[4] Quoted, ibid. p. 299.   [5] Ibid. p. 309.

a different proposition from America pursuing a virtuous republican policy of isolation—and the change was attributed to ascendant democracy. Tory imperialists, already on the defensive against the anti-colonialist Little Englanders, denounced the republican roughnecks who aided the Canadian rebels after 1837, and who provoked the successive *Caroline* and McLeod incidents. Demagogues, they claimed, had hotted up the crisis over the Maine border, and popular pressure upon the government prevented the resolution of diplomatic disputes over the right of search—a matter of special interest to the anti-slavery zealots amongst the British gentry. It is true that Croker, and the party leaders, were willing to compromise over such issues as the North-East boundary, and later defended the Webster-Ashburton settlement against British and Canadian critics.[1] But the reputation of American democracy suffered a shock in these years which was not repaired by negotiation; and many more English opinions were alienated in the subsequent era of further American expansion.

It was widely believed that the President in the United States was being seduced into dangerous policies by the insidious flattery he received from a glory-seeking mob, as in the case of Jackson;[2] or else that he was overawed by the power of the populace, as in the case of Van Buren and Polk. According to the diplomat Foster, the trouble began when Jefferson, at the time of the split between Federalists and Republicans, built up support by courting the 'democratical party': 'He flattered the low passions of a mere newspaper-taught rabble, and seemed pleased to mortify men of rank and station . . . unless they paid him servile court.' By personally assuming republican manners, by setting the capital in an agrarian locality, by his theories of popular rights, he had opened the way to full-blooded, and now tyrannous, democracy.[3] (In this respect, if not in their interpretation of the framing of the constitution,

---

[1] See *QR*, Vol. 67, No. 134, Mar. 1841, Art. 8 (U.S. Boundary Question), by Croker; and *QR*, Vol. 71, No. 142, Mar. 1843, Art. 12 (Treaty of Washington), also by Croker. He applauded the success of the mission led by Lord Ashburton, a close friend of his. Disraeli also defended the treaty against Palmerston's vitriolic charge that it was a capitulation.

[2] E. S. Abdy, no Tory, was critical of the atmosphere he found at Washington during Jackson's term: '. . . an American need not go to St. Petersburgh or St. James to find a courtier. I was, indeed, not a little surprised at the gross flattery with which this old man was fed. What a subject for Lucian or Le Sage! Here were the vices of a court in all their deformity; arrogance without dignity, and adulation without refinement. . . .' Quoted from *Journal of a Residence and Tour in the U.S.* (London, 1835), in *QR*, Vol. 54, No. 108, Sept. 1835, p. 401.

[3] Foster, op. cit.; see *QR*, Vol. 68, No. 135, June 1841, p. 26. This article scooped the other periodicals, for Lockhart was able to consult Foster's MS. jottings and diaries.

Englishmen and Americans were substantially agreed in their historical stereotypes.)

As the United States intruded into the British sphere of influence in Central America, as Texas was annexed to the Union in 1845 and war broke out with Mexico in 1846, as a serious Anglo-American crisis arose at the same time over Oregon, genuine alarm was felt in Britain at the aggressive temper of transatlantic democracy. The Wild West received its first gust of real publicity in this decade, but stories of frontier lynchings and gun law did not increase confidence in the responsibility of majorities. Under their rule, politics seemed more turbulent, sectional animosities more bitter. Culture continued to lag behind European standards, and a materialist ethos seemed to hold the nation in thrall. America was obviously undergoing great changes, but Britain's cultured minority looked upon them with intense unease.

Americans themselves were plagued by doubts and questionings about the character of the age, and the Tories drew upon these as excellent propaganda. In 1838 the *Quarterly* commissioned an article upon the affair of Texan independence from Benjamin Bussey Thatcher, a Northerner, a convinced opponent of slavery and editor of the *Colonizationist* (which favoured expatriation of negroes to Liberia as a solution of the slavery problem).[1] Thatcher impeached the South for attempting to open a new slave market, and for encouraging American adventurers (motivated by ideas of profitable land-speculation) in a 'high-handed theft'. The slogan of 'liberty for the people' of Texas, he alleged, was a cloak for grossly materialist ends; and he quoted extensively from W. E. Channing, and other anti-annexationists, to show the extent of indignation amongst righteous Americans about the episode. These sentiments were well calculated to appeal to the opponents of slavery who formed a significant portion of Tory opinion. The crusade of philanthropic aristocrats against American slavery was often, as Dr. Clare Taylor points out, 'a backhanded way of hitting at America'. Enslaved Africans were regarded as 'a proof of the inherent falsity of American democracy'[2]

[1] *QR*, Vol. 61, No. 122, Apr. 1838, Art. 3 (Texas). Thatcher was not an abolitionist, and he strove to dissociate his journal from William Lloyd Garrison and his followers. Thatcher visited England in 1836–8, contributing another article, upon 'Atlantic Steam Navigation', to the *Quarterly* in 1838.

[2] Clare Taylor, 'Notes on American Negro Reformers in Victorian Britain', *Bulletin of the British Assoc. for American Studies*, New Series, No. 2, Mar. 1961, pp. 45, 46. The *Quarterly's* tactics on Texas, it should be noted, were in striking contrast to those of the *Edinburgh Review*, which was still in 1841 defending independence in the hope that the new Republic, under the British wing, might become a buffer state between the U.S. and Latin America. See *ER*, Apr. 1841, Art. X, by Charles Buller.

and of the prevalent prejudice of sacred majorities. Anti-slavery interests
in Britain consistently opposed the extension of Southern influence into
Texas and Mexico in the 1840's, lobbying against the trading, banking,
and cotton interests, which favoured American expansion.[1] They lost
their fight, but they mobilized much middle-class and evangelical, as
well as upper-class and high church, opinion against democracy in the
process.

James Fenimore Cooper, who suffered from public opinion at home,
became bitter about its parochial and partisan character; and his complaints duly appeared in the Quarterly.[2] So did the criticisms which
Horace Mann levelled against American society in order to draw attention
to his campaign for educational reform. It was symptomatic of English
conditions that, whilst educationists and reformers (such as George
Combe and Richard Cobden) were stimulated by Mann's brilliant new
understanding of school problems, and by the 'Massachusetts system'
which he fathered,[3] the Tories were exclusively interested in his con-
demnations of untutored majority rule. Mann, like Channing and others,
was appalled by the violence and corruption of politics and dismayed by
materialism and the low standards of business ethics. He feared that
America was too subject to the 'ignorant rapacity of mob-rule', enforced
upon politicians by means of pledges and the threat of removal from
office. Conscience had flown out of the window, to be replaced by
popular whim. Mann had unbounded confidence that education could
provide the enlightened, and moral, public opinion upon which republicanism depended. But Croker, who introduced Mann's ideas to
conservatives in Britain,[4] had none of this confidence. He gave little
account of Mann's educational ideas, because, in Croker's view, the
problems which faced America, and would face a democratic Britain,
far outstripped the abilities of 'the schoolmaster and the lecturer'.[5]

[1] See F. J. Klingberg, 'Harriet Beecher Stowe and Social Reform in England',
Am. Hist. Rev., XLIII, Apr. 1938, p. 544. This article has a discussion of the role
played by Shaftesbury, and the Stafford House group, in anti-slavery in the 1850's.
(pp. 547–8.)

[2] QR, Vol. 59, No. 118, Oct. 1837, p. 356. The review, by Croker, contained a
vituperative attack upon Cooper, who had alleged that anti-American propaganda
had been 'prepared under the direction of the government, and inserted in the
Quarterly Review' during Gifford's editorship. This was a 'CALUMNIUS FALSEHOOD',
according to Croker. (p. 361.)

[3] See Thistlethwaite, pp. 144ff. Mann's name was probably brought to the notice
of the Tories during his visit to England in 1843.

[4] See QR, Vol. 71, No. 142, Mar. 1843, Art. 10, pp. 523–8.

[5] It is worth noting that even George Combe, a warm friend of America, agreed
with Mann's indictment of 'an ignorant and ill-willed multitude' (Combe). Combe's
views were printed by the QR, Vol. 68, No. 136, Sept. 1841, pp. 305–11, in a review of

Let us look somewhat more closely at the charges of corruption levelled at the American party system. To Tories the American style of politics was unfamiliar and disturbing. They recoiled from the pervasive election-eering spirit—from the press campaigns, the constant appeal to the people from the hustings and the assembly, the new scale of intrigues and canvassing for votes. Few British constituencies experienced such phenomena until much later in the century. (The City of London and Westminster, with their Wilkite agitations, were exceptions which may have seemed very American.) That public attention should be continually engrossed in politics was thought to be unhealthy, and conservatives regarded the intrusion of party-spirit into private life as an invasion of individual liberty.[1]

As propagandists, however, the Tories seized upon the issue of corrup-tion in American politics. If its existence could be established, then the Benthamite justification of universal suffrage and ballot—that they were checks against the venality which marked aristocratic governments—fell to the ground. The faith of the Benthamites in the purity of American elections was strong, but was in fact (until 1832) based upon the limited evidence of liberal travellers, such as Hodgson, Vigne, and Ouseley. The Tories scoured a wider field to get contradictory testimony, and they came closer to the facts of life, despite a constant tendency to exaggerate depravity.

The most abundant examples of influence at elections were found in the eastern cities, especially in New York and Philadelphia. Even Cobbett had declared that he had witnessed, in one week in Pennsylvania, more bribery, corruption, and place-hunting than 'during the several years in which he resided near the Treasury in London'.[2] Fearon, the 'democrat fieffé', described elections in Philadelphia, even before 1820, as loathsome affairs, involving open corruption.[3] Further details of venality from Faux and Neal were used in the 1820's to discourage reformers.

The Tories, on the other hand, were embarrassed in their quest for bribery and corruption, because they had no desire to prove that wealth

---

his *Notes on the U.S.A., etc.* (Edinburgh, 1841). For a standard Tory attack upon the 'iron grip' of public opinion, see Thos. Ryle, *American Liberty and Government Questioned* (London, 1855), pp. 58ff.

[1] See *QR*, Vol. 41, No. 82, Nov. 1829, pp. 432–3, by Barrow. The misgivings of De Witt Clinton on this topic were widely publicized in Victorian Britain. Nominated as a peace candidate for the Presidency in 1812, he was regarded as a friend of Britain; and long extracts from his speeches against perpetual elections in New York were used by Basil Hall, and by Alex. Crombie in his anti-ballot pam-phlets of 1837 and 1838.

[2] Quoted, without documentation, by Barrow, *QR*, Vol. 21, No. 41, Jan. 1819, p. 163.

[3] *Ibid.* p. 144.

enjoyed an illegitimate advantage in the United States. This might have shattered Bentham's cherished view that democratic devices were sufficient to secure common, rather than minority, interests. But it was not a very good argument against democracy in the eyes of property-holders, who had been constantly assured that the well-born and monied groups in America were persecuted and powerless. Hence the Tory press emphasized the spoils system at a time when it was hardly noticed by other groups. Place-giving, rather than money-giving, was the most current form of bribery, according to William Jacob. The effect was, not to give power to the propertied or to variegate the interests represented in assemblies (as bribery in Britain did), but to confirm the ascendancy of a single democratic party.[1] (It is noticeable that when conservatives argued in this way, they did not consider the crucial effect of sectional representation as a diversifying influence in national politics, although they always examined sectionalism as a factor when discussing schismatic tendencies in the Union.) In the 1820's attention was also drawn to the caucus system, which had grown up alongside the spoils system. Whigs like Mackintosh and Tories like Jacob were well aware of the exact nature of the caucus (although the meaning of the word was to be deliberately stretched in the 1870's in order to discredit Joseph Chamberlain's National Liberal Federation); but the Tories were more alarmed by it. The choice of President, especially, they complained, was dictated by a small party group who 'recommended' the candidate: 'The President thus becomes dependent on his party; and provided the suitor for office be supported by them, his morals, his talents, and his knowledge are secondary considerations.'[2]

Not until the rise of 'machine politics' in the large cities, during the twenty years before civil war, were British moderates seriously alarmed by American trends. By 1840 immigration and urbanization were obviously facilitating the work of political wire-pullers. Before this, corruption was commonly attributed to the Union's cheap-government policy[3] except by classical economists and utilitarian radicals, who

[1] See Jacob's attack on Presidential patronage in 1819, QR, Vol. 21, No. 41, Jan., p. 5. In 1832 Jacob alleged that Jackson had replaced 'every agent of the executive to the lowest throughout the land' to repay his partisans (an historical exaggeration which he probably imbibed from the anti-Jackson press in America). QR, Vol. 48, No. 96, Dec. 1832, pp. 522–3.

[2] Jacob, in QR, Vol. 21, No. 41, Jan. 1819, p. 4.

[3] See Foster, op. cit.; quoted in QR, Vol. 68, No. 135, June 1841, p. 45. He pointed out that between 1787 and 1812 seven American judges had been impeached, a Secretary of State bribed by the French, a District Attorney had fled New York with 50,000 dollars of public property, and a son of the Secretary to the Treasury had been convicted of swindling. So much for the virtue of public men in republics!

continued to regard economy as an undiluted virtue. Thomas Hamilton preferred to blame the division between executive and legislative powers for aggravating the situation. Ministers, he thought, should have to justify their actions at the bar of the assembly, as in England, instead of sheltering under the Presidential cloak. Jobbery and trickery would then be severely restricted.

Instead, as even admirers of America had to admit in the 1840's, fraud and venality were increasing. George Combe cited instances of evasion of electoral laws, and, in his lectures to American audiences upon education and phrenology, exhorted the nation to cleanse its Augean stables. Your faults, he justly declared, 'are carefully collected, blazoned, and recorded in Europe—not to *your* disparagement alone, but . . . to the unspeakable injury of the cause of liberty all over the civilized world'.[1] The bitter attacks of Americans like Channing and Mann against the morality of the age of expansion and the 'machine' were also widely publicized in England. According to Mann, vast sums were spent on bribery and propaganda at elections; pressure was brought to bear upon voters; double voting and ballot-rigging were common; cart-loads of voters were transported, at party expense, from state to state and election to election; fraudulent sequestration of votes had been proved against returning officers—'I tremble', said Mann, 'at the catalogue of national crimes which we are exhibiting before heaven and earth'.[2]

This adverse publicity about the United States helped immensely to bolster the English opposition to the campaign for the ballot which raged between 1832 and 1840. The Tories maintained that the ballot obviously did not prevent intimidation and fraud in America, that it did not ensure secrecy, and was not highly esteemed by Americans. They could point to the dislike for the ballot of Louis Maclane, the Minister to England, and of aristocratic travellers such as Edward Stanley, who, with Charles Russell, James Barlow Hoy, Sir Robert Wilson, and Peel, spoke regularly against American precedent in the annual debate on George Grote's motion.[3] The Whigs, whose support was required,

---

[1] *Notes on America*, quoted by Lockhart in *QR*, Vol. 68, No. 136, Sept. 1841, p. 309. 'In no country which I have visited', wrote Combe, 'has such an array of delinquencies, committed by men in confidential public situations, been exhibited. . . .' (Quoted, p. 310.)

[2] Quoted, *QR*, Vol. 71, No. 142, Mar. 1843, p. 526. Marryat made similar charges in his *Diary in America* (London, 1839), II. 217–28.

[3] See *Lillibridge*, pp. 19–23, for an exhaustive account of the Tory reaction to the American ballot between 1832 and 1840. The periodicals were strangely reticent on the subject, although Croker was critical in *QR*, Vol. 61, No. 122, Apr. 1838, pp. 526–7. See also Rev. A. Crombie, *Letter to Henry Wm. Tancred . . . on the Ballot* (1837), and *Letter to Geo. Grote . . . on the Ballot* (1838).

were suspicious of the American parallel: Sidney Smith wrote a pamphlet which derided it, *The Times* equivocated, Lord John Russell was sceptical[1] —and open voting had triumphed by 1840.

4. *Atlantic Links*

So far it is apparent that the conservatives had advanced a consistent opposition, at almost every point, to the solid phalanx of Radical approval of American politics. For the vision of a democratic millennium they substituted the picture of tyranny by the majority. Instead of a harmony of interests, they saw schismatic sectionalism. Attention was drawn to the mediocrity of American politicians; the ballot as a panacea was ridiculed; and an attempt was made to prove that democratic politics were corrupt. The influences of an unrestricted press and popular education were disparaged. Yet in many ways the Tories had affinities and sympathies with Americans, especially with American conservatives and conservative thought. These links were never as direct or as enduring as those between reformers in both countries. But their existence qualifies any assertion that Tory attitudes towards America were unrelievedly hostile.

Just as there was social intercourse between reformers in Britain and the United States, there was contact, on a smaller scale, between the upper classes of each nation. English Tories, like English Radicals, tended to mix with those people in the new world whose habits and sentiments were similar to their own. Thus they frequently returned to England bolstered in their adverse opinion of raw democracy by the verdict of American conservatives—of those whom they believed to be the most responsible and informed classes in the Union. Thomas Hamilton was impressed by the graces and acquirements of the 'top people' in America, and by their sense of grievance against Jacksonian democracy. He encountered this resentment in the polite society which lionized him in Boston, Philadelphia, New York, and Baltimore and thought that here, but for the sanctions of majority opinion, existed a class which would welcome monarchy.[2] Hamilton felt a sense of fellowship with other leading Americans—with cultured men of letters such as George Ticknor of Harvard, who had studied at Göttingen and Berlin and was a friend of William Hamilton; with the *North American Review* circle; with Edward

---

[1] See Rev. Sidney Smith, *Ballot* (London, 1839), pp. 16–18; *The Times*, 8.3.1830; and Russell's speech, reported in the *Weekly Chronicle*, 3.7.1842 (referred to in Lillibridge, p. 130).

[2] *Men and Manners*, p. xvii. Similar sentiments were expressed by Sir Francis Head in *QR*, Vol. 63, No. 125, Jan. 1839, pp. 25–26.

Livingston, framer of the penal code of Louisiana, and a Benthamite; and with the intellectual John C. Calhoun. Other travellers, including Basil Hall, Marryat, and Godley, were equally impressed by American *élites*.

The Tory press delighted in pointing to the paradoxical existence of aristocratic groups and sentiment in a professed democracy, for this seemed a convincing demonstration of society's inexorable tendency to hierarchy.[1] There was disagreement, however, about the real strength of American *élites*. William Maginn, who was the brilliant but unpredictable editor of Toryism's errant *Fraser's Magazine*, believed that a small patrician band controlled the ultimate destiny of the Union—although at present it humbly abstained from plebeian politics:

They appear to us to be the most singularly situated order in the world—the highest aristocrats conceivable in the midst of a brawling democracy, which they look upon with the profoundest disdain at heart, though offering to it, when necessity leads them to speak on political subjects at all, the humblest tribute of lip homage. . . .[2]

Many Tories, including Croker, prophesied the meteoric rise of such groups to power when the inevitable disintegration of the Union took place. Basil Hall, however, thought that the egalitarian laws of property in America effectively prevented the consolidation of any aristocracy of talent or wealth.[3] There was, he saw, no distinct classification in America's fluid society, nor were there established relations between men as in England. This was widely suggested as one reason why wealthy Americans envied the advantages which affluence and rank commanded in the old world.[4]

Social intercourse was, of course, a two-way affair. During and after the 1830's an increasing stream of rich and distinguished Americans made the now convenient voyage across the Atlantic. They scrambled

[1] Barrow wrote a good deal on the theme that 'Distinctions exist to an extent rather ludicrous under a free and popular government'. *QR*, Vol. 21, No. 41, Jan. 1819, p. 141. For example, in Boston, he noted: 'There are the first class, second class, third class, and the "old families". Titles, too, are profusely distributed.' (Ibid.) Much fun was made in England of the American love for titles and ostentation.

[2] *Fraser's Magazine*, Vol. 5, Apr. 1832, p. 343. (Trollope and Paulding on America).

[3] See Hall's review of Trollope, in *QR*, Vol. 47, No. 93, Mar. 1832, p. 43. Indeed the evidence was overwhelming in favour of the view that aristocratic influence was vastly overshadowed by the universal power of democratic laws and manners. Chevalier, Tocqueville, and Beaumont each noticed the 'rude demands' made by egalitarian democracy upon the upper classes.

[4] Fenimore Cooper was lucid on this topic in his *Residence in France, etc.* (Paris, 1836).

to obtain invitations to the coronations of William IV and Victoria, and they attended the levees and social occasions sponsored by royalty and the aristocracy. Some, like Richard Rush, who succeeded John Quincy Adams as Minister to Britain in 1817, were to republican eyes almost indecently impressed by the brilliant society of Whigs and Tories.[1] Certainly Washington Irving (described by the *Westminster Review* as an 'ignorant puling sentimentalist' who 'has a manifest preference for British institutions')[2] and the diplomats Rush, Albert Gallatin, and Louis Maclane felt more at home in London's polite society than amongst the new industrialists, the dissenters, and radical reformers of the provinces. (Not indeed until the tenure of Van Buren, a Jackson-man, at the Court of St. James were American Consulates established in the chief manufacturing towns of the North.) Conservatives were wont to regard this sort of man as America's cream,[3] with whom, despite their republicanism, they felt many ties of common interest and outlook.

This sense of affinity became applied to the Federalist party in American political history, for that group was seen to inherit the tradition of caution and responsibility, of concern about the unfettered power of the multitude, that marked the thinking of the Founding Fathers. Fifty years after the great secession, and after the experience of jacobinism in Europe and Jeffersonian democracy in America, Toryism was ready to stifle its eighteenth-century opposition to the Republic's first statesmen. The Federalists, on the eve of their extinction as an effective force in American politics, were receiving greater homage in England. Jacob commended their writings because, as he put it,

. . . we wish to convey to the minds of our readers the feelings of that party in America, which has been the most averse from the irreligious and levelling principles of the Jacobins, and which contains the most respectable portion of the American people. They were never deeply smitten with the charms of the French Revolution; they wished to avoid the war with England; they were eager for the return of peace, and desirous that such improvements might be made in their system of government, as should strengthen the executive power, remunerate more

---

[1] See his rapturous description of drawing-room society, in his *Memoranda of the Court of London*, quoted in Beckles Willson, *America's Ambassadors to England, 1785–1928* (London, 1928), p. 141. Rush (1817–25) was on particularly amiable terms with the Tory leaders, especially Liverpool (whom he held in high respect) and Castlereagh (who invited him regularly to his country seat).

[2] *WR*, Vol. 2, No. 4, Oct. 1824, p. 339.

[3] See Lockhart's remarks, in *QR*, Vol. 64, No. 128, Oct. 1839, p. 316. More Americans 'of mature years and tastes, of high attainments, character, and honour' were coming to Britain: 'how different from the raw, petulant striplings that used to excite our astonishment. . . .'

liberally the officers of government, render the judges less dependent, and have a President sometimes chosen from the other states as well as from Virginia. . . .[1]

The centralism of Alexander Hamilton, his independence of the mob, his concern for the interests of property and intelligence, received unanimous Tory approval. He was regarded by most as the greatest practical philosopher produced by the age of the Revolution, and one who was never deceived by 'the flimsy dogmas of human perfectibility, which dazzled the weaker vision of such men as Jefferson and Madison'.[2] John Adams was less well known than Hamilton until the 1840's, when his *Letters* were praised by the Tory press.[3] Croker assessed Adams as a man of respectable talents with sound political instincts: 'a friend of liberty, but not less the advocate of order and discipline in the state'.[4] Robert Southey was influenced by the ideas of Timothy Dwight, the President of Yale, who was renowned in America for his splenetic identification of Jefferson's Republicanism with French jacobinism during John Adams's administration. Southey read Dwight's *Travels in New England* in 1823, and very many of his subsequent references to America were based upon this book. In the 1830's, when the House of Lords seemed in peril, the moderate ideas of John Adams and Gouverneur Morris respecting second chambers were seized upon. Morris had come out long ago in favour of an hereditary Senate, and Adams in his *Defence of the Constitution* . . . had advocated an aristocratic upper house to neutralize the popular assembly. Radicals were duly reminded of the fact.[5]

Extreme Tories, in the crisis years immediately after 1832, were especially attracted by the eloquence and power of Fisher Ames. His stubborn conservatism, his distrust of man and utopias, touched a responsive chord in their breasts. The *Works of Fisher Ames*, which had been published in Boston in 1809, was edited and presented to the English

[1] *QR*, Vol. 21, No. 41, Jan. 1829, p. 19. The Democrats, he alleged, were supported 'by means of a majority composed of the lower classes, including the Irish and English recruits, and the paupers existing on charity. . . .'

[2] Thos. Hamilton, *Men and Manners*, quoted in *Blackwood's*, Vol. 34, Sept. 1833, p. 295.

[3] See Croker's review in *QR*, Vol. 69, No. 137, Dec. 1841, Art. 8. The work reviewed was *Letters of John Adams, addressed to his wife*, ed. by Chas. Francis Adams (Boston, 1841).

[4] *QR*, ibid. p. 270. Adams's example, Croker hoped, would help to 'moderate and control that spirit of unbounded democracy which has been growing, we fear, in America. . . .'

[5] For example, Ewbank publicized Morris's ideas in 1835 in his introduction to Fisher Ames, *The Influences of Democracy on Liberty, Property, and the Happiness of Society, etc.* (London, 1835), pp. 19–20, n.

public in 1835 by Henry Ewbank, the Ultra-Tory M.P. Circumstances were timely, Ewbank had decided, to exhibit 'a living picture of Democracy by the hand of a master':

> . . . if the testimony of an eye-witness—an American Republican—and a most ardent lover of liberty—is entitled to any attention, thinking men will perhaps pause before they sacrifice themselves to the Juggernaut of self-government, or give way to the specious, but false opinion, that the transfer of political power to the people is necessarily attended by an increase of liberty.[1]

The edition promptly received the imprimatur of Croker and the *Quarterly*.[2] Ames had been desperately concerned for the sanctity of property in a licentious democracy, ruled by passion and not by reason. He was preoccupied, until his death in 1808, with the ominous rise of Jeffersonianism, which he viewed as a challenge to the true ideals of that Revolution which he had helped to accomplish. Jefferson he suspected of trying to carry the Revolution of 1787 a step further by abolishing all institutions likely to encourage respect for hierarchy and tradition. Faction was rendering ineffectual the checks and balances devised by the architects of the constitution as 'professed means of ensuring to the nation, rulers, who will prefer the durable good of the whole, to the transient advantage of the whole or a part'.[3] The legislator, the administrator, and the judge, Ames believed, were becoming instruments of the majority; and public liberty would soon be no longer safe. Then men, not laws, would govern, and government would be a despotism beyond rule, rather than a republic confined to rule. Ames, who read the ancients and Hobbes, was a pessimist who believed that the people were incapable of rational judgement and easy prey to those who appealed to their appetites.[4] Their rule, he reasoned, was unlikely to be a moral one, and very likely to end in military despotism. Ames's blunt vehemence against democracy was in the Tory tradition, and was excellent propaganda at a time when the centre in British politics was having second thoughts about America.

After the fading of the Federalist star, the Tories looked for American allies less from the sphere of politics, and more from that of the judiciary. Chief Justice Marshall and Justice Story of the Supreme Court received

---

[1] Ibid. p. 10 (introd.). Ewbank rigorously selected from the original papers, condensing the whole into 199 pages.

[2] *QR*, Vol. 53, No. 106, Apr. 1835, Art. 10, by Croker.

[3] Ibid. p. 37. (The words are those of the American editor of the *Works*, summarizing Ames' ideas.)

[4] 'The more free the citizens,' he wrote, 'the bolder, and more profligate will be their demagogues, the more numerous and eccentric the popular errors, and the more vehement and pertinacious the passions that defend them.'

the plaudits of both conservatives and Whigs. Sir John Taylor Coleridge, nephew of the poet-philosopher, and an eminent jurist, was especially impressed by Story's ability and character.[1] Coleridge took the view, widespread amongst British lawyers of all political leanings, that the American judiciary was an invaluable drag-wheel to the chariot of democracy. Story's complaints about majority rule in the United States were given wide currency in England in the early 1850's. He gave warning of the threat posed to the independence of the judiciary by popular jealousy and pointed out that democratic control over stipends and tenure of office was in America providing the means of shackling judges to the will of the masses. The charge was a shocking one, not only to a tradition-bound legal profession, but to almost all informed opinion. Benthamite reformers were committed to ridding the law of formalism and pedantry, but even they were aghast at democratizing it.

After about 1830, it would seem that the affinities of conservatives in Britain and America became much more tenuous. As Jeffersonian, and then Jacksonian, dogmas captured the political arena, as an orthodoxy of approval for existing institutions settled upon Americans, British conservatives looked increasingly to the American past, to the age of questioning after 1776. Their search for kindred spirits in contemporary America became progressively more difficult. Federalists and Republicans might be separated by some ideological test, but Whigs and Democrats appeared indistinguishable. No convincing polarization of opinion could be made in such a welter of sectional and class alignments as emerged after Jackson's election in 1828.[2] Relationships were more easily discovered in the sphere of law, and with the social *élites* of Boston and Philadelphia. Useful propaganda could be culled also from the American humanitarians, the college teachers, the abolitionists, the opponents of expansionism; and even from the more thoroughgoing reformers, who,

---

[1] See Coleridge's article upon Story in *QR*, Vol. 92, No. 183, Dec. 1852, Art. 2. Story was 'an excellent judge, a remarkably successful teacher of the law, and he ranks very high amongst the jurists of this, perhaps we may say, of any age'. (p. 29.) The two men corresponded, and Coleridge, like most self-respecting intellectuals, had read Story's main writings.

[2] See, e.g., J. R. Godley, *Letters from America* (London, 1844), II. 51. Godley, a conservative, stressed that in the United States all men were agreed upon the great principles of government, and that hence no valid demarcation could be made between parties (in 1842). He thought the Whigs were more conservative than Democrats or 'Locofocos'—but differences emerged only when principles were put into practice. Sometimes it was, he thought, simply a matter of persons and place. Nevertheless, the party system produced, not harmony, but extreme animosity. He suggested, interestingly, that, in a situation where basic principles were retained within 'the trammels of received formulae', natural differences of personal temperament and intellect found expression in party warfare.

in their various ways, asserted their dissatisfaction with the existing character and morality of American society. But, except in their broad spirit of criticism, most of these people were poles apart from the British Establishment, and the use made of their dissent by this ruling group was usually made in an alien spirit. They gave approval to the wealthy classes as a responsible group, but it was becoming clear that the American rich were committed to the existing system, and were determined to attain their ends through it. Moreover, of those rich men who stayed in America at least, their affinity was rather with the English industrialist class. Even hidebound American conservatives were sometimes disconcertingly insular and nationalist in outlook, and their frame of reference was quite separate from that of English Tories. The movements of the Right in both countries exchanged ideas, and felt a regard for each other, but their interrelationship was much more sporadic, and much less important, than that of the reformers of each nation.

5. *Democracy versus Whig Checks*

. . . In church and in state America presents the *reductio ad absurdum* of Whiggism. (Lockhart.)

As we have seen, the English Whigs were particularly impressed by the built-in checks and balances of the American *polis*, and they preferred to explain American stability in terms of these Whig, rather than of democratic, principles. This raises the question whether the Tories took a similar stand, especially in view of their separate political tradition. The short answer is that they were divided upon the subject. The British Right had, on the whole, a friendly regard for the conservative aspects of American politics, which included the Whig aspects. As this chapter will attempt to show, such an appreciation dates from at least the 1820's, and is not, as Pelling has suggested,[1] a development of the 1880's. It existed, however, under the shadow of a more pungent fear of 'pure democracy' than was felt by later generations. All obstructions to popular fury were regarded as desirable, but frail and hardly to be relied upon. Many Tories, in addition, found American checks and balances simply too Whiggish for their liking and preferred more traditional methods of bridling popular movements.

The heart of the problem that faced conservatives was whether to take a Whig or a Tory view about the nature of authority in America. Whiggism approved the constitutional division of powers, which prevented supreme power being placed in any single repository; it approved

[1] Henry Pelling, *America and the British Left* (London, 1956), pp. 5–6, 51–52.

the weakness of government in a society largely self-regulated, and the balancing of interests, classes, and regions against each other. The basis of the doctrine, an ingrained pessimism about the nature of man, was congenial to Tory thought, and so was its objective, to hamstring democratic uprisings and usurpations. Some Tories, indeed, were unreserved in their enthusiasm for transatlantic checks and balances, despite the historical opposition of their party to the doctrine in England.

The traditional antipathy towards a written constitution provided no obstacle to admiration of that of America. In the absence of a rich and complex system of social institutions imposing their own inhibitions, a fundamental law limiting men's actions was acceptable. Indeed, the Tories were not, like the Whigs, embarrassed in this matter by any contrary loyalty to the doctrine of parliamentary supremacy. They approved the practical wisdom of the Founding Fathers; and, without undue trouble, could come to regard the provisions of the constitution as a rough approximation to a set of moral mandates, permanently imposed upon the citizens. As a consequence, British Tories always resisted any proposal that the constitution of the Union should be made easier to amend (an issue on which the Whigs, wedded to parliamentary supremacy and the right of assemblies to change any law, disagreed amongst themselves—Senior, for instance, believing that the rigidity of American forms was an obstacle to necessary change). The Radicals were sometimes taunted with the fact that America's constitution was anti-democratic upon this very point of amendment.[1]

Those who commended higher law usually commended the federal system of government, which they interpreted as a mechanical obstruction to omnipotent and centralized majority rule, and as a device for compartmentalizing regional discontents. Edward Stanley, who toured the United States in 1825, declared that the virtue of the government at Washington lay in 'the looseness of its connection with its subjects'.[2] Matters of popular interest, likely to stir dangerous popular passions, were, he argued, matters for the state governments. Turbulence was thus, by virtue of the federal system, localized, and divisive sectional interests were absorbed as they could never be in a unitary state. Stanley, at the time a Whig, had little sympathy with Burke's mystic reverence

---

[1] See *QR*, Vol. 45, No. 89, Apr. 1831, p. 305. Reformers were asked whether they were aware of 'that powerful conservative principle so wisely embodied in . . . the American constitution, for the express purpose of guarding against the encroachments to which that constitution must otherwise have been liable, from the innovating spirit of a popular legislature invested with unlimited power'. Croker also used the argument in *QR*, Vol. 46, No. 92, Jan. 1832, p. 584.

[2] Stanley, *Journal*, p. 332.

for unplanned constitutions, but instead heartily approved of artificial and rational safeguards against anarchy.[1] Croker was a more fervent disciple of Burke, but he at times took a similar view to that of Stanley. His appreciation of federalism in America was more influenced by French history, for Croker was convinced that the worst excesses of the Terror had been exacerbated by the centralized form of government. Federalism, in his view, prevented the control of national government by city mobs. It preserved the state from 'sudden shocks and local impulses'. In America, he wrote:

The several states are so distinct in position, and so diversified in interests, that they serve to balance and control each other, and cannot, within any reasonable probability, be ever universally and simultaneously affected by any one popular paroxysm. If Virginia and Carolina should go mad, New England and the Jerseys are in their senses. . . . The assemblage in the supreme legislature of so many constitutional powers, each with different interests, views and principles exhibits in practice something of the same system of combination and check which existed in the British House of Commons, while under its old constitution.[2]

This was high praise from Croker, and aptly illustrates the gap that could exist between Radical and Tory interpretations of American politics.

Some people pinned their hopes upon bi-cameral institutions as a check upon majority rule. (Conversely, most Radical thinkers ignored the manifestly undemocratic nature of bi-cameralism, as a prejudice to their use of American example.) William Jacob had a good deal of faith in the American Senate. Lower assemblies throughout the Union, he believed, were filled with men who 'have flattered the lowest passions of the populace, or intrigued with their voluble leaders'. The Senate was, on the other hand, 'the concentration of the aristocracy of the state-governments which it represents', and had on occasions 'been found highly useful in calming and suspending the will of the people when clamourous to their own injury'.[3] He applauded the view of Gouverneur Morris, expressed at the Federal Convention, that the Senate ought to exist to save the people from themselves—but thought it ominous that Morris had been cast into the political wilderness for declaring such an

[1] For example, he wrote of American government that it 'harmonises with the people . . . there are none of the imaginary checks and balances, the virtual representations, the conflicts between theory and practice, which we see in our own Constitution, and which, however some of them "work well", are not the less practical inconsistencies.' Ibid. p. 331.
[2] QR, Vol. 53, No. 106, Apr. 1835, p. 556. He re-emphasized the manageability of state divisions in June 1849: QR, Vol. 85, No. 169, p. 267 (Democracy).
[3] QR, Vol. 21, No. 41, Jan. 1819, pp. 2–3 (Bristed, Statistical View of America).

obvious truth. In 1819, however, he was reasonably satisfied with the general character of Congress. Although sometimes misled by 'the abstract reasonings of theorists, and the violence of party spirit', it was normally a cautious body, mindful of usage and precedent and solicitous of the rights of property. Other reviewers agreed with Jacob about the Senate, Benjamin Bussey Thatcher describing it in 1838 as one of the constitution's 'most important, and its very most conservative, ingredients'.[1]

To the pro-American brief for federalism, bi-cameralism, and checks could be put the reply that, in a politically homogeneous society such as the transatlantic, even the most ingenious artificial checks could not effectively contain the ascendant spirit of democracy. Tories, mindful of their traditions, were especially sensitive to such a rejoinder, and Tory opinion constantly shifted around the issue. For one thing, the domestic interests of the party were doubtfully served by reiterating Whig propaganda about America. Brougham, Merivale, and others emphasized the Whiggish nature of the principles accepted at Philadelphia in 1787, because those principles, and especially the general clause about the need to qualify popular power, were a guarantee of the permanence of the 1832 settlement in England. True-blue Tories shared the anti-democratic sentiment, but opposed its use to justify the rule of the middle class. They held that 1832 was not a truly conservative solution of the problems posed by the unreformed parliament. Abuses should have been remedied without subverting confidence in national corporations and institutions, or destroying the constitutional balance of classes. Whigs and liberals might profess a doctrine of checks against further democracy; but the Tories thought the mere profession inadequate unless coupled with a genuine endeavour to preserve the established institutions and usages beloved by Burke and the eighteenth century. They did not, in fact, want to see in England what they believed had happened in America, i.e. democratic theory overlaid by a veneer of Whiggery. Representation must, at all costs, be grounded upon constitutional principles; checks would not then be so necessary.

This argument was supported by pointing to the failure of checks alone in the United States to restrain popular passions. As sectionalism increased, British confidence even in the federal system declined. The first convincing accounts of tensions within the Union reached England in the mid-twenties, and steadily became more alarming until 1861. John Neal, as early as 1825, could point out antipathies between slave-holders in the South and abolitionists in the North, between manufacturing,

[1] QR, Vol. 61, No. 122, Apr. 1838, p. 358 (Texas).

commercial, and agricultural interests. He pointed to the separate economic interests of East, West and South, revealed in their differences over tariff policy; and drew attention to the strength of resentment against federal authority in many states.[1] The United States, it seemed clear, was expanding too fast to allow the reconciliation of widely diverse interests, despite the peculiar excellencies of the federal system. Predictions were rife in Britain during the whole of our period that the American Empire was about to break up into states of a more manageable size.

Faith in bi-cameralism also waned. As people came to believe in the truth of Tocqueville's analysis of the monolithic democracy of the United States, they recognized the absurdity of equating upper houses there with the House of Lords in Britain. Their mode of recruitment, their composition, was entirely dissimilar; they expressed different theories of government. Could one rely, in a full-blooded democracy, upon elective institutions, even the Senate (where Senators were elected until 1913 by State legislators, not by 'ill-informed' voters) as a check? This question was asked with increasing frequency as time went on.

The Senate [said *Blackwood's*] is under the control of the popular voice; it has no distinct part of the community to stand upon, its members have no peculiar character, it is destitute of moral weight and power, it cannot act as a check upon, and a counterpoise to, the other body, neither can it make any effectual stand against it on great public questions.[2]

This was an exaggeration of historical reality, but it indicated accurately enough Tory distress about a system that refused to grant separate representation to a noble estate, or to the closest approximation to one that could be found in the new world. The failure of Alexander Hamilton and John Adams to obtain a concession to this viewpoint at Philadelphia was deeply regretted by Tories. The institution of high property qualifications, or life election for Senators, might, they thought, have gone some way towards creating a permanent class interest at variance with that of the majority.[3]

---

[1] *Blackwood's*, Vol. 18, Sept. 1825, pp. 355–68. Robert Southey also criticized federalism for encouraging the proliferation and sub-division of states, thereby loosening the bonds of 'an union which is already too relaxed'. QR, Vol. 30, No. 59, Oct. 1823, p. 34.

[2] *Blackwood's*, Vol. 18, Sept. 1825, p. 347 (The Nobility).

[3] Thos. Hamilton took this view in *Men and Manners*, p. 256. The bi-cameral system was 'founded in wisdom' but was vitiated by its dependence upon democratic theory. Senators, he said, were 'creatures of public favour' and, unlike British peers, had no 'direct and personal interest in maintaining the privileges of their branch of the legislature'. See also Thos. Ryle, *American Liberty and Government Questioned* (London, 1855), pp. 59–60.

Richard Chenevix expressed the opinion of the sceptics when he announced that America's nominal checks, 'although they look pretty enough on paper, are, in practice, all trodden under hoof by the class which there assumes the government of everything'.[1] Genuine freedom, as Chenevix said over and over in his articles, involved a multitude of restraints; and it was obtained only in a society where such restraints were built in, where sacrifices were habitually made for the public good. His ideal was the obligatory system of feudalism or the English manorial system, and American democracy was the very negation, he said, of this. Macaulay, whose attitudes towards America were on the whole more Tory than Whig, took a not too dissimilar stand. He placed great importance upon the fact that supreme power in England lay in the hands of a class 'numerous indeed, but select; of an educated class; of a class which is, and knows itself to be, deeply interested in the security of property and the maintenance of order'. In America no such group stood between the government and the potentially discontented masses. Distress there would produce spoliation, and spoliation further distress. 'There is nothing to stop you', he wrote to H. S. Randall, the biographer of Jefferson: 'Your Constitution is all sail and no anchor.'[2] Henry Hart Milman, the Dean of St. Paul's and historian of Christianity, agreed:

There is no great repressive, no controlling power, nothing to drag the wheel of popular rule, either in the Constitution of the Federation or in the States. In each the Senates must obey the mighty will of the masses.[3]

Believing this, some in the party which had in the past defended the prerogative of English kings wondered whether they ought to defend the power of the American President. This betokened a desire to solve the problem of too-powerful majorities in a traditional Tory fashion—by strengthening the Executive power so that it would become insulated from outside pressure. At the same time legislative and judicial power would be pruned. The Tories looked for a man of character who, given the power, could rise superior to contending democratic factions to uphold the permanent interests of the nation. The idea was an interesting throwback to notions current at the time of George III's accession, when

[1] QR, Vol. 43, No. 85, May 1830, p. 225 (Political Condition and Prospects of France).
[2] Macaulay to Randall, 8.1.1859, in Sir Otto Trevelyan, ed., Life and Letters of T. B. Macaulay (New York, 1877), II. 407–12 (App.). Macaulay's letters to Randall were published by the New York Public Library in 1925 as a pamphlet, Macaulay on American Institutions, and soon afterwards printed by the thousands as propaganda against President Roosevelt and the New Deal.
[3] QR, Vol. 85, No. 196, June 1849, p. 221 (Lyell's Second Visit to the United States).

it was hoped that a powerful monarch would, in the national interest, chasten squabbling Whig oligarchies.

It was natural that this argument should be coupled with an attack upon the American, and Whig, liking for weak government. There had been, as yet, no wholesale conversion of conservatives to the doctrine of economic individualism. The Tory view of society and politics was still essentially patriarchal. Tories had a Hobbesian fear that a people free of paternal government control would revert to a turbulent state of nature in which selfish motives had free reign. In such a situation no harmony of interests such as some philosophers predicted would exist. Robert Southey, amongst others, pointed to the American West to illustrate the point— its near-anarchy and lack of benevolent social institutions were due in his opinion to unlicensed individualism; and its example strengthened him in his resistance to the utilitarian reliance upon self-help as a solution to pauperism in England:

The experiment, in reality, which our brethren in America are trying, is to see, with how little government, with how few institutions, and how cheap a rate men may be kept together in society. Is this a safe experiment? Can it possibly be a successful one? Can it tend to reform and to exalt the manners and morals of the people. . . . Time will tell whether a people can become powerful without an efficient government; whether they can be prosperous without a liberal public expenditure. . . .[1]

In Southey's view republican government, more than other forms, presupposed the existence of positive virtues in the body politic, because the people and rulers were more closely associated. The guidance of a benevolent government, cherishing goodness and punishing evil, was therefore indispensable.[2] From Timothy Dwight's writings he became convinced that an increase of Presidential powers was the only means of obtaining such a government without changing American society.[3]

Other critics, believing in Alexander Hamilton's dictum that 'the vigour of government is essential to the security of liberty', regretted that the founders of the constitution had shorn the executive of its powers

[1] Southey in *QR*, Vol. 30, No. 59, Oct. 1823, p. 36, p. 40.

[2] It must be the business of government, he said, 'not to relax its own duties in reliance upon it [i.e. the goodness of the people]; to provide ways for making men good, not to rest in the assumption that they are so'. Ibid. p. 36.

[3] Dwight advocated strong government as a protection of the rights, peace, and civilization of ordinary people, always at the mercy, otherwise, of bad men. A weak Executive would never awe bad men, but *they* might awe the Executive. He appealed to the Puritan tradition of strong, even tyrannical, rule—believing that only thus was New England able to enjoy her present high standards in education and religious aci lities.

to the point of emasculation. Thomas Hamilton wrote of the President that 'He stands in circumstances too precarious to admit of his boldly adopting measures of enlarged and liberal policy, or attempting to stem the tide of ignorance and prejudice . . . The President is a kind of King Log . . . [unable] to resist the inroads of mere wanton innovation.'[1] He thought that the fathers had been unnecessarily fearful of dictatorship. They had pared effectively the claws of a possible Caesar—certainly one could only laugh at the idea of tyranny 'organized by a quad-rennial President with a salary of 5,000 a-year, an army of 6,000 men, and without independent and unshackled patronage of any sort!'[2] But Executive government had been virtually strangulated in the process. Basil Hall agreed.[3]

The theory of separation of powers, even, incurred conservative displeasure, because it imposed legal checks against Presidential power as much as against the power of democratic assemblies. William Jacob took this view. Ignoring Blackstone, he described the division between legislative and executive branches, supposed to be a cardinal principle of the English constitution, as an idle theory got up in radical circles during the English Revolution.[4] (As the theory, during the eighteenth century, cloaked the encroachment of parliamentary, and hence Whig, power at the expense of royal prerogative, his antipathy was understandable.)[5] He alleged that these ideas, transported to America, had served to per-petuate the executive branch in weakness;[6] while encouraging non-co-operation and jealousy between Congress and White House.[7] It was strange to see Bentham and Jacob, at about the same time, denouncing the separation of powers in America, but for totally opposite reasons— Bentham because he believed it detracted from the power of the majority, who ought to control an omnipotent Legislature; and Jacob because he

[1] *Men and Manners*, pp. 258–9.
[2] Ibid. p. 257.
[3] QR, Vol. 41, No. 82, Nov. 1829, quoted p. 426. 'The power of the chief magistrate', he said, 'has been gradually abridged, till his actual authority, either for good or for evil, has been almost annihilated.'
[4] QR, Vol. 21, No. 41, Jan. 1819, p. 4.
[5] Cf. QR, Vol. 76, No. 151, June 1845, pp. 24–26. The writer, an advocate of strong government in the U.S., argued that, in England, Whig opposition to authority, professed as a concern for the ancient constitution, had been an excuse for the revolutionary constitutional changes of 1688 and 1832. Appeal to antiquity, he concluded, was not a conservative sentiment, but an innovatory one.
[6] QR, Jan. 1819, op. cit., pp. 3–5, where Jacob, like most Tories, attacks the failure of the Confederacy interregnum as a failure of Whig ideas about government.
[7] Jacob deplored the exclusion of able men in the Executive from seats in the Congress. Like Bagehot after him, he preferred the English ministerial system as more efficient and less confusing than the American. Hamilton raised similar objections, *Men and Manners*, pp. 260–1.

thought it detracted from the power of an Executive which might be an independent bastion against the majority.[1]

The idea of a strong Executive, and more government, as a solution to the problem of democracy was, nevertheless, open to serious objections. A President with enlarged powers, in a full-blooded democracy like the American, might be a less effective check than written ones; for how, in the absence of an aristocracy or established institutions, could he avoid being a cypher of the people? This would simply give the multitude more power, while lessening constitutional impediments to its exercise. The alternative and also great danger was that a popular President might become a Caesar, playing first upon the passions of the people, then abrogating all civil and political liberties to assume supreme power. This cycle of change was generally assumed at the time to have been the history of republics. Many observers were therefore concerned at the popularity in the United States of successful military leaders, who might become dictators. It was true of course that, by tradition, the Tories abhorred the doctrine of lawful resistance to authority. Their memory of republicanism was that of the Commonwealth—'of all tyranny the worst'[2]—hence they were readier to tolerate other forms of arbitrary authority. Chastened during the long Hanoverian rule, this viewpoint received a more decisive setback during, and after, the era of Bonapartism. The nineteenth century produced new forms of absolutism from which even Tories shrank as an alternative to democracy. There was also, during Victorian years, an opposition generated against strong central rule by virtue of Benjamin Disraeli's new statement of conservatism.[3] It was probably for these reasons that Tories could be found raising cries of alarm when military leaders with large followings assumed the Presidency—Andrew Jackson, the hero of New Orleans, in 1828, and

[1] Croker apparently feared that Bentham, rather than Jacob, was right. He approved separation of powers, writing that a separate Executive and upper house 'have hitherto been in practice a more efficient check on popular impetuosity than our own Monarch and House of Lords'. QR, Vol. 85, No. 169, June 1849, p. 267.

[2] Blackwood's, Vol. 14, Dec. 1823, p. 667 (Whig and Tory).

[3] The logic of Disraeli's philosophy would probably have led to a commendation of weak government in American circumstances, had he followed up the issue. The Americans had in fact succeeded in doing what he feared the Whigs were trying to do in England—weakening (the Americans beyond repair) great national institutions which guarded the practical liberties of the people, viz. Crown, Church, Universities, Corporations, and Magistracy. Disraeli feared that, if this should be accomplished, the mass of individuals would be faced with a corruptive, pervasive and central bureaucracy. Any shift in the United States, he might have argued, away from weak government would have precipitated just such a situation. See Disraeli, Vindication of the English Constitution (London, 1835), in Wm. Hutcheson, ed., Whigs and Whiggism, etc. (London, 1913), pp. 215-18.

Zachary Taylor, the hero of Buena Vista, in 1848. *Blackwood's*, reflecting on the eve of Jackson's election in 1828, thought it a bad sign that 'This people, the most unmilitary among civilized nations, is proud of its military achievements, and pants for military renown'.[1] Southey warned Americans that 'so surely as ambition shall introduce a military spirit, the cradle will be made ready for an *Imperator*'.[2] He had difficulty in finding a happy mean between excessively weak and over-strong government for the United States. In a non-corporate and non-pluralist society he was very aware of the dangers of tyranny:

It is true that there is nothing to pull down in America; no temple for Erostratus to destroy. But the very levelness of the political platform may excite in some Pharaoh the ambition of constructing a pyramid upon it. Ambition, even if it be not the besetting sin of republics more than of monarchies, acts in them, when once they are possessed by it, with greater force, and has fewer obstacles in its course.[3]

Conservatives were therefore faced with a dilemma. America in many ways represented to them the sort of society that Englishmen would have if Radicals, Whigs, and economists had their way. And they were baffled in seeking satisfactory Tory, or even Whig, solutions to the problems of such a society. Emotionally many preferred the 'strong government' solution to that of checks, but both presented formidable difficulties. Ultimately, to save America from democratic anarchy, or tyranny, conservatives could only propose to change American society, to introduce an aristocracy on British lines, or, more plausibly, on a basis of property and education. This of course was also an argument for the *status quo* in England. The criticism of feeble government in America was both a product of tradition and a useful counter-attack upon the ideas of *laissez faire* liberals and utilitarians. Here, if the nettle had been grasped, was Toryism's chance to embrace a twentieth-century view of a positive and responsible state; and American example could well have provided a catalyst in such a shift of ideas. Southey, for one, appears to have been moving tentatively in that direction. But the possibility of such a radical development of thought, although it was compatible with some aspects of Old Toryism, was in reality infinitesimal. The

[1] *Blackwood's*, Vol. 24, Nov. 1828, p. 633 (Notes on the U.S.A.).

[2] R. Southey, *Sir Thomas More: or Colloquies on the Progress and Prospects of Society* (London, 1829), II. 196.

[3] Ibid. p. 196. A general who conquered Quebec or Mexico for the Americans, he predicted, 'might pass from the Presidency to the Throne with as little opposition as Buonapart' (p. 200). He stated the essence of the dilemma when he wrote that 'a weak government cannot enforce obedience at a distance; a strong one cannot exist without establishments which the American people will not willingly support' (p. 196).

conservatives were deeply divided upon the role of the state in industrial England. Many Canningites and Peelites (who were not as well represented in the Tory press as they were in Parliament) leaned towards economic individualism,[1] and tended to be complacent about minimal government and public economy in the United States. They were the real friends of America in Tory ranks, for they approved, although not always overtly, of its atomistic society and emphasized the economic links which bound England to the Union. But even the hard core of Tories who professed to believe in the customary and non-competitive state were ambivalent when faced with concrete problems such as the condition-of-England question. They frequently asserted their belief that paternalistic government, and the regulation of affairs, was necessary to solve the problem of poverty. But, in practice, they had usually strong local attachments, and an instinctive antipathy to centralized governmental interference with property.[2] Thus they were not fitted for setting the theory in motion. Their 'strong government' cry, as applied to both Britain and the United States, turned out to be an eighteenth-century one, inapplicable to the practical problems of the nineteenth century.

6. America: the Acquisitive Society

If conservative attitudes towards authority in America were coloured by antipathies towards *laissez faire* ideas in England, a similar motive lay behind their dislike of many other aspects of America's acquisitive society. Indeed, it was the relatively concerted opposition of true-blue Tories to the materialist and bourgeois values of American culture that distinguished them from the mass of other groups. This anti-commercial motive has, I believe, been insufficiently noticed by scholars, who have tended to accept English criticism of such values in the early nineteenth century as unsystematic and springing from a sense of national superiority rather than from theoretical motives. This was probably true of most Whig and liberal comment, for the political interest of such groups did not on the whole lie in criticism. The economic ideas they espoused were those of the classical economists, and America seemed to exemplify their system of independent economic effort. The United States was manifestly of the new steam age. Its society seemed more streamlined, less restrictive, more dynamic than that of England; its values were

[1] For an admirable discussion of the deep belief of the mid-Victorians in individual effort as a character-forming influence, and state-sponsored charity as a demoralizing one, see W. L. Burn, *The Age of Equipoise* (London, 1964), Ch. 3, esp. pp. 113-29.

[2] See David Roberts, 'Tory Paternalism and Social Reform in Early Victorian England', *Am. Hist. Rev.*, LXIII (1958), 323-37.

commercial and modern; even its political system could be interpreted (and was) as the rule of a great middle class. Britain's new industrialists and manufacturers, her merchants and free traders, Whigs, Benthamites, and a large section of the Radicals—those, in short, who welcomed the rise of the middle class in England and accepted its dogmas—acquiesced in the dominant values of American society. They, unlike the Tories, were blind to all but the most obvious moral defects of such a society. So even were those Radicals and Chartists who dedicated themselves to redressing the 'condition of England'. To smear America, in their eyes, was to question democracy, and they were committed to the view that political reform in Britain was a panacea for deep-seated social problems. Socialist ideas of economic determinism and projects for more thorough-going social change had some, but very few, converts before 1850. Again, these people were preoccupied with the concept of America as a pre-industrial, egalitarian, working-men's utopia and were reluctant to admit that it was in any way an acquisitive and competitive, rather than a co-operative, society. Thus only those Tories and intellectuals to whom such middle-class and Chartist ideas were anathema were inclined to attack American social values.

In what follows I want first to trace some themes on which the con-servatives found themselves rather on the defensive against the new industrial, commercial-Whig ethic. Against the intruding, questioning, materialist and empirical spirit of the age, the typical conservative was forced, willy-nilly, into an overt justification of an order which had hitherto been accepted on trust. His position as natural governor, his role as arbiter of political truth, no longer went unchallenged. Against the new political economy, and a rational utilitarianism, he had to find convincing arguments in favour of the Corn Laws and protection, of a top-heavy and expensive public administration, of a religious establish-ment. In retaliation—and to recount this constitutes the second task of my argument—the conservative turned splenetically upon the defenders of industrialism and the industrialist ethos, claiming that compassion, duty, and civilization had passed away with the fading of agrarian England. The criticism awoke a sympathetic response in the breasts of all those who felt disquiet—whether on grounds of personal or group hardship, temper-ament, philosophy or aestheticism—about the Victorian machine age.

The Tories fought a steep uphill fight against the praise of the economists and Cobdenites for America's fluid economic structure. Free traders emphasized that, in the Republic, no customary restrictions imposed by an outdated Establishment impeded the path to economic strength. Ideas and prosperity, they held, accompanied the free flow of commerce between states and regions.[1] The Tories, in the early years, countered by pointing to the Union's protectionist policy, set up in 1816. 'How can we be called bigoted, illiberal, and unenlightened', asked *Blackwood's* on behalf of the Corn Law champions, 'when we join in creed with such a people?'[2] The existence of the 'American system', protecting home manufacturing and markets, was used to discount idealistic free-trade ideas that a world-wide customs union was inevitable if other nations should abolish internal barriers to trade. It was argued that countries like the United States would simply capitalize upon the funds, labour, and skills exported from free-trade Britain to build up competitive and subsidized industries. During the twenties the reviews, which represented Ultra-Tory and rural opinion on this matter, were in favour of a stringent mercantilist policy toward the United States. They wanted the British carrying trade restricted to British (even European) bottoms. They advocated a tightening of the law to prevent the migration to America of capital, machinery, and artisans with vital industrial skills.[3] These feelings received intermittent official approval during commercial wrangles with the Adams administration of the twenties. In general, however, the practical politicians—Huskisson, Liverpool, Peel—had a finger on the pulse of industrial England, and were consequently opposed to economic warfare with America. The position of such men was strengthened at the expense of the Corn Law apologists with the continuing consolidation of Anglo-American trade, and with the rise of anti-tariff opinion in the Republic during the 1830's. When Peel and his followers finally split with the protectionists in 1846 over the repeal of the Corn Laws, their action was hailed with delight by the many free-trade converts in the new world. The Tory rump was left resentfully with the conviction, confirmed by the Walker tariff of 1846, that the United States was rapidly joining the free-trade camp.[4]

England's business classes were highly appreciative of America's

[1] See, e.g., Richard Cobden, *England, Ireland and America* (London, 1835), p. 136.

[2] Vol. 24, Nov. 1828, p. 635 (Notes on America), by David Robinson. 'Our Free Trade people', he added, 'are shocked at the barbarous folly of America, and they are wroth beyond measure at the injuries she has inflicted on them.' For the economic policies of the *Quarterly*, see Frank W. Fetter, 'The Economic Articles in the *Quarterly Review* and their Authors, 1809–52', *J. of Pol. Econ.*, LXVI (1958), pp. 47–64, and LXVI (1958), pp. 154–70.

[3] See *Blackwood's*, Vol. 24, Nov. 1828, pp. 621–38. *Blackwood's* wanted emigrants to be diverted to the British colonies and colonial industries. The latter (e.g. Canadian fisheries) ought to be positively encouraged, by bounty if necessary.

[4] Croker argued, however, that the Walker tariff was not in fact based upon free-trade principles. He admitted the scaling down of tariffs, but saw in the retention of a variable *ad valorem* duty a protectionist principle. *QR*, Vol. 78, No. 156, Sept. 1846, p. 538 (Close of Peel's Administration).

cheap government as well as of her internal free trade. The example of cheap administration encouraged reformers of all colours, including respectable manufacturers as well as republican Radicals, to attack the nepotism and sinecurism of the British system. It led directly to criticism of the Establishment and the Crown.[1] During the Victorian age administrative retrenchment and rationalization took place at central and local levels, despite Tory objections that reform was based upon Benthamite and Yankee misconceptions. Stringent economies were never taken, however, to American extremes, for which, no doubt, conservative propaganda and instincts were partly responsible. Cheap public service, in the Tory view, was 'the most ruinous *cheap* article that can be speculated in'.[2] It repudiated the wholesome aristocratic tradition of honourable rewards for service. It also bred inefficiency and corruption. Under such circumstances, men of talent or riches were not tempted into office, but, as in America, sought success in business or commerce. The Tories were distressed by what they believed to be the wrong priorities accepted by Americans. Only meagre rewards, without honours, could be won honestly in politics or executive office, in the judiciary or armed services. Leading public men received little recognition once their services had been dispensed with. Washington had been buried without honours; Jefferson, Monroe, and Jackson had ended their days in poor circumstances. National pride notwithstanding, American Ambassadors abroad received inadequate public assistance to maintain the dignity of their establishments.[3] How, it was asked, in a nation which revered money-making, would it be possible to obtain eminent public servants in this way? 'A nation, to have the choice of the market of ability,' declared *Blackwoods*, 'must outbid all competitors.'[4] England, ultimately, accepted

[1] See, for example, Cobden's passionate advocacy of 'strict economy' in his *England, Ireland and America* (London, 1835), p. 138. If, he stated, economy was found to be inconsistent with the maintenance of monarchical and aristocratic institutions, 'then we answer, let an unflinching economy and retrenchment be enforced. . . .'

[2] *Blackwood's*, Vol. 18, Sept. 1825, p. 343, by Robinson.

[3] See Foster's criticisms, quoted in *QR*, Vol. 68, No. 135, June 1841, p. 45; and Croker in *QR*, Vol. 68, No. 136, Sept. 1841, Art. 7.

[4] Vol. 18, Sept. 1825, p. 342. 'America', the article continued, 'has scarcely had one public servant who has risen above mediocrity since the Revolution . . . *cheap* statesmen—*cheap* heroes!—the nation bantering, and over-reaching, and buying *cheap* genius, knowledge, skill, wisdom, industry, blood, and suffering of the individual. . . .' (p. 343.) A great debate went on in England about the truth of claims made for the cheapness of government in the U.S. Croker argued that the Radicals twisted American statistics by failing to consider the duplication of institutions under federalism, and neglecting other expenses (e.g., judicial), which were not enumerated in Federal accounts. He also emphasized the greatly different circumstances of the American continent *vis à vis* those of Europe, and thought that English government was as relatively inexpensive as American. *QR*, Vol. 46, No. 92, Jan.

this Tory view. Public service continued to be rewarded even in the case of the Dissenters, the industrialists, the self-made men, with titles and status, and established things were conserved.

The gap between upper- and middle-class temperament was clearly revealed over the issue of religious disestablishment. Britain's industrial middle class was predominantly Dissenting, and the sects had close and cordial relations with their fellow-believers in the United States. Dissenting admiration for the American church system, for the voluntary principle in religion, was intense, and helped enormously to encourage campaigns against state sponsorship of the church in England.[1] In one sense this religious struggle was part of a wider capitalist and commercial attack upon medieval establishments. Tory defences of the state church were, conversely, associated with the aristocracy's struggle for power against the new men of the steam age. Defence of the established church was conceived as a central duty of conservatism, and a political as much as a religious act; because 'the Church of England was the central institution of Toryism—the state in its religious aspect, and the divine principle in monarchial government'.[2]

The Dissenters, as it turned out, lost their fight to abolish state-sponsored Anglicanism; but the Tories were never able to turn the American religious example successfully in their own favour. Tory publicists tended to take the High Anglican attitude of distaste for a Nonconformist America. Political conservatism, indeed, outstripped opinion within the Church of England in its insularity. The vocal Evangelical wing within the church—in many ways Dissenting in outlook and having roots among commercial and artisan classes whose allegiances were not Tory—had many links with America, and was much more pro-American.[3] Tory propaganda was quite often exaggerated, as well as being supercilious, about the American churches, and thus had little

---

(Continued from p. 155)

1832, pp. 594–8. Sir James Graham, in the 1840's a Peelite, disagreed in 1830, and strongly advocated a streamlining of Britain's consular service in line with cheap American administration. See Hansard, New ser., XXV, 257. For Lillibridge's rather critical interpretation of Tory attitudes on this, see *Beacon of Freedom*, op. cit., pp. 17–19.

[1] See *Thistlethwaite*, op. cit., Ch. 3.

[2] G. H. Guttridge, *English Whiggism and the American Revolution* (California, 1942), p. 2.

[3] See *Thistlethwaite*, op. cit., pp. 82–85. Evangelicalism, as Thistlethwaite points out, 'was essentially rebellious and disruptive, and brought considerable strength to the mobilized forces of Dissent'. Evangelicals cared little for the church or for the state as a divine institution. Their business was with individual rather than corporate religion. (pp. 82–83.)

effect upon those who were in close and real touch with brethren over-seas. The most effective criticism was directed against revivalist and other extremist movements among frontier farmers and city proletariat. The respectable middle class in England shared Tory fears on this subject, but alarm did not extend to crusading Methodists and evangelists who imported American techniques to aid their own missions. An alternative charge, that indifference and unbelief were rife in America, was widely publicized by the Tory press in the unsettled years after Waterloo, and again with the expansion of the frontier in the late thirties, but it was received sceptically by liberals and Nonconformists and was qualified as knowledge about the United States increased.[1]

More plausible was the contention that schismatic sectarianism, which could spill over into politics, was increased where the state enjoyed no union with the church. Under the American voluntary system, Thomas Hamilton alleged, 'differences of religious opinion rend society into shreds and patches',[2] and he explained that an established religion encour-aged the creation of stable opinion. The Americans missed the moderating influence wielded in England by a cadre of University-educated clergy. Henry Hart Milman, one of the church's most distinguished theologians, and a brilliant Oxonian, agreed. Milman was somewhat sceptical of the popular notion that religious toleration was the necessary result of Nonconformity and the proliferation of sects. He suggested that individual sects were jealous and authoritarian to a degree unknown in the established church. He concurred in the opinion of the eminent geologist Sir Charles Lyell, reached after his second visit to the United States in 1845–6, that '. . . the strength and repose of a great establish-ment are, in some respects, more favourable to private liberty. If less favour is shown to those without, there is usually more liberality to those within.'[3] For this reason Milman favoured the co-existence of independent sects and an established church; and he used Lyell's evidence about American practice to oppose those Anglicans who unwisely desired the

---

[1] In 1820 Southey, filching his testimony from John Bristed's voluminous *Resources of the U.S.A.* (London, 1818), complained that one-third of Americans were destitute of religious ordinances and that atheistic societies flourished. (*QR*, Vol. 23, No. 46, July 1820, pp. 550–2.) Ten years later Tories had to admit the strength of religion in the East, although frontier religion, with its camp-meetings alternating with indifference, still came under fire. Opponents credited this state of affairs, how-ever, to physical conditions, not to the voluntary principle.

[2] Quoted in *Blackwood's*, Vol. 34, Sept. 1833, p. 299.

[3] Sir Chas. Lyell, *A Second Visit to the United States . . . 1845–1846* (London, 1849), quoted in Milman's review, *QR*, Vol. 85, No. 169, June 1849, p. 198. Milman was pleased and impressed by the book, which contained a long section on the merits and demerits of America's voluntary system. (See pp. 193–203.)

separation of church and state.[1] Milman wrote many articles in this spirit during the years of challenge to the church between 1835 and 1850, consistently, although amiably, resisting the use of American precedents. In this he was aided by such staunch defenders of the established order as J. J. Blunt,[2] and by more vitriolic pamphleteers like J. G. Lorimer of Glasgow.[3]

American experience was also relevant to the debate about 'congregationalism' which split the Church of Scotland in the early forties and threatened to become an issue in the Church of England. In 1843 Thomas Chalmers, with a large following of Scottish Evangelicals, seceded from the established Church of Scotland to found the Free Church of Scotland. The cause of the schism was alleged infringement of the right of a majority of heads of families registered in the parish to veto the choice of minister made by a lay patron.[4] Such insistence on democracy in ecclesiastical matters was opposed by moderate Presbyterians, and it alarmed most Anglicans and Tories (although it gratified the English Congregationalists). In the midst of the controversy, in 1841, Croker came forward with warnings against the congregational principle taken from the dire spectacle of American sects.[5] Milman too used that example to exert pressure upon the separatists within his own church. He warned them that disestablishment would result in greater dependence upon the congregations, and would produce 'a Cadmean army of sects, not yet compelled as in America, and wearied out into mutual toleration!'[6]

The voluntary secession of Chalmers's Presbyterians from the benefits of state patronage was a shock to the Establishment. It was already faced by the polemics of Edward Miall's *Nonconformist* and Edward Baines's *Leeds Mercury*; and in 1844 the Anti-State-Church Conference met in London. Moreover, Chalmers had, besides Dissenting support, the sympathy of some High Churchmen, including the Bishop of Exeter, who feared the bondage of the church to a secular state in any union.[7] Some would have preferred to re-create the church in the image of the American Episcopal Church. For this very reason orthodox Tories were very chary of praising too generously their co-religionists in the Republic.

[1] Ibid. *QR*, p. 199.

[2] See, for example, Blunt's article, 'The Life of Dr. Adam Clarke', in *QR*, Vol. 51, No. 101, Mar. 1834, pp. 140–2.

[3] Lorimer's pamphlets: *The Past and Present Condition of Religion and Morality in the U.S.A.—an Argument not for Voluntary, but for Established Churches* (London, 1833) and *Church Establishments Defended* (London, 1834), were standard Tory texts.

[4] See Élie Halévy, *History of the English People in the Nineteenth Century* (London, 1961), IV. 71–77.

[5] *QR*, Vol. 69, No. 137, Dec. 1841, p. 251.

[6] *QR*, Vol. 85, No. 169, June 1849, p. 199.   [7] Halévy, op. cit., p. 74.

J. R. Godley was enthusiastic in the cause of the Episcopal Church, and his book on the Union enjoyed considerable Anglican approval. Godley, probably unique in being at one and the same time a disciple of Wakefield and the Tractarians, believed that the tie to the state hampered the reorganization and revitalization of the church. The Episcopal Church, he pointed out, although still in communion with England, was self-governing, self-reliant, and in closer contact with its laity.[1] Disestablishment in England, in his view, would infuse similar new life into the home church.

So far we have been watching conservatism on the defensive against restless innovation and the apparently resistless sweep of new and disturbing ideas. But the gigantic economic revolution which made Britain the world's workshop also made her the seed-bed of ideas and ideologies in reaction against the machine morality, ranging from Owenite Socialism and the near-Marxism of Hodgkin and Thompson to Carlyle's German statism and the romantic conservatism of Coleridge and 'Young England'. To redefine America in relation to this welling reaction enabled Toryism to snatch the initiative, and to offer a more generous interpretation of its own aims. The switch to the offensive was begun by laying open the vices of America's open economic society. The Tories advanced criticisms, later almost the prerogative of Socialists and British Labour, that economic individualism led to a national prostration before the dollar idol. This criticism depended upon a rare enough awareness that American democracy, even Jacksonian democracy, was not, in economic terms, a levelling utopian movement. This view emphasized that Americans respected the natural differences between men, differences which could find their level in free economic interplay; Americans wanted equality only before the law, and in the distribution of official favours. The Tories sometimes played down these qualities in American life, for they were too acceptable to much English opinion. Stress would be laid, instead, on the fact that Americans, once they were rich, were unable to purchase social privilege and encountered popular antagonism. Yet it seemed at times that the wealthy were not pariahs, but the gods of public opinion. Some Tories accepted this view wholeheartedly, for it enabled them to scorn uncritical Radical admiration for the United States as an egalitarian paradise. David Robinson of *Blackwood's* pointed this out:

Does the want of title place the rich men of America, or any other republic, on a level with the poor ones? . . . In America, that Elysium of English philosophers,

[1] 'Everywhere there are signs of a superintending authority; new dioceses are admitted, new parishes formed in proportion to the extension of the demand for them; domestic and foreign missions are maintained and regulated . . . each emergency is met as its arises.' Quoted from *Letters from America* (London, 1844), by C. E. Carrington, *John Robert Godley of Canterbury* (Christchurch, 1950), p. 22.

society divides itself, as far as practicable, into ranks, as it does in this country. There are the same pride, the same keeping apart from inferiors, the same struggles for precedency, there as here. The chain of ranks is shorter, from its not possessing the links formed by a nobility; but as far as it reaches, it is similar to that which exists in England. There is practically an aristocracy in America, which is as ambitious of standing at the head of the community, and as anxious to engross the utmost degree of influence and power, as our own aristocracy.[1]

Pursuing this logic to its conclusion, Robinson denied that the Americans were true democrats. True democrats, in his conception, abhorred all gradations in society, and would have destroyed them:

All men cannot be made rich, therefore they should make all men poor. They should prohibit people from deriving fortunes from public services, trade, bequests, and everything else. They should continually take money from those who accumulate it, and bestow it on those who do not accumulate.[2]

Robinson hated such a communist system. It was, he thought, impossibly theoretical; it flew in the face of nature, which approved the principle of hierarchy.[3] But English Radicals, he contended, ought to recognize the American dilemma—to accept honestly the inconsistency between the formal language of democracy and an actual system of economic hierarchy.

This was far from being an attack upon the aspirations of working-men intended to justify a natural bourgeois order. Tories had as much dislike of that concept as of egalitarianism. The morality of the market-place, in the conservative philosophy, required constant check:

The great object of trade and profession is, not merely to gain bread, but to acquire fortunes. . . . Men can scarcely pursue such an object the greater part of their lives without attaching too much value to money, and too little to everything that may stand in the way of getting it. They are exposed to everything that can tempt them to be mercenary, dishonest, and dishonourable. . . . the unremitting pursuit of personal gain must tend powerfully to stifle many of the feelings on which the weal of the state depends.[4]

---

[1] *Blackwood's*, Vol. 18, Sept. 1825, p. 341 (The Nobility). The actress Fanny Kemble, who professed a sentimental and backward-looking conservatism, noted the same phenomenon when she compared the levelling spirit of American democracy with 'the separating and dividing spirit of American society'. *Journal of Frances Ann Butler* (London, 1835), quoted in *QR*, Vol. 54, No. 107, July 1835, p. 54.

[2] *Blackwood's*, ibid. p. 341.

[3] Theorists, he said, mistakenly treated man as raw material to be shaped in a desired pattern—'With the name of Nature eternally in their mouths . . . they make it their study to thwart and trample upon her. . . .' Ibid. p. 340.

[4] Ibid. p. 345.

Yet in America there was virtually no counteracting force to the com-mercial. As early as 1825 Robinson believed that the United States was 'an unrestrained commonwealth of traders':

Its government has generally manifested, in its dealings with other states, the shirking, low cunning, and mean trickery of the petty tradesmen. Interest has been with it everything, and honour nothing. Without an aristocracy, its ministers have been slaves to the passions and interests of the traders.[1]

Sir John Barrow felt that Americans were consumed with a restless ambition to multiply their material goods, a motive which took prece-dence over more altruistic feelings.[2] As a disappointed emigrant had remarked to William Faux: 'Liberty here means to do each as he pleases; to care for nothing and nobody, and cheat everybody.'[3] Lockhart too recoiled from the doctrine of rugged individualism. In 1832 he read the *Recollections* of Timothy Flint, a Presbyterian clergyman from New England who had for many years attempted, unavailingly, to import Christianity into a remote part of the Mississippi valley. Lockhart, moved, was led to remark that

. . . we have here but one more instance of the practical effect of a social system which trusts everything to individual free will. Any attempt to provide the means of regular religious instruction for the multitudinous population scattered over the woods and prairies of the west, would be an unwarrantable infringement of the rights of the America citizen. . . . In church and in state America presents the *reductio ad absurdum* of Whiggism.[4]

Robert Southey looked at the problem in a broader context. America, he thought, was part of a civilization which bred the peculiar vices of the commercial ethic:

The truth is, that America neither is, nor can be any more exempt from those evils which are the original sin of the trading system, than from the original sin of human nature itself. Commerce has everywhere its Helots. . . . The evil is not affected by any form of government. It is the same under the despotisms of Italy and the Peninsula, the limited monarchy of England, and the representative republics of the United States.[5]

Yet Southey was capable of arguing for comprehensive government as a protection against warring individualism.[6] One defect of the American

[1] Ibid. p. 346.
[2] QR, Vol. 29, No. 58, July 1823, p. 359.
[3] Quoted, ibid. p. 359.
[4] QR, Vol. 48, No. 95, Oct. 1832, p. 207.
[5] QR, Vol. 30, No. 59, Oct. 1832, p. 29.
[6] Ibid. pp. 30–31, 36.

constitution, he felt, was that it provided no such protection. Southey, unlike some of his compatriot Tories, refrained from advising that a titled nobility should be introduced into America as a solution to materialism. He was, by Tory standards, dangerously pro-American; and his philosophy included the proposition that the legitimate ends of government were attainable under many forms of government, including the republican. He wished to see the acceptance in America of some principles counter to those prevailing—for instance, a stronger Presidency. But he insisted that such adaptations must be gradual and a response to evolving circumstances. To advocate violent changes in the form of American government was not, he believed, the proper duty of true conservatives.

This counsel of restraint became less popular during the age of geographical and technological expansion in America. The process of unregulated expansion, the working out of Manifest Destiny, had no mystical attraction for Tories. They deplored the involvement in finance, business, and speculation which it necessitated; they attacked the materialist culture which it produced. In the words of Gustave de Beaumont:

The relations of man with man have but one object—money; one sole interest—to get rich. The passion for money is born along with the dawnings of intellect. . . . Money is the god of the United States, just as Glory is the god of France. . . . But at the bottom of this violent passion it is impossible to discover any moral sentiment. Restricted to the relations of mere interest, American society is grave without having the imposing character of virtue.[1]

On the occasion of the Texan affair in 1837, W. E. Channing, in a pamphlet publicized by the *Quarterly*, wrote that Americans were consumed by a 'degrading passion' for gain. Under this influence, the higher virtues and simplicity, the stern uprightness, the respect of man for man 'which are the ornaments and safeguards of a republic' had given place to 'selfish calculation and indulgence, to show and extravagance, to anxious, envious, discontented strivings, to wild adventure, and to the gambling spirit of speculation'.[2]

The Tories sought proof of these charges in the sordid history of financial malpractice and land-jobbing. The reviews cited innumerable

[1] *Marie* (Paris, 1835), quoted in *QR*, Vol. 53, No. 106, Apr. 1835, p. 299. Cf. Fearon: 'Gain is the education—the morals, the politics, the theology, and stands in the stead of the domestic comfort of all ages and classes of Americans; it is the centre of their system.' *Sketches in America, etc.* (London, 1818), quoted in *QR*, Vol. 21, No. 41, Jan. 1819, p. 151.
[2] *QR*, Vol. 61, No. 122, Apr. 1838, quoted p. 348 (Texas), by Thatcher, from Channing, *Letter to the Hon. Henry Clay on the Annexation of Texas to the U.S.* (Boston, 1837).

instances of knavery, embezzlement, absconding, and bankruptcies. They noticed the preoccupation of politicians with questions of banking and the issue of money. 'Wild-catters' opposed hard-money theorists; the nation seemed caught up in a debate about the merits of currency and credit systems. The courts were bogged down with questions of contracts; and Englishmen were dismayed to see, in many states, the tolerance of the law and society towards the condition of insolvency. Abstract justice, apparently, was being trifled with for the benefit of business.

Education was criticized because it did not prevent, indeed encouraged, the perversion of the young to the pursuit of material success. No alternative values gained expression through a leisured class, for no class existed which did not 'dwell constantly on subjects connected with profit and loss'.[1] In America opprobrium was levelled against idleness in all forms—the tyranny of public opinion thus preserving the commercial ethos which had brought results. Politicians were subservient to an electorate which John Stuart Mill had correctly labelled bourgeois; and political office was attained by a corruptive competition whose prototype was surely commercial. Even the clergy, added the critics, were infected by a surrounding materialist culture. Was not piety confined to the Sabbath? How often were topics such as business ethics or negro slavery dealt with from the pulpit when the congregation was antagonistic? Were not the pulpits, as well as the churches, emptied when rich new areas, or gold, were discovered? The church in America was regarded as simply another profession, an avenue to better things.[2]

From such appraisals of an open economic society the inference was usually drawn that an aristocracy had valuable social functions. Society, ran the argument, was naturally hierarchical, but it required a privileged class at the top in order to preserve other standards, and pursue other interests, than those of an efficient business class. A nobility, because it was independent of the everyday pursuit of wealth, was independent of the vices of the world of commerce—of avarice and the 'sleepless regard for personal interest', of inhumanity to fellow-creatures, of disregard for civilization and culture.[3] People like David Robinson argued that the English nobility, despite some characteristic vices, was generally high-minded and subject to a rigorous code of honour, self-imposed. Aristocratic government appeared to its apologists to be a trust shouldered on

[1] QR, Vol. 41, No. 82, Nov. 1829, p. 437 (Travels in North America), by Barrow.

[2] See, e.g., Lockhart on commercialism and the clergy in QR, Vol. 53, No. 106, Apr. 1835, pp. 302–5. For Hall's criticisms of materialism as taken up by the Quarterly, see Vol. 41, No. 82, Nov. 1829, pp. 437ff.

[3] See Robinson's very able exposition of this theme in Blackwood's, Vol. 18, Sept. 1825, pp. 335–51 (The Nobility).

behalf of the people; society was conceived as an exercise in mutual duties and obligations. In so far as the middle class aspired to titles and prestige within the Establishment it was obliged to pay respect to such views, to conform to some extent to established and socially beneficial usages.[1] In short, rank and privilege were civilizing influences in a mercantile age.

Tory criticism, then, only partly resembled modern Socialist criticism of American capitalism. In a sense there was a surface affinity springing from the similarity between Socialist planning and the old mercantilist idea of state control (so directed, however, as to encourage and protect national and vested interests). Both views repudiated *laissez faire* theory about the limited state and unrestricted economic activity. A deeper Christian repugnance to unlicensed and selfish commercial competition also underlay both views. On the other hand, Tory disquiet had its roots in feudalism and the ideals of chivalry, in rural manorialism. Conservatives criticized a materialist and bourgeois America, not in order to advocate a collective economic plan for society, but as a nostalgic plea for aristocracy and Old England.

Jacksonian America, again, was obviously not America of the Gilded Age. It was still the society of open opportunities, the era of 'rural capitalists and village entrepreneurs', not of monopoly and big business. The upper classes in Britain had a conception of the United States as an unrelievedly acquisitive civilization; but they had, rightly, little concept of the country as an industrial hell which ground the faces of the poor, as supposedly did the factory system of Britain. Radicals and liberals were agreed in praising the amelioration in the condition of the labouring class in America; and the liberals claimed it to be the product of commercial virtues (a claim which was not very plausible when made about England). The Tories were obliged to appeal in reply to loftier and less obvious ideals than material success (as do critics of the capitalist system today in the face of the affluent society). They had to follow Carlyle in saying of the Americans:

Their quantity of cotton, dollars, industry and resources, I believe to be almost unspeakable; but I can by no means worship the like of these. What great human

---

[1] Robinson wrote: 'It is . . . of the first importance that a balance of feeling should be created against that generated by business, that effectual means for nurturing and promoting, amidst the more influential part of the community, generosity, chivalrous honour, high feeling, and the opposite of almost everything that business inspires. It is essential that in the intercourse between the men of trade and the great landlords, etc., the former should be the inferiors—should be the relievers, and not the givers, of example.' Ibid. p. 345.

soul, what great thought, what great noble thing that we could worship, or loyally admire, has yet been produced there? None. . . .[1]

[1] *Latter Day Pamphlets* (1872), p. 18 (written in 1850). Not all Tories, as indicated earlier, were anti-commercial. Peel, as far as is known, made no complaint against bourgeois values in America. Ashley was friendly towards America; he was obsessed with the iniquities of slavery, and fearful of Socialist doctrines in Britain, and apparently did not consider the anti-humanitarian aspects of unrestrained competition in the Republic. He was, instead, impressed by material prosperity there, and by the nation's inherent conservatism: 'They may, and will, have party strifes and struggles for the possession of place and power; but what social question remains? There is no Church to be invaded; no aristocracy to be pulled down; no king to be replaced by a president; efforts at organic changes would seem to be impossible, nor will the bane of Europe, the Socialistic principle, become, for many generations at least, a continuous and concentrated question.' Entry in his diary, 20.6.1852, in Edwin Hodder, *Life and Work of the 7th Earl of Shaftesbury* (London, 1887), p. 454. *Fraser's Magazine*, which was a vitriolic opponent of *laissez faire*, failed to profit by an attack upon its results in America, to which few references are made.

CHAPTER V

THE INFLUENCE OF ALEXIS DE TOCQUEVILLE

1. *Tocqueville and the British Intelligentsia*

ALEXIS DE TOCQUEVILLE, whose name has already been impossible to repress, is a figure of critical importance in such a study as this. Political scientists today commend his *Democracy in America*, both as a commentary upon the Jacksonian political scene and as political philosophy. But it is important to remember that his book was always regarded as a classic. It profoundly influenced British opinion about America, and about democracy, at a time when liberals and conservatives were bitterly wrangling about both subjects. Before 1835, when the *Democracy* first appeared in translation, the most striking accounts of America had been written by Radicals or Tories with axes to grind. As John Stuart Mill complained: '. . . for many years every book of travels in America had been a party pamphlet, or had at least fallen among partisans, and been pressed into the service of one party or the other . . .'[1] Tocqueville created an essentially new image of America, and American democracy. He raised the debate to a more serious level by presenting new evidence in an objective spirit, by asking new questions, and by clarifying the issues. For many informed Englishmen, America became America as seen by Tocqueville. This is not to deny that resistance was generated to Tocqueville's ideas in various quarters, but the resistance was itself shaped in relation to his own orthodoxy.

Henry Reeve's translation of Part I of *De la Démocratie en Amérique* burst upon the English literary world in 1835 and met with instant success, being widely reviewed and soon running through a number of editions. Contemporaries obviously felt that here was a new revelation about America, presented with the clarity of an astute political philosopher. John Stuart Mill, then at the height of his power as a spokesman of

[1] *ER*, Oct. 1840, reprinted in Mill, *Dissertations and Discussions* (London, 1859), II. 2.

the Philosophical Radicals but sensitive to new insights, was deeply impressed, and wrote in his *London Review*:

The book has at once taken its rank among the most remarkable productions of our time; and it is a book with which, both for its facts and its speculations, all who would understand, or who are called upon to exercise influence over their age, are bound to be familiar. It will contribute to give to the political speculations of our time a new character. . . . The book is such as Montesquieu might have written, if to his genius he had superadded good sense, and the light which mankind have since gained from the experiences of a period in which they may be said to have lived centuries in fifty years.[1]

Mill's endorsement, together with the near-universal praise of the major periodicals, urged with their then almost magisterial authority, set the seal on the book's success in England. (It was of course immediately successful in America and Europe as well, and won a prize in 1836 from the Académie française.)[2] The eagerly awaited Part II appeared in 1840 and was given a critical attention reserved for important works of speculation. Although the deeper philosophy of this volume did not satisfy all tastes, Tocqueville's argument was carefully expounded in most of the journals, which invariably gave long extracts from the original, for Tocqueville was eminently quotable, although he did not always endorse the ends to which his words were put. Even the Tory *Blackwood's* extended tolerant approval to a work which was by no means obviously anti-democratic:

The clearness with which he analysed and exposed to view the working and tendencies of the democratic state of society exhibited in the United States carried all his readers with him. Whether they liked or disliked the inferences to which his remarks seemed to point, they acknowledged, either promptly or reluctantly, that his statements, and his comments upon them, were fair, luminous, and most eminently instructive.[3]

The first sense of the enduring worth of the *Democracy in America* remained undissipated by time, or so it seemed to Henry Reeve, writing in 1861. He felt that the work, over twenty-five years, 'has gained in interest from the inexhaustible depth, the unflinching truth, and the extraordinary foresight which are its characteristics. It is, and will remain, by far the

---

[1] *London Review*, Vol. 26, Oct. 1835, p. 94.
[2] See J. Lively, *The Social and Political Thought of Alexis de Tocqueville* (Clarendon Press, Oxford, 1962), p. 2. This excellent work is recommended for a wider theoretical analysis of Tocqueville's significance.
[3] *Blackwood's*, Vol. 48, Oct. 1840, p. 463. For similar praises, see *Blackwood's*, Vol. 37, May 1835, pp. 758, 766.

greatest work of political philosophy of this age, for it embraces futurity itself, and that with no uncertain range.'[1]

In the compact world of the British intelligentsia in the 1830's and 1840's there was ample opportunity for the spread of Tocqueville's ideas. Personal contact added to the effect of the written word. Tocqueville visited England in 1833 and 1835, and made the acquaintance of a number of important thinkers and leading politicians to whom he conveyed some of his impressions about the new world. On his first visit Tocqueville made himself known to Nassau Senior, with whom he maintained a lifelong friendship; he met Edward Bulwer Lytton, the Radical M.P. and author of a now-forgotten classic, *England and the English*; and he discussed government with Lord Radnor, a Whig, and Sir John Bowring, editor of the *Westminster Review*. The precocious and cosmopolitan Henry Reeve he met in Paris in March 1835. On his return to Britain in May 1835 Tocqueville was a celebrated writer, and was feted in London society. He became the centre of attraction in the polished Whig society of Lansdowne and Holland Houses. According to Reeve, an eye-witness:

. . . his manners and his powers of conversation ensured him a cordial reception; he found there not only the easy citizenship of good breeding, but the same deep interest in the progress of mankind, and the same ardent attachment to every great and free object which had become the ruling passion of his life. His own ideal of social excellence and political greatness lay precisely in the combination of aristocratic tastes with popular interests, and in that independence of position and character which is never more complete than when it is united to a high sense of the duties . . . of property and station. That is what he found in the Whig society of this country.[2]

Tocqueville may have obtained different impressions when he was received among the Benthamites who were wont to gather at Senior's house in Kensington. In London he came to know John Mill; the Grotes and J. A. Roebuck; Henry Hallam, the learned Whig historian of England; Sir George Cornewall Lewis, the classical scholar and enigmatic administrator-politician; and the 'enthusiastic but paradoxical' Monckton Milnes, M.P., poet, and social butterfly *par excellence*. He also met John Austin, the Benthamite student of jurisprudence, and Sir James Stephen (permanent head of the Colonial Office from 1836 to 1847, and as such ridiculed by Charles Buller as 'Mr. Mother-Country'

[1] *ER*, Vol. 113, Apr. 1861, p. 431. *Tait's Edinburgh Magazine* was the most unfavourable about Part II.
[2] *ER*, Vol. 113, Apr. 1861, p. 442.

for his *de facto* control over colonial policy). The letters and autobiographies of the time show abundantly the considerable impression made by this young Frenchman of aristocratic lineage but with startling ideas about democracy. Symptomatic of the high regard in which he was held was the fact that he was invited to give evidence before the 1835 Select Committee on Bribery at Elections, probably at the instigation of George Grote.[1] Peel used his testimony freely in a debate upon bribery five months later in the Commons. Tocqueville maintained many of the contacts he made in England. He corresponded regularly with Senior and Reeve, frequently with Mill, and occasionally with the Grotes and Lewis. The Seniors, the Grotes and Monckton Milnes often visited the Tocqueville estate in Cherbourg. In this way his new ideas on democracy and politics were kept before his British friends, who passed them around in correspondence, reviewed them in the journals, and, undoubtedly, discussed them socially.

It seems likely that the gregarious Henry Reeve was a leading disseminator of Tocqueville's ideas in England. As the translator of the *Democracy*, Reeve became closely acquainted with Tocqueville's thought, besides becoming a close friend and admirer of the author. Widely travelled, urbane, and something of a prodigy in his youth, Reeve was exceedingly well-connected and mixed freely in English and French society.[2] In 1837, through Lord Lansdowne's patronage, he obtained the important post of Clerkship of Appeals to the Judicial Committee of the Privy Council. From 1840 he became a critic and leader-writer for *The Times*; he was Registrar of the Privy Council from 1847 and editor of the *Edinburgh Review* from 1855 until 1895. Here was a man, imbued with Tocqueville's ideas upon America, who lived, according to his biographer, 'with his fingers on the keys of public opinion, directing it, leading it, guiding it with a power which was none the less real because few recognized it or knew of it'.[3] His ideas are considered at greater length later in this chapter. Among others who owed intellectual stimulus

---

[1] Tocqueville's evidence is reprinted in Tocqueville, *Journeys to England and Ireland*, ed. J. P. Mayer (London, 1958), Appendix, pp. 210ff. For his reception in England see also J. K. Laughton, *Memoirs of the Life and Correspondence of Henry Reeve* (London, 1898), Vol. I; A. Zemach, 'Tocqueville in England', *Review of Politics* (July, 1951); and S. Drescher, *Tocqueville and England* (Cambridge, Harvard University Press, 1964).

[2] He was related to the influential Austin family, and became a protégé of Lord Lansdowne. He knew most of the Benthamites and Whigs, and among Frenchmen, knew D'Eichthal, Cousin, Victor Hugo, Lamartine, Balzac and Montalambert. His work for the Privy Council brought him into contact with Greville, Brougham, and Lyndhurst, among others.

[3] Laughton, op. cit., I. v. Reeve's counsels, we are assured, 'had a large but unreported share in the decisions of Cabinets'. Ibid. p. vi.

to Tocqueville were, as we have seen, the younger Mill, who was
certainly influential in propagating the new ideas within the important
Benthamite *salon*. It is at least relevant to note here the extraordinary
effectiveness of this circle as a political and intellectual pressure group
in Victorian England. Influence was wielded by means of what Professor
Samuel Finer has called a process of irradiation—by working through
personal contacts, family connections, and social intercourse in informal
as well as specialist bodies, by methods of conversion, recruitment, and
proselytizing manipulated by and from a missionary clique. Many of
Tocqueville's English friends were either members of this clique or else
exposed to it, and it seems not unreasonable to conclude that his influence
upon these people was considerable and infectious. Nassau Senior was a
fringe member of the group, and his reaction, showing sympathy with
Tocqueville's liberalism but alarm at some of his conclusions, was
perhaps not untypical. Senior described Part I to its author as 'one of the
most remarkable books of the age'; but, from his correspondence with
Tocqueville, it appears that Senior's main interest was in the economic,
rather than in the political, analysis.[1] In his own writings upon the
United States he frequently referred to Tocqueville as an authority;
but, as we have seen, his assessment of American politics was emphatically
not in Tocqueville's tradition. Nevertheless, it is interesting to note that
Senior took a Tocquevillian standpoint in the 1850's when interest in
reform was revived. Although sympathetic to Aristocracy in its present
clash with Democracy, he was above all 'for the winning horse': '. . . if
Democracy is to prevail I shall join its ranks, in the hope of making its
victory less mischevous'.[2]

2. *The New Revelation*

It was part of Tocqueville's significance that he forcibly brought America
into the great debates upon liberalism which rent Europe in the nineteenth
century. He suggested that western society was in transition from a
corporate condition to that of an industrial egalitarian democracy. This,
he said, was a Providential fact, the result of irreversible historical forces.
Feudalism had exemplified a society based upon a coherent theory of
inequality, but ever since the rise to power of the commercial and
business orders there had been a growing tendency towards 'the equali-
zation of social condition'. Clashes between kings and nobles had first

[1] See a letter from Senior to Tocqueville, 17.2.1835, in M. C. M. Simpson, ed.,
*Correspondence and Conversations of Alexis de Tocqueville with Nassau William Senior
1834–1859* (London, 1872), I. 2.
[2] Senior to Tocqueville, 19.2.1852.

accelerated this tendency; then the rise of technology and bureaucracy, the spread of knowledge, and the success of Protestant individualism had enabled a democratic revolution to occur throughout Christendom. In Tocqueville's view the gradual development of social equality in the modern mass society had the character of a law of nature: '. . . it is universal, it is durable, it constantly eludes all human interference, and all events as well as all men contribute to its progress'. He therefore regarded as obsolete the debate being waged between the adherents of democracy and aristocracy: 'Necessity and Providence have decided that for us', as Mill put it. Choice was possible only between a well- and an ill-regulated democracy, 'and on that depends the future well-being of the human race'.[1]

With this historical interpretation constantly in mind, Tocqueville proceeded to examine the United States as a specific form of what would ultimately be the universal condition of mankind. 'I confess', he wrote, 'that in America I saw more than America. I sought the image of democracy itself.' By studying empirically the structure and dynamics of American society, he hoped to gain insight into the potentialities of democracy for good or ill; he thereby hoped to give man a chance to exert some control over his future, within the framework of historical laws. He believed that generalizations could be legitimately made from the American condition, although he was nevertheless aware of America's peculiar historical and geographical situation. Indeed he saw in the very novelty of American experience some valuable lessons to be learned by Europe.

Tocqueville viewed the democratic process as a levelling and broadening influence in terms of power, knowledge, and prosperity.[2] Extremes of condition disappeared, to be replaced by standardization and homogeneity. As Reeve explained: '. . . multitude is substituted by the democratic change for magnitude; whatever existed with greater intensity for the few, is diluted for the many; and the standard dimension is changed from that of depth to that of extent'.[3] Tocqueville, an aristocrat by birth and sympathy, was uneasy about the disappearance of the

---

[1] Mill in *London Review*, Vol. 26, Oct. 1835, pp. 91–93. This review article is hereafter referred to as Mill, *London Review*, 1835.

[2] Tocqueville was not semantically clear in his use of the term 'démocratie', and his readers were often confused as to its exact meaning. The senses in which he used the word varied from the concept of a limited system of political democracy to a wider concept of the egalitarian society at large. By it he often meant the entire structure of bourgeois, capitalist society. The Tories had a sound criticism when they objected that Jacksonian democracy had inegalitarian characteristics which Tocqueville underestimated.

[3] *British and Foreign Review*, Vol. 10, No. 20, p. 548.

aristocratical cultural dimension, but justified it as the historical price to be paid for the realization of a more widespread social justice. Democracy at its best, he was convinced, could substitute for the noble virtues the civil virtues of human welfare and peace, practical morality and social sympathy. Like Bentham and the Mills, he saw as the advantage of a well-regulated democracy, such as the United States, that its systematic and perpetual end was the good of the immense majority, or at least its interest. By means of reason, rather than blind tradition, popular obedience and attachment to the law was obtained. The majority, said Tocqueville, respected authority because, through universal suffrage and elections, authority was clearly seen to emanate from the people, from themselves. He agreed with the criticism that republics were less expert than aristocracies in administration. He thought that America lacked a states-man class, that it had no traditions of continuity and expertise in administration, that it often followed hasty and shortsighted policies. But a democracy of this type had one overriding virtue, that it escaped the exclusiveness and class spirit of aristocratic government.

The opponents of democracy preferred to seize upon Tocqueville's criticisms of majority rule—as we have seen, his doctrine of the 'tyranny of the majority' was widely publicized in upper-class circles. Many commentators suggested that this tyranny was a threat to property and person, but Tocqueville emphasized that it was primarily a threat to the independence of thought: Democratic societies, he argued, tended to atomization. At first, this resulted in anarchic individualism of opinion, for the older authorities, such as tradition, had been discredited. But soon a democratic tradition was built up. Society succumbed to the logic of numbers, and a new authority—that of the majority—replaced the old. In the United States the majority combined all the powers of society, and virtually constituted public opinion. The existence of social equality only served to emphasize the essential insignificance of the individual and to underline his final dependence upon the majority. The deviant must conform or submit to the sanctions of social ostracism, or worse. The result was to promote a permanent 'courtier spirit' in society, to encourage the majority in perpetual adoration of itself. Average standards were embraced; genius, distinction, and difference were resented and discouraged. This, for Tocqueville, amounted to a stultification of the human personality. Thus he explained the mediocrity of American culture (although he allowed some credit to its provincial condition). Literature, art, and philosophy suffered through a constant reference to the market criteria of the many. Widespread education, wealth, and leisure created a demand for the products of the intellect; but the values to which creation must conform were, by virtue of popular tastes, vitiative of real achievement. Quality was sacrificed for quantity, permanence for topicality, deep meditation for immediate entertainment.

Tocqueville was a Frenchman, well aware of France's revolutionary history, and he was therefore deeply concerned at the tendency of democracy to degenerate into despotism. In the circumstances of the nineteenth century he feared that 'democratic despotism' would be more pervasive than any known hitherto. In the new democracies, where the older corporate hindrances to autocracy had been swept away, society became dangerously atomized. The individual was weak, and dedication to equality kept him so. Unless alternative safeguards were devised, there would be no resistance to the despotic tendencies of the modern age. Tocqueville was wary of the bureaucratic centralism which was being adopted by most countries to meet expanding social needs. He perceived that the demands of technology and the requirements of the new industrial age encouraged the creation of an all-powerful state, omniparticipant in the lives of its citizens.[1] He foresaw that egalitarian dogmas could breed despotism, for the values of freedom and equality were by no means necessarily compatible. He thought that it was equality rather than liberty which distinguished democracies. The citizens might cherish freedom (and it was Tocqueville's contention that they must do so if the potentialities of the new age were to be realized); but their passion for equality was 'ardent, insatiable, incessant, invincible'. Thus they would endure poverty, barbarism, and even servitude under a despot, rather than lay down their right to 'equality of social condition'.

Tocqueville hated despotism of any kind: '. . . for myself, when I feel the hand of power lie heavy on my brow, I care but little to know who oppresses me: and I am not the more disposed to pass beneath the yoke because it is held out to me by the arms of a million men'. He regarded himself as a liberal of a new species—one who combined a humanist concern for the individual with a deep sense of social justice for the masses.[2] Personal and social fulfilment he believed possible only in the presence of liberty, but liberty in the present age, he also believed, must be co-existent with, and an element of, the new egalitarian society. It must be achieved within the historical framework of the levelling, democratic process, for he regarded that process as prerequisite to the decent existence of the people. He had faith that the amalgamation of the

[1] For the administrative implications of Tocqueville's thinking, see L. Smith, 'Tocqueville and Public Administration', *Pub. Admin. Rev.*, II (1942), 221–39.

[2] See A. Salomon, 'Tocqueville, Moralist and Sociologist', *Social Research*, II (1935); and his 'Tocqueville's Philosophy of Freedom', *Review of Politics*, I (1939), 400–32.

two sets of values would ensure a continuous vitalization in the new society.

Tocqueville suggested a number of safeguards for the preservation of a desirable form of democracy with a liberal character. Here the crucial experience was American, although Tocqueville always insisted that national varieties of democracy must derive from their own history and needs. In his view American democracy exemplified a way of life in a spirit of freedom; it seemed to demonstrate the possibilities of free institutions which embodied the mores of the nation, whereas France indicated the dangers of a divorce between forms and values. He saw that American liberalism sprang out of a complex of historical, social, religious, and geographic considerations: out of the frontier, the traditions of local self-government, religious dissent, and the heritage of English common law. He advised strife-torn Europe to look at some of the controls which prevented extremism in the new world. He advocated administrative decentralization after witnessing the merits of municipal self-government in the townships of New England. Believing the strength of a free people to reside in the *commune*, Tocqueville looked upon democracy in the locality as the school and safety-valve of demo-cracy in the state. As in the United States, the people became accustomed to administering the business of society without outside assistance; and this was an important lesson in public responsibility as well as a means of personal fulfilment.[1] The individual, through his experience in local affairs, was made aware of his place in the public *cosmos*: his sphere of reference and his knowledge were enlarged, and his selfish materialist interests tended to be balanced by public-spirited ones.[2] The active faculties of groups and associations in the community were fostered in the same way. In short, demagoguery was avoided by a training in communal obligation. Thus, as Mill said, democratic institutions were Tocqueville's remedy for the worst mischiefs to which democracies

[1] As Monckton Milnes wrote of Tocqueville in 1861: '. . . he considered the art of government to consist in enabling society to understand itself, to submit to its own obligations, to regulate its own affairs and to work out its own destiny . . . he was ambitious to assist, eager to co-operate, and ready at any personal sacrifice to encourage others to produce the greatest possible good to themselves.' QR, Vol. 110, Oct. 1861, p. 524.

[2] Give the citizen a public duty, 'whether as vestryman, a juryman, or an elector; and in that degree, his ideas, and feelings are taken out of their narrow circle . . . he is made to feel that besides the interests which separate him from his fellow-citizens, he has interests which connect him with them; that not only the common weal is his weal, but that it partly depends upon his exertions.' This is Mill paraphrasing Tocqueville in the *ER*, Oct. 1840, reprinted in *Dissertations and Discussions*, op. cit., p. 15. This article is hereafter referred to as Mill, *ER*, 1840; and the page numbers will refer to *Dissertations and Discussions*.

were exposed. In countries where everything was done *for* the people, and nothing *by* the people, he was certain that the superficial love of freedom would never survive the practical habit of slavery.

Tocqueville had also a Whiggish appreciation of American checks and balances. He warmly approved the federal system, which countered the menace of legislative supremacy at the centre; and he concurred in the separation of powers. He commended a constitution which caused legislation to be referred to a fundamental law, interpreted judicially. Tocqueville saw little likelihood of the judiciary usurping power—the legal profession was, he thought, a very conservative social group—and a bulwark was thus ingeniously set up against both mob-rule and Caesarism.

Tocqueville believed that Christian morality, in a broad rather than a sectarian sense, was indispensable to genuine democracy; and he suggested that the viability of American democracy owed much to the expression of this morality in institutions and social life. Here in the Union, largely because of Puritanism and the Pilgrim tradition, there was no European divorce between liberalism and religion. He advised European liberals to espouse a less secular creed, to recruit support from popular religion.

3. *Interpretations*

Tocqueville was quite clear upon his standpoint in the great political debate of his age. As he declared to Stoffels (who had imagined the tendency of his theories to be radical, almost revolutionary):

I have sought to show what a democratic people is in our days, and by this delineation, executed with rigourous accuracy, my design has been to produce a two-fold effect upon my contemporaries. To those who make to themselves an ideal democracy, a brilliant vision which they think it easy to realise, I undertake to show that they have arrayed their picture in false colours; that the democratic government they advocate, if it be of real advantage to those who can support it, has not the lofty features they ascribe to it; and, moreover that this government can only be maintained on certain conditions of intelligence, private morality, and religious faith, which we do not possess; and that its political results are not to be obtained without labour. To those for whom the word 'democracy' is synonomous with disturbance, anarchy, spoliation and murder, I have attempted to show that the government of democracy may be reconciled with respect for property, with deference for rights, with safety to freedom, with reverence to religion; that if democractic government is less favourable than another to some of the finer parts of human nature, it has also great and noble elements; and that perhaps after all it is the will of God to shed a lesser grade of happiness on the totality of mankind, not to combine a greater share of it on a smaller number, or to raise the few to the verge of perfection.[1]

Yet, as Tocqueville regretted, there were few who understood this position, and many who greeted his work favourably because they found in it arguments suitable to their 'passion of the moment'. Writing to Henry Reeve in 1837 of the various complexions thrust upon the *Democracy*, he quipped:

It makes a collection of portraits which I like having. Up to now, however, I have received none which resembles my real self. They insist on making me a party man, and I am not. They give me passions, when I have only opinions, or rather the only passions I have are love of liberty and human dignity. . . . They endow me alternatively with aristocratic and democratic prejudices.[2]

Reeve in 1861 testified to the contradictory receptions accorded the *Democracy* in opposing political camps:

It was hailed with equal satisfaction by the ardent friends of democracy and by those who dread the exclusive predominance of democractic power. The former were gratified by M. de Tocqueville's admission of the predominance of this great element in modern societies, and by his prediction of its future dominion over the world. The latter were no less struck by the acuteness with which he pointed out its tendency to favour absolute government, and to degrade the noblest faculties of man. His doctrine of the universal extension of social equality was applauded by Mr. Mill and Mr. Grote; his doctrine of the tyranny of democractic majorities was quoted with extraordinary effect by Sir Robert Peel, when he was laying the foundations of the great party of conservative resistance, after the popular movement of 1832.[3]

For some therefore Tocqueville's very impartiality lent itself to selection for party ends. They often praised his magisterial disinterest; for example the *Quarterly Review* noted in 1861 that 'the effect of this permanent study, discreetly used and sanely regulated, stood out in strange contrast to the diffuse fancies and distracted notions of the political sciolists of our age';[4] but the profundity of Tocqueville's vision only served to render more subtle its assimilation to political ends.

(i) *John Stuart Mill and America as a Middle-Class Democracy*

John Stuart Mill came to be regarded in the decades following the Great Reform as one of England's great seminal minds. He was at the

[1] Letter to Stoffels, quoted by Reeve in *ER*, Vol. 113, Apr. 1861, pp. 430–1.
[2] Tocqueville to Reeve, 22.3.1837; first published in A. H. Johnson, 'Correspondence of Tocqueville and Reeve', *ER*, Oct. 1923, p. 288.
[3] *ER*, Vol. 113, Apr. 1861, p. 430.
[4] Vol. 110, Oct. 1861, p. 519, by Monckton Milnes.

same time the foremost interpreter of Tocqueville in Britain, and his authority gave a great impetus to Tocqueville's reputation. Mill clarified the ideas of the *Democracy* for the benefit of English minds and stated their implications for English politics. What scholars have perhaps underestimated is that Mill subtly amended Tocqueville's analysis, and the effect was to render his work more acceptable to the English middle class.

Mill read the *Democracy* during a critical stage in the evolution of his own political thought, and the book hastened him on the way to the ideas set out in his *Representative Government*.[1] Between 1829 and 1835 Mill had begun to question orthodox Benthamite Radicalism. In 1832 he attacked the Radical theory that representatives ought to be pledged to their constituents. He began to explore the means by which the ablest few should govern *for* the many in a democracy, and to move away from his father's preoccupation with the need for checks upon the power of any set of rulers. Mill agreed with Burke that the will of the people must, in the end, be supreme; but he thought that the test of what is right in politics should be the *good* of the people, not the *will* of the people.[2] Like Tocqueville, Mill was concerned with a central problem of democracy, how to impose restraints upon popular rule in the general interest, a problem which Bentham and his disciples avoided. Mill was also aware of another problem that Tocqueville was to examine closely, that of the flattery of majorities by 'every factious minority, every separate class, every adventurer' with an interest to fulfil. Only intelligent leaders, Mill felt, could combat 'the formidable array of human weaknesses and passions which would be at work to make a Representative Democracy (what it has so often been asserted to be its own essence) a mere mob-government'.[3]

In 1835, when Mill first read Tocqueville, he had just launched the *London Review* as a vehicle for his New Radicalism. As has frequently been pointed out, this was for him a time of intellectual eclecticism. He had read and been influenced by the St. Simonians, by Robert Owen and the early English Socialists, and by Coleridge. He found immediate stimulation in Tocqueville's analysis of transatlantic democracy, sympathizing with the Frenchman's liberalism and responding to his sociology:

M. de Tocqueville's is, in our eyes, the true view of the position in which mankind now stand: and on the timely recognition of it as such, by the influential classes of

---

[1] Mill, *Autobiography* (repr. London, 1924), p. 161.
[2] See *Examiner*, 1.7.1832, pp. 417–18; and 15.7.1832, pp. 449–50.
[3] Ibid. 15.7.1832, p. 450.

our own and other countries, we believe the most important interests of our race to be greatly dependent.[1]

Mill came to regard himself as something of a disciple of Tocqueville: '. . . if there was any one of the leading intellects of this age to which I could flatter myself that my own had a kind of analogy it was probably yours', he wrote to him in 1840.[2] Mill read Part II in 1840, and informed its author that

You have changed the face of political philosophy; you have carried on the discussions respecting the tendencies of modern society, the causes of those tendencies, and the influences of particular forms of polity and social order, into a region both of height and of depth, which no one before you had entered, and all previous argumentation and speculation in such matters appears but child's play now. I do not think that anything more important than the publication of your book has happened even in this age of great events.

Mill accepted most of Tocqueville's theses. He agreed that history was leading inevitably towards greater democracy and gave evidence to show that England was involved in the process. He thought that Tocqueville's attempt to guide democracy to desirable goals was a valid one, and he was impressed by such American safeguards as administrative decentralization and a tradition of communal self-government. Although Mill was not, in the thirties, as pessimistic as Tocqueville concerning the frailties of democracy, he extended a guarded approval to such propositions as 'tyranny of the majority', the want of merit in public men, and democratic tendencies to cultural mediocrity. On these subjects, however, Mill constantly found himself wallowing in Tocqueville's intellectual wake. Part II, which disappointed some people, made a profound impression upon Mill; and he lamented to the author that 'although my own thoughts have been accustomed (especially since I read your First Part) to run very much in the same direction, you have so far outrun me that I am lost in the distance . . .'[3] At least until the publication of his Logic,

---

[1] *London Review*, 1835, p. 91.

[2] Mill to Tocqueville, 30.12.1840; in Tocqueville, *Oeuvres Complètes: édition définitive*, ed. J. P. Mayer (Paris, 1954), Vol. VI, *Correspondance Anglaise* (hereafter referred to as *Oeuvres*, ed. Mayer). Mayer's introduction to Vol. VI gives a useful summary of the early relationship between Mill and Tocqueville. There is a virtual translation given in Mayer, 'Tocqueville and Mill', *Listener*, Mar. 1950.

[3] Mill to Tocqueville, 11.5.1840, *Oeuvres*, ed. Mayer. (The letters are listed chronologically.) Tocqueville, in his turn, was gratified by the care and penetration of Mill's review of Part II in the *Edinburgh*; he even spoke to Mill of binding the article with his own copy of the *Démocratie*. See Tocqueville to Mill, 18.12.1840, ibid. (The preceding extract is from Mill to Tocqueville, 11.5.1840.)

Mill retained this sense of Tocqueville's elder status in the field of their mutual concern.

Despite this respect, Mill was never the acquiescent disciple. He freely interpreted Tocqueville's ideas to fit the English situation, and in doing so he drew a picture of the United States as an essentially *bourgeois* republic. Mill and Tocqueville had taken a radical step in asserting the triumph of the democratic over the aristocratic principle; but Mill at least made the idea less dangerous by making it attractive to the English middle class.

He did so in a number of ways. He proposed that the process of democracy in America was equivalent to the English process of commercialization. Mill alleged that Tocqueville had bound up in one abstract idea—Democracy—the whole of the tendencies of modern commercial society. The tendency to equality of social condition was in this view simply a tendency of the commercial civilization:

When a nation is advancing in prosperity—when its industry is expanding and its capital rapidly augmenting—the number also of those who possess capital increases in at least as great a proportion; and though the distance between the two extremes of society may not be much diminished, there is a rapid multiplication of those who occupy the intermediate positions. There may be princes at one end of the scale and paupers at the other; but between them there will be a respectable and well-paid class of artisans and a middle class who combine property and industry. This may be called, and is, a tendency to equalisation.[1]

Democratic societies were therefore societies in which the preponderant social condition approximated to that of the middle class. In this view, the United States was a typical democracy, wherein all were equal because all were middle-class. Thus Mill could conclude that

. . . to most purposes in the constitution of modern society, the government of a numerous middle class is democracy. Nay, it not merely *is* democracy, but the only democracy of which there is yet any example; what is called universal suffrage in America arising from the fact that America is *all* middle class; the whole people being in a condition, both as to education and pecuniary means, corresponding to the middle class here.[2]

Mill suggested perceptively that many of the so-called egalitarian traints which Tocqueville discovered in America were in fact universal commercial characteristics; they were to be found in England as well as in the United States. As an example he cited the brooding spirit of restlessness abroad in both nations, a spirit of aspiration and acquisitiveness, 'that treading upon the heels of one another, that habitual dissatisfaction of each with the position he occupies and eager desire to push

[1] Mill, *ER*, 1840, p. 63.   [2] Ibid. p. 21.

himself into the next above it'.[1] Mill cited other changes stemming from the same cause: a greater mobility of individual relations, the corruption of the permanent ties of an older type of society, and a resultant shackling of the individual to the mass. But the mass in England, as in America, was pre-eminently the middle class, only now through technological change attaining emancipation from the aristocracy. Its wants were now of crucial economic importance. Its opinions were dominant and constituted a new 'despotism of the majority'—'not the less irksome because most of the tyrants may not be manual labourers'.[2] Its taste determined the nature and value of art and literature; hence, said Mill, there was now a greater amount of mediocre work, and fewer devotees of thought for its own sake. Finally, the supremacy of the middle class had been secured politically at the time of the Reform Bill. Mill thus discerned more than capricious identities between English and American experience. He appealed to all competent observers:

. . . whether in nearly all the moral and intellectual features of American society, as represented by M. de Tocqueville, this country does not stand next to America? whether with the single difference of our remaining respect for aristocracy, the American people, both in their good qualities and in their defects, resemble anything so much as an exaggeration of our own middle class? whether the spirit which is gaining more and more the ascendancy with us, is not in a very great degree American? and whether all the moral elements of an American state of society are not most rapidly growing up?[3]

Mill clearly was not altogether happy about such a situation. He regarded the rule of the middle class in England much as Tocqueville regarded the rule of the many in America—with respect for its salutary influences and suspicion for its frailties. Mill, like Guizot, believed that the dominance of any single element in society was ultimately detrimental to the growth of that society. The advance of commerce and industry—and thus of democracy according to Tocqueville's concept—was coming to be accepted as a 'law of progress', but Mill was sceptical that such an association of ideas would continue to seem plausible. He admitted that the growth of commerce in Europe had been 'one of the greatest instruments not only of civilization in the narrowest, but of

---

[1] Ibid. p. 65. Mill thought that the existence of a nobility encouraged such ambitions by the rewards which it offered to wealth: '. . . it perhaps required the example of America to prove that the "sabbathless pursuit of wealth" could be as intensely prevalent, where there were no aristocratic distinctions to tempt to it.' (p. 56.)

[2] Ibid. p. 76. Even the aristocracy, Mill claimed, was succumbing to the yoke of bourgeois opinion: 'No rank in society is now exempt from the fear of being peculiar, the unwillingness to be, or to be thought, in any respect original.' (p. 67.)

[3] Ibid. p. 65.

improvement and culture in the widest sense'. But he predicted that it would remain so only so long as the environment in which it flourished was diverse and many-sided: '. . . so long as other co-ordinate elements of improvement existed beside it, doing what it left undone, and keeping its exclusive tendencies in equipoise by an opposite order of sentiments, principles of action, and modes of thought . . . But example and theory alike justify the expectation, that with its complete predominance would commence an era either of stationariness or of decline.' Such homogeneity and stagnation, particularly in the spheres of philosophy, morality, and culture, seemed to Mill the real defect of American democracy. As he wrote in his article 'The State of Society in America', the faults of the Americans were the faults of the middle class everywhere:

. . . a general indifference to those kinds of knowledge and mental culture which cannot be immediately converted into pounds, shillings, and pence; very little perception or enjoyment of the beautiful, either in nature or in the productions of genius, along with great occasional affectation of it; the predominant passion that of money—the passion of those who have no other; indifference to refinements and elegancies for their own sake, but a vehement desire to possess what are accounted such by others.[1]

Mill's solution to the problem was not unlike that suggested by Tories such as Robinson. Mill declared that deviant ideological forces should be encouraged as a counterbalance to the sole sway of the commercial spirit: '. . . in order to the formation of the best public opinion, there should exist somewhere a great social support for opinions and sentiments different from those of the mass'. He thought that, in England, such support might come from an agricultural, a leisured, and a learned class.[2] England's possession of such classes, he believed, was the greatest natural advantage she enjoyed over America, 'and we believe that the interests of the time are greatly dependent upon preserving them'.[3] Indeed Mill contended against the 'propitious circumstances' doctrine on these grounds. America, he said, was 'in many important points, nearly the

---

[1] *London Review*, Vol. 2, Jan. 1836, p. 375. Both Mill and Tocqueville were agreed on what was then an unusual point, 'that the real danger in democracy . . . is not anarchy or love of change, but Chinese stagnation and immobility'. See Mill to Tocqueville, 11.5.1840, *Oeuvres*, ed. Mayer.

[2] Mill said that the agricultural class accepted authority and kept local attachments, unlike the manufacturing classes. But he did not regard the American agriculturalists as a counterpoise to the business class, because they shifted constantly and were 'to all intents and purposes a commercial class'. (This, true up to a point, surely neglects some aspects of the sectional clash between the rural Mid-West and the commercial oligarchy of the East.)

[3] *ER*, 1840, p. 76.

most unfavourable field in which democracy could have been tried'.[1] Her frontier conditions obstructed the advance of civilization; her provincial circumstances encouraged mediocrity in intellectual life; while 'everything in the position of America tends to foster the spirit of trade, the passion of money-getting, and that almost alone'. Democracy would have a fairer trial there, he predicted, when education and prosperity should create a leisured class and a more diverse culture, in the English tradition.

The English middle class was much less likely to concern itself with these misgivings, which in some sense were as old as Christianity, than to reassure itself that democracy could be interpreted as the natural rule of the propertied classes. The United States was already admired for its open society and its economic structure. American politics—which had hitherto been suspect in the eyes of those who did not accept Radicalism— acquired a new gloss of respectability from Mill's analysis. His doubts and qualifications served to channel speculation into what was becoming a familiar, and therefore manageable, debate—the merits or otherwise of the steam age. The Radicals were disconcerted to find that Republican democracy had been filched from their political armoury, and to find the formidable authority of Mill and Tocqueville ranged behind the backs of their bourgeois opponents. Instead of Tocqueville's radical-sounding 'equality of condition', there was now Mill's 'homogeneity of rule by the middle-class'. Working-men had imagined the Republic to be peopled by Radicals. Mill informed them that 'America is a republic

---

[1] *London Review*, Vol. 2, Jan. 1836, p. 380. The article contains a very interesting discussion of democratic causation. For example: 'America has been discussed, as if she were nothing but a democracy: a society, differing from other human societies in no essential point, except the popular character of her institutions. The friends or enemies of parliamentary reform have been more or less in the habit of ascribing to democracy whatever of good or evil they have found or dreamed of in the U.S. . . . But the Government is only one of a dozen causes which have made America what she is. The Americans are a democratic people: granted; but they are also a people without poor; without rich; with a "far west" behind them; so situated as to be in no danger of aggressions from without; sprung mostly from the Puritans. . . . with boundless facilities to all classes for "raising themselves in the world".' (p. 371.) He ascribes their prosperity to rapid accumulation of capital beyond the increase of population; and their education to an English middle-class tradition. But high wages and universal reading are pre-conditions for democracy: '. . . where they co-exist, all government, except the government of public opinion, is impossible.' Mill concludes that much of what is good and bad in America is the result of non-democratic causes; its system must be studied with much more discrimination to separate essentials from non-essentials. Mill wrote this article after reading Part I of Tocqueville, but he is noticeably more optimistic about the benevolent influence of democracy than the Frenchman; he is still affected by the Benthamite tradition.

peopled with a provincial middle class'.[1] Nor did the preoccupation of both Mill and Tocqueville with the need to restrain pure democracy meet with Radical favour. Both stressed the importance of popular participation in public affairs, but until the 1840's Mill was satisfied with the £10 householder franchise for England. He saw little likelihood of universal suffrage being a success, for the majority would be degraded *proletaires*, labouring in abject poverty and swilling away their earnings in gin. Such people, until they were made wiser and better, might safely be excluded from sovereignty, although society might not escape their Swing outrages and Wat Tyler insurrections.[2] The franchise, he thought, could be given to skilled artisans and the upper ranks of the working class—such people, in Mill's view, were aspiring to middle-class status. Only as the working class did so aspire to better conditions, and higher education, should its opinions 'tell, according to its numbers, upon the affairs of the country'. Mill's overriding idea about government in England was that it was progressing from the rule of the few to the rule, not of *the* many, but of many—'from an aristocracy with a popular infusion, to the régime of the middle class'.[3]

Mill's theory of representation logically followed. Tocqueville actively encouraged Mill to explore further the dangers of *delegation*, which he had begun to appreciate in the early thirties. Tocqueville wrote to Mill in 1835, commending the distinction which the latter had drawn between 'delegation' and 'representation':

Rest assured, my dear Mill, that on this occasion you have mooted a most important question. . . . it is much less essential for the partisans of democracy to find means of governing the nation, than to teach the nation to choose the men most capable of governing; and to exercise sufficient influence over the general nature of their government without interfering with their individual acts, or means of execution. This is the problem. I am quite convinced that the fate of the modern world depends on its solution.[4]

Mill was already arguing that the people should not themselves govern,

[1] Ibid. p. 374. 'Subtract from the British empire London and Edinburgh . . . leave . . . the merchants of Liverpool, the manufacturers of Manchester, the bar of London spread over the whole of England, and the physicians, attorneys and dissenting clergy; then raise the working classes to the enjoyment of ample wages—give them universally the habit of reading, and an active interest in public affairs; and you will have a society constituted almost identically with that of the United States. . . .' (p. 374.)

[2] See Mill's article on 'Civilization' in L & WR, Apr. 1836, reprinted in *Dissertations and Discussions*, in Mill, *Works*, IV (New Universal Library, London, undated), pp. 139–40. Mill argued that, if the people were prepared for power, aid ought to be given to the democratic movement; if they were unprepared, their ultimate supremacy must be recognized, and the utmost done to prepare them.

[3] ER, 1840, p. 21.

[4] Tocqueville to Mill, 5.12.1835, *Oeuvres*, ed. Mayer.

but should ensure security for good government by retaining ultimate control and sanctions.[1] The best government, he said, was self-evidently government by the wisest, and therefore by the few. The people's interest lay in choosing the ablest rulers, and allowing them to exercise their ability for the good of the people, with the minimum restraint. This was the solution to the 'tyranny of the majority'. Mill saw that, as a solution, it depended upon the good sense of the people; but he was still Benthamite enough to hope that the people would reject any alternative arrangement as a mistake of interest.[2] Mill's theory of 'enlightened' democracy, of an almost Platonic rule by the best men, was reassuring to the middle class; for they did not doubt that such an *élite* would be provided from their own ranks.

In his writings upon the United States, Mill emphasized the bourgeois respect with which property was there held. Following Tocqueville, he specifically denied that 'tyranny of the majority' meant economic tyranny. Where 'equality' implied practical equality of economic opportunity, the many were unlikely to oppress the few economically:

That the security of person and property are the first social interests not only of the rich but of the poor, is obvious to common sense. And the degree of education which a well-constituted democracy ensures to all its citizens renders common sense the general characteristic. Truths which are obvious, it may always be expected that the American democracy will see.[3]

Only where the poor were so poor as to have no reasonable expectation of improvement, claimed Mill, were property rights endangered. Democracy might be dangerous, then, in the crowded and poor countries of Europe, but never in a prosperous middle-class community. Mill's tone might be more like that of George Grote than of Mackintosh upon this subject, but his conclusions were more Whig than Radical.[4]

[1] Both men believed that a governing class not accountable to the people must serve separate interests. The people must thus retain final sactions; 'but this is the only purpose for which it is good to entrust power to the people'. Mill, *London Review*, 1835, p. 110.

[2] Tocqueville was more pessimistic. He was not sure that the people would see that their interest lay in representation rather than pledges. His sociologist's analysis of America made him more aware of the situational factors which encouraged 'tyranny of the majority'. Mill's analysis was basically ideological; he was still affected by the Radical's incurable optimism about mankind.

[3] *London Review*, 1835, p. 118. See also on this topic, Mill, *ER*, 1840, pp. 36–37. These ideas preceded his much later conclusion that Socialism was equality 'logically carried out'.

[4] However, Mill thought that, even where the poor had power and were led by their grievances to make laws of economic redress, the danger was not so much of spoliation of property as of 'undue interference' with contracts, and of laws founded on mistakes of political economy (for example, a minimum wage or a tax on machinery). *ER*, 1840, p. 37.

Both Mill and Tocqueville employed empirical and utilitarian standards in their appraisal of the new world, and this appealed to the middle class. So did much, although not all, of Tocqueville's political philosophy. His view of America was constructive and non-partisan. His idea of a 'well-regulated' democracy was not revolutionary or visionary except in teleogical terms: it was essentially an idea of *cosmos*, of integration in society; he was sensitive about the need for order, interdependence, and obligation, as well as about the need for change and variety. On the whole, these qualities in Tocqueville were satisfying and comforting to the English middle class; even though his ideas were closer in various ways to the thought and feeling of Burke than to the atomistic individualism of some liberals.

I do not want to suggest that Mill's influence was unequivocally calming and conservative. There were tensions and ambivalences in his thought about democracy at this stage in his life which he did not always recognize, and which were susceptible of various interpretations. For instance, he styled himself as far more the left-wing democrat than Tocqueville,[1] yet his concept of democracy was essentially a middle-of-the-way, middle-class one. His extremism, as compared with Tocqueville and the English upper class, consisted in a more vehement rejection of aristocracy. Mill dissented from Tocqueville's adulation of the aristocratic virtues of government, and acidly questioned the nobility's supposed qualities of prudence and skill:

The only steadiness which aristocracy *never* fails to manifest, is tenacity in clinging to its own privileges. . . . In all other matters, the opinions of a ruling class is as fluctuating, as liable to be wholly given up to immediate impulses, as the opinions of the people. Witness the whole course of English history. All our laws have been made upon temporary impulses. In what country has the course of legislation been less directed to any steady and consistent purpose?—except, indeed, that of perpetually adding to the power and privileges of the rich. . . . And as for the talents and virtues of those whom aristocracy chooses for its leaders, read Horace Walpole or Bubb Doddington, that you may know what to think of them.[2]

Anti-aristocratic sentiment was of course by no means anathema to the middle class, but Mill frequently said things which gave little comfort to the interests of industry and business. Democracy, he said, would inevitably become middle-class. But he also asserted that the middle

[1] See Mill's second letter to Tocqueville in 1835, *Oeuvres*, ed. Mayer, p. 299.
[2] *London Review*, 1835, p. 116. The converse of this position was that Mill was more inclined than Tocqueville to regard the vices of democracy as temporary and not congenital. For example, he suggested that the mediocrity of American politicians was due to such factors as the attractions of business, and the lesser need for administration.

class of the day had a positive responsibility to ameliorate the condition of the working class—to create, in short, a society like the American, where *all* enjoyed middle-class status and all were therefore prepared for power. He insisted that such altruism was justified, if only in terms of self-interest, but this did not gild the pill. There were alarming intimations in Mill's thought that democratic evolution might attain a separate dynamic out of the numerous, but less enlightened, working class. Tocqueville had said, and Mill agreed, that even a dominant middle class could not impede the ultimate triumph of numbers: '. . . is it credible that the democracy which has annihilated the feudal system, and vanquished kings, will respect the *bourgeoisie* and the capitalist? Will it stop now that it has grown so strong and its adversaries so weak?'[1] Mill stressed that Britain had only gone part of the way along the American road to homogeneity of social condition. He praised England's plural society, but he recognized that it could breed class conflict. In 1840—the time of Chartism, of embryonic Socialism, of Owenism, and the cooperative movement—it seemed to Mill that the masses were intruding into older spheres of economic and political activity. The common people had multiplied in number. It was generally acknowledged that knowledge and intelligence were spreading to the lower ranks. Workingclass propaganda was gaining in influence through the popular press; labourers and artisans were forming trade unions for industrial purposes; and their political power was 'increasing and likely to increase'. Mill liked to look upon such developments as part of a general progression to a state of bourgeois welfare and enlightenment; but it was not clear to the commercial classes of 1840 that a violent challenge to the existing order was not also part of its potential. It was not the intention or the general tenor of Mill's political thought to suggest such dismal prognostications; and the American parallel seemed to indicate the possibility of class collaboration. But the spectre of class war remained a permanent qualification to optimism and a stimulus to the institutional safeguarding of democracy.

(ii) Henry Reeve: a Whig View

Henry Reeve, at the time a precocious young man of letters, met Tocqueville in Paris in March 1835. He read the *Démocratie* hot from the Paris press, and was at first alarmed by its arguments. But he soon came to a more favourable opinion, describing the book to his mother as 'perhaps the most important treatise on the Science of States . . . since

---

[1] Quoted by Mill, *ER*, 1840, p. 12.

Montesquieu'.[1] He laboured over his translation during the summer of 1835, and by so doing underwent a valuable discipline in Tocqueville's methods and opinions. As he later wrote: 'My own opinions were no doubt affected by the influence of that pure and subtle intellect; and the highest merit I would venture to claim for them is their conformity with his principles.'[2] As we have seen, Reeve, as an intimate of both the Benthamite and Whig *salons*, and as an important figure behind the political scene in the 1840's and 1850's, had ample opportunity to propagate Tocqueville's ideas in England. He favourably reviewed Parts I and II of the *Democracy* for the *British and Foreign Review* in 1836 and 1840. He maintained a regular correspondence with Tocqueville, keeping abreast of his rapidly evolving thought. Although a busy man, Reeve found time to translate *L'Ancien Régime* when it was written. During the fifties he prepared critiques of Tocqueville's collected works, and he wrote the memorial articles of 1861 and 1865 for the *Edinburgh Review*.

Nevertheless, Reeve's acquiescence in Tocqueville's thought was only partial, and his response was typical of the traditional school of Whiggism. Henry Reeve was an aristocrat by sympathy, if not by descent.[3] He was a cosmopolitan liberal who favoured the cause of liberty in Continental Europe; but he was not a democrat, and he was completely unsympathetic towards plebeian aspirations in Britain itself. Reeve responded warmly to Tocqueville's very personal brand of liberalism, to his regard for the individual human personality; and he was vastly impressed by the brilliant and dispassionate analysis of transatlantic democracy offered in the *Democracy*. But, as Reeve once said, Tocqueville was writing the book of the People for France and the world, just as Machiavelli wrote the book of the Prince for Caesar Borgia. Reeve never overcame a distaste for the fact that such a book needed to be written, for he distrusted the People and their 'darker sophistries and more pressing tyranny'.[4] Like the Tories, he was reluctant to grant that the day of the aristocracy—with its noble culture for the few, its intense cultivation of the highest faculties of man—was over, to be replaced by the era of the mob and the industrial middle class. Reeve agreed that Tocqueville's doctrine of the inevitability of democracy was difficult to deny in America, France,

[1] Letter to his mother, Paris 25.2.1835, in Laughton, op. cit., I. (The letters are arranged chronologically.)
[2] Reeve, *Royal and Republican France* (London, 1872), quoted in Laughton, I. 50.
[3] His grandfather established the family fortune by astute management of his corn mills in Essex. His father was a medical man who was acquainted with the *Edinburgh* circle—Jeffrey, Brougham, Horner, and Smith—and who married into the influential Taylor family of Norwich.
[4] Reeve's preface to *Democracy in America* (London, 1835), p. v. See also Reeve to Tocqueville, 22.2.1840, *Oeuvres*, ed. Mayer.

and most of Europe; but he was hopeful that in England democracy would be modified in interaction with the peculiar national heritage.

These divergent ideas even became part of the translation of the *Democracy*, although scholars have rarely noticed the fact. Tocqueville was aware that he was more of a friend and counsellor of democracy than his youthful translator, and he had cause to admonish Reeve on the point in 1839:

I think that, influenced by your opinions, you have, in your translation, unwittingly coloured too highly all I say against democracy. I pray you, resist this temptation and preserve the impartiality of my book in its theoretical judgment of the two societies, the old and the new, and moreover my sincere desire to see the new establish itself.[1]

This indeed was the core of the matter. Reeve was not willing to pay the historical price to be paid for achieving a well-regulated democracy: the necessity of countering its vices, and the inevitable sacrifice of the aristocratic virtues. Reeve knew only French democracy at first hand, and he recoiled from its 'fierce revolution' and 'spirit of strife'.[2] He was aware of Tocqueville's central argument that French democracy exemplified the weaknesses, American democracy the strengths, of popular government. He admitted that France lacked 'the wholesome restraint of earnest religion, the machinery of local institutions and combined enterprise, the protection of extensive public education or the tradition of self-government' enjoyed by America. Tocqueville preached the necessity of larding the egalitarian society with these liberal elements. But Reeve was both less confident of the validity of American panaceas and more sanguine of guiding aristocracy to meet the new situation in Britain.

Reeve pointed out that Tocqueville's generalizations about America had been deduced from undeniable conditions of social equality. England, he objected, was, unlike France and America, still an inegalitarian society. The habits and manners of the English people were still monarchical rather than republican. Moreover, England had not America's vast

---

[1] Tocqueville to Reeve, undated, 1839, in A. H. Johnson, 'Correspondence of Tocqueville and Henry Reeve', *ER*, Vol. 238, Oct. 1923, pp. 288–9. For Francis Bowen's criticisms of Reeve as a translator, made in Bowen's American translation of the *Democracy* in 1862, see E. Phillips Bradley, ed., *Democracy in America*, by Tocqueville (New York, 1945), Appendix II.

[2] He believed that Englishmen would read in the example of France 'the fate of those who would launch the vessel of state, without due pilotage, on more tumultuous seas: they may trace the gradual infiltration of democracy into the minds of men and into the frame of society, till the former lose their noblest powers and impulses, the latter its security from oppression'. *British and Foreign Review*, Vol. 10, 1840, pp. 544–5. Reeve never visited the U.S., but he was acquainted with literature about the new world, translating, besides Tocqueville, Guizot's *Washington*.

territory in which to try the dangerous experiment of democracy. Thus Reeve was sceptical about the relevance of Tocqueville's analysis to English conditions (an objection which Tocqueville upheld, to a point). Reeve admitted that English society was in flux—one had only to look at the intelligence, energy, industry, and accumulating wealth of the nation, he said, to reject any theory of an immutable, fixed constitution, to repudiate the doctrine of final measures in politics. But Reeve saw no overwhelming evidence that aristocratic principles were permanently irrelevant to the new conditions. The future could lie in an adaptation of these principles to new needs:

For if we be destined to prolong the existence of British institutions, based, certainly, on aristocratic principles, it must not be by a reaction arising from timourous prejudice against democratic innovation, but by a high and enlightened determination to vindicate the true application of those principles, to cast out their abuses, to repress their evil tendencies, and to confer upon them the power, without which all their dignity is adventitious—the power derived from the just fulfillment of the law of duty, directing all things to the public good.[1]

Reeve described himself as a 'constitutional' reformer, determined to distinguish the value of institutions from the delinquencies of individuals who worked them. This he regarded as a far more profitable endeavour than the immediate and uncritical acceptance of American-type democracy; for as he wrote:

If the institution itself be destroyed, it may never be replaced, and upon its ruins must necessarily arise that purely democratic form of government, which— unsuited as it may prove to the present habits and manners of the people, and not adapted, perhaps, under any circumstances, to a redundant population within a confined space—may bring with it anarchy and terrorism, instead of that partial success, which the confirmed manners, and the local advantages of the Americans, have shown to be not inconsistent, for a time, with equality and democracy.[2]

On a higher plane aristocracy was justifiable for its spiritual values— values whose loss, for Reeve, transcended the egalitarian compensations set out by Tocqueville. Reeve, like Carlyle and the Tories, despaired of

[1] *British and Foreign Review*, ibid. p. 545. In a letter to Tocqueville, 7.12.1852. Reeve wrote: '. . . it has been given to the English Aristocracy to march with the times, and even to take the lead.' *Oeuvres*, ed. Mayer.

[2] *British and Foreign Review*, Vol. 2, 1836, p. 327. He agreed with Tocqueville that democracy had to be studied, but to be met 'before the unhallowed rites of destruction have begun . . . before the vertigo of conquest has seized the lower orders, or the palsy of dejection fallen upon the aristocracy'. (Preface to the *Democracy*.) Reeve went to the other extreme from Mill in defending the aristocracy against Tocqueville's criticisms (e.g., that the nobility lacked sympathy with those outside the pale of their caste—this was an exaggeration, said Reeve).

finding high spirituality in the industrial middle class. He was, for a Whig, surprisingly acrimonious and outspoken in his dislike of this group:

That bastard aristocracy which M. de Tocqueville predicts may arise from the manufacturing powers of our age, has all the harshness of contrast, with none of its humane corrections—all the hideous consequences of the property of man in man, without even the interested sympathy of the slave-owner in the negro. Such an aristocracy would indeed be the worst of all changes, even from the worst democracy. . . .[1]

There was a tension in Reeve's thought whenever he tried to weigh the merits of aristocracy versus democracy in Tocqueville's terms. He felt bound to admit the force of the humanitarian and liberal arguments which Tocqueville used to defend the existence of greater social equality in society:

Yet we pause before we adopt so sweeping and disastrous a conclusion, confident that on however broad a scale this system may be applied to the moral, intellectual and political conditions of life, there will ever remain above the law of society minds and qualities which are a law unto themselves—the indomitable energy of virtue, the aspiring flight of genius, or if even these fail, the desperate activity of passion: in these things men are not equal.[2]

The attempt to clamp society in an egalitarian straightjacket led directly to the culture of materialism and mediocrity, and such a culture was ultimately degrading of mankind's highest aspirations, even in America:

The paltry indulgences of animal life, the mere pursuit of self-interest . . . cannot satisfy minds which are not devoid of cravings for the highest intellectual enjoyment. . . . Man can only improve by humility, by the love of superiority, and by respect for what is higher than himself: but these qualities are the reverse of the democratic virtues of reliance on self, emulation pushed to jealousy, and disdain of authority.[3]

Reeve therefore believed that 'the great principles of science and abstruse truth' would languish in America. He was pessimistic about the efficacy of Tocqueville's counterweights to democratic vices.[4] His inclination was

---

[1] *British and Foreign Review*, Vol. 10, 1840, p. 571.
[2] Ibid. p. 550.   [3] Ibid. p. 571.
[4] For instance, Reeve questioned whether the growth of 'associations' in America was a protection for a free society. Associations, he said, lacked individual responsibility; they were led by interest rather than by principle or regard for the general good; and they were uncontrolled in a democratic system. In 1856 Reeve wrote to Tocqueville thus: 'Twenty years ago, when you were writing your apology for American Democracy I was not always of your opinion; I had less faith than you in those institutions; and today I have still less. . . .' Reeve to Tocqueville, 1.5.1856, *Oeuvres*, ed. Mayer.

to reject the Frenchman's quasi-determinism[1] and to reassert an older patriarchal solution of 'the difficulty of God's various allotments to men'.

(iii) Tory Impressions

Tocqueville's book was reviewed widely, and in most cases favourably, in the Tory periodicals. Outside speculative circles it was pressed quite openly into the service of the Tory party. Peel, as John Mill remarked, 'praised it, and made the Tories fancy it was a Tory book' ('but I believe', he added in 1840, 'that they have found out their error'.[2]) In 1835 Peel quoted extensively from Tocqueville's Democracy during the Commons debate upon bribery at elections.[3] Two years later, in his inaugural address as Lord Rector of the University of Glasgow, Peel presented his audience with heavily biased selections from the Democracy in order to give a panegyric upon the political status quo in Britain.[4] At Cambridge University, where Professor William Smyth delivered lectures upon America, Tocqueville's study was projected in such a conservative fashion that protests arrived from the United States. The American historian Jared Sparks, a friend and correspondent of Tocqueville and a later President of Harvard College, remonstrated with Smyth: 'I think too much confidence is placed in M. de Tocqueville's ideas of the "tyranny of the majority" . . . in practice we perceive no such consequences as he supposes.'[5]

[1] Tocqueville often wrote upon the dangers of historical doctrines of necessity, and Reeve used the master's warnings to criticize the so-called inevitability of democracy. Reeve was more confident that the individual could master his destiny; he hated the idea that the only space left to the free will of man was to make the best of a democratic lot. As the years passed Tocqueville's determinism, although providential, became stricter and gloomier. He wrote in the 1850's: 'What I called "the bottom I cannot touch" is the wherefore of the world; the plan of creation of which we know nothing, not even in our bodies, still less in our minds—the reason of the destiny of this singular being whom we call Man, with just intelligence enough to perceive the miseries of his condition, but not enough to change it. . . .' Quoted by Reeve from the Oeuvres Complètes, etc. (Paris, 1864), in ER, Vol. 122, Oct. 1865, pp. 458, 476.

[2] Mill to Tocqueville, 11.5.1840, Oeuvres, ed. Mayer, p. 328. Tait's Edinburgh Magazine, a liberal journal, wrote in similar vein: 'Sir Robert, finding some of the harsher lineaments of democracy portrayed in lines equally harsh by M. de Tocqueville, speaks patronisingly of that author: but Sir Robert, no more than Pilate, cares for an exposition of "what is truth"; we shall hear no more eulogies of M. de Tocqueville from such a suspicious quarter, now that he has professed himself a democrat, anxious to turn democracy to the best account.' Vol. 3, 1840, p. 507.

[3] See Tocqueville, Oeuvres Complètes, etc., ed. Beaumont (Paris, 1864), I. 36.

[4] See A Correct Account of Sir Robert Peel's Speeches at Glasgow January 1837 (London, 1837).

[5] Sparks to Smyth, 13.10.1841; published in H. B. Adams, 'Jared Sparks and Alexis de Tocqueville', John Hopkins University Studies, XVI. No. 12, 44. For eight

Tocqueville, despite Peel and Cambridge University, presented a challenge to the conservative style of thought. There was in his thinking much that was congenial to the Tory mind—his sympathy with the advantages of a patriarchal corporate society; his feeling for law, tradition, and order; the sense of reverence in his liberalism; his distaste for democratic vices and his distrust of utopianism.[1] Nevertheless, the central tenet of his theory was a rejection of the present utility and relevance of aristocracy. Tocqueville was aware of his standpoint between 'the plaintive murmurs of the dying past and the undistinguishable tumult of the advancing time'; but his utilitarian concern was with the future, and was thus in the final analysis profoundly repugnant to the aristocrats.

The Tory reaction to his influence was thus understandably ambivalent and ranged from harmless reiteration by people like Basil Hall to outright rejection of basic premises by *Blackwood's*. Hall's readable account of Part I, which appeared in the *Quarterly Review* in 1836, was unexceptionable in its fidelity to the original.[2] He acquiesced in Tocqueville's praise of the inbuilt checks of the American system, and came to believe only less vehemently than Mill that Tocqueville's was the true account of American society:

He has not only shown us the country, but explained to us the reasons why it exists in the present state; and for the first time, so far as we are aware of, not only the true situation of that extraordinary people, but the true causes of their social and political situation, are clearly developed.[3]

Hall was less certain than Tocqueville of the irresistibility of democracy in Europe, but he had no qualms about having the Frenchman's ideas on the subject broadcast in Britain. He recommended the production of a cheaper edition, 'in order that the interesting information and practical

---

(Continued from p. 191)

letters from Tocqueville to Sparks and Charles Sumner, see R. L. Hawkins, 'Unpublished Letters of Tocqueville', *Romanic Review*, XIX (1929), 195ff. Sparks in 1833 welcomed the *Démocratie*, and compared it favourably with the English press, 'teeming with . . . misrepresentation and spleen on America'.

[1] 'Whatever might be his views on that unpractical speculation, the ultimate destiny of the human race, he regarded with open contempt all "phalansterism"and similar projects for the immediate or rapid perfectibility of mankind.' *QR*, Vol. 110, Oct. 1861, p. 525 (by Richard Monckton Milnes).

[2] It is somewhat surprising that Hall, an aristocrat, whose book of American travels (1829) excited the utmost indignation in the U.S., should have been so temperate. He acknowledged, however, that the *Democracy* had weeded out many of his long-cherished fallacies, and 'substituted solid reasons for believing that to be right which we had believed to be wrong and vice versa'. *QR*, Vol. 57, Sept. 1836, p. 133.

[3] Ibid. p. 135.

wisdom with which it abounds may be placed within the reach of those classes where prejudice and error take the firmest stand'. Hall, like Peel, was satisfied with the non-revolutionary character of Tocqueville's work; he did not perceive any necessity for qualification.

The reaction of *Blackwood's* to the *Democracy* was politically significant. Part I was reviewed in 1835 by a Mr. O'Donnel, who was a regular contributor but about whom little is known. O'Donnel opened with an ingenious attack that cut at the very roots of Tocqueville's method. He denied the validity of Tocqueville's attempt to universalize the conclusions he had reached upon the new world. This was a resurrection of the argument used by Alison when discussing Thomas Hamilton's book in 1833. Generalizations, according to Alison and O'Donnel, ought not to be made from one set of peculiar national conditions to fit another. The commonest fallacy into which spectators of the American scene fell, said O'Donnel, was to assume that American society constituted a tangible product of theory; that it exemplified a general principle rather than a uniqueness of condition: 'Reasoners, considering state organizations as wholes, and finding theories in them, by a common mistake regard them as resulting therefrom.'[1] Yet there was no necessary reference from existing structure to predetermining plan, and in fact governments should be analysed 'not in their finished states, and as a result of *plans*, but in their beginnings and growing details, and as the result of *peculiarities*'. In such an analysis, 'the gross deceptions which sprang from invidious comparisons between state and state would fall to the ground, and each would see that in its peculiar self resided its *peculiar* sources of amelioration and well-being'. Comparison was legitimate only when there was complete parity between the countries being compared. This condition was never fulfilled; hence 'a *just* comparison between nation and nation, with a view to proposing one, in any singular particular, as a model for the other may be pronounced impossible'. Nations could be understood only by the historical view; the scientific study of states to create a Science of Society was chimerical.

O'Donnel went on logically to deplore any reform that was not an entirely indigenous reform: '. . . the habit which nations have of looking *out of themselves* for reforms, has occasioned more disorder and misgovernment . . . than all other causes put together.'[2] This was an

---

[1] *Blackwood's*, Vol. 37, May 1835, pp. 758ff, for this and following quotations.

[2] Ibid. p. 759. The subject of reform, he added, should be separated 'from all the foreign associations, prejudices and perversions with which it is oftentimes mixed'. It is interesting to note how the debate which now revolves around such subjects as 'Comparative Politics' was anticipated in some ways in the political speculation of the 1830's.

attempt to lessen by one the species of weapon in the Radical arsenal; although the Tories themselves refused to abide by the logic of their argument when they enthusiastically drew anti-democratic lessons from the American experience.

The Tories had no objections to many of Tocqueville's conclusions respecting America. *Blackwood's* warmly approved his respect for the 'scriptural piety' of the Americans, past and present, and agreed that it was a key to republican stability, though for Tocqueville's Christian Deism O'Donnel preferred to substitute the Protestant religion, alone in history 'the mother of civil liberty'. The party of the landed gentry applauded Tocqueville's recommendation of decentralization and the virtues of local government. But they were careful to point out that the spirit of civic responsibility which Tocqueville found in New England had grown slowly throughout American history; it sprang from ancient Anglo-Saxon tradition, and had *not* been created by legislative enactment.[1] This was a thrust at the Municipal Reform Act of 1835; but it readily became an argument for precluding any directive reconstruction of society in favour of natural and organic social evolution.

Freedom [wrote O'Donnel] naturally grows out of the *infancy* of states; not from speculative wisdom, but from the simple wants of man; and . . . history will teach us to add, that when the natural action of these wants have been frustrated, or that men rebel in wantonness, so that speculative wisdom or theories come to usurp their place, the result aimed at is never attained. There is then a disproportion between men and their aims.[2]

Legislation could only formalize changes which had slowly evolved through time—'it is vain to attempt to force them'.

O'Donnel had his own theory of 'propitious circumstances'. Universal suffrage, he argued, was neither inappropriate nor hurtful in the virtual universality of condition that prevailed in the United States. The whole population was 'one industrial class', that of manual labour: '*Hands* have been alone wanted, and therefore *hands* alone counted.' Numbers were the great desideratum in such a situation, and numbers alone deserved to be represented. Under conditions of minimal government, suited to a pioneering society, tensions were avoided—'men in large spaces jostle

---

[1] It was typical of the Tory view that local institutions were pictured as virtually the only centres of order in the Union: '. . . beyond the township all is agitation, confusion, violence, and constant change; society seems to be brought to the brink of dissolution; but in the very height of each crisis every man falls back upon his city, town, or hamlet, and there recognizes an authority of which he individually forms a constituent part, and is an administrator, and he obeys, and the danger passes off as if by magic.' Ibid. p. 760.

[2] Ibid. pp. 760-1.

not against each other, especially when their work is a common one, their interest a common one . . .' O'Donnel, however, foresaw insurmountable difficulties for democracy once emancipation took place from frontier conditions:

When the great work of *hands* shall be completed, *hands* will lose their predominating value; when the all-absorbing necessity of MANUAL *industry* shall be abated, and it continues no longer to resolve all classes of society into *one*, many distinctions, as yet hardly known and all connected with or arising from *intellectual superiority*, will emerge. The question then will be, shall all these yield the political arena completely to a numerical majority . . . ?[1]

Whereas Mill could envisage increasing (bourgeois) homogeneity in America's future, unless there were safeguards, O'Donnel predicted that transatlantic society would become more complex and more heterogeneous. The one saw democracy as the natural government for the future, the other thought such a government would become increasingly inadequate. O'Donnel pointed out the pernicious effect of majority rule even in the favourable environment of the West. Had Tocqueville not shown that intelligence was sacrificed to ignorance in the nation's assemblies? Did he not demonstrate the oppression of an egalitarian society over will and opinion? Was not in America 'the minority struck with a fiat of moral annihilation?', and did it not lay down 'as an axiom, which lies at the heart of all pure democracy, that there can be no superiority, either intellectual or moral, that is not given or expressed by a major number . . . ?' It was unthinkable that such stultifying values would be tolerated in the complex and variegated, higher-order civilization of the future. If America was to transcend her mechanistic materialism, democracy could not last:

If her mind is to rise from the earth and have *its* wants, its labours, its delights, and to bring all the results of its researches to adorn, dignify and liberalise the otherwise grubbing pursuit of society; if she is to consider man not a mere work-day labourer, but an inquisitive intelligence, and this world, not so much a material as a spiritual laboratory; then she must find some other interpreter than bare numbers to express her will.[2]

O'Donnel was indefinite in suggesting an alternative to representative government as a solution to the problem, but he was unimpressed by Tocqueville's premise about the inevitability of democracy, or by the relevance of that system to an evolving society. Like Reeve, he was refusing to abandon the values of aristocracy for those of equality. Tocqueville was, in Laski's phrase, an aristocrat admitting defeat; but England had many aristocrats who refused to do the same.

[1] *Blackwood's*, Vol. 37, May 1835, p. 765.   [2] Ibid. p. 766.

Part II of the *Democracy*, which appeared in 1840, was much more abstract and philosophical than Part I, and the Tories became more openly critical. Some became more friendly towards America, which they now began to see, in many aspects, as a conservative society. Tocqueville's catastrophic vision of an America driven by an egalitarian dialectic was said to be overdrawn, to be much too theoretical in the French fashion. Conservatives alleged that Tocqueville was confusing the American kind of democracy with that of France: 'One cannot read a single chapter of his work', commented *Blackwood's*, 'without being struck by the conviction that all his observations, touching all people, are made from the meridian of Paris.'[1] French democracy was admitted by all to be doctrinaire, visionary, abstruse: it sprang from the French Revolution, which 'aimed at the universal; its most potent spellword was the *regeneration* of man'.[2] According to O'Donnel, who wrote a second article on Tocqueville for *Blackwood's* in 1840, French democrats tested institutions by ideal standards; and the French ideal was a doctrine of equality both uncompromising and unpractical. Inevitably, he argued, any attempt to translate the ideal into reality became an attempt to reverse the natural human order. Thus he explained the French passion for transforming society. American democracy was said, on the other hand, to have a profoundly different spirit. The Tory argument was similar to the Whig insistence upon the common cultural qualities of Americans and Englishmen. American politics were more like British than French politics. American democracy was piecemeal and practical, earthy and concrete in the English tradition, not abstract and visionary in the French style:

The words democracy and equality have a noticeable diversity of signification in the apprehension of the Frenchman and of the American. The former sees in them . . . an ideal; he maintains and defends them continually by abstract reasonings. The latter is quite insensible to these subtle perceptions. . . . He understands them only as practical things, and values them solely on account of their practical effects. Indeed, equality in the United States should more properly be called rude and

---

[1] *Blackwood's*, Vol. 48, Oct. 1840, p. 470. 'In France he seems to fancy he has discovered the *Catholicon* passion of all nations, and this notion . . . falsifies radically all the dubious and frightened deductions he has drawn from it.' Basil Hall, on the contrary, regarded Tocqueville's nationality as a distinct advantage. Like Shaw, he suggested that the British and Americans were separated by a common language: 'There is undoubtedly much in the current language of American society which conveys to an Englishman's mind a very different class of impressions from what the self-same words do to the understanding of a native. . . . The Englishman never suspects that he is taking up a wrong idea; the Frenchman distrusts himself and inquires.' *QR*, Vol. 57, Sept. 1836, p. 135.

[2] *Blackwood's*, ibid. p. 467.

exuberant freedom; for it wants the chief mark—passionate blindness—by which M. de Tocqueville has discriminated equality from liberty. It has in America arisen out of, and is associated with, no eccentric agitations of the spiritual man, but comes entirely from the *terra firma* man. . . .[1]

In the view of men like O'Donnel, Tocqueville had failed to consider sufficiently the Anglo-Saxon character of the Americans, which was a more important fact than the superficial identities between French and American democracy: 'We maintain especially that the description he has given of democracy and equality only describes the French conception . . . and that in England, and more positively in America, this French idea is sternly reprobated and repudiated.'[2] The empiricist frame of mind seemed an obviously conservative influence to O'Donnel. All was safe and right in societies where men devoted their energies to the pursuit of everyday interests. Dangerous social convulsions always occurred 'out of the irresistable predominance of some new *spiritual* principles, and never out of the common energies and activities of men, however high-wrought, enterprising and ambitious these may be'.[3] (He would surely have regarded the Civil War as a product of absolute moralism prevailing over the counsels of pragmatism.) O'Donnel felt that Tocqueville might have been less pessimistic about the future if he had realized 'that the *Real* in the two freest countries on the face of the globe, is much more than an over-match for the *Ideal* in France, and is able to counter-balance and counteract its effects very sufficiently'.[4]

Like the argument of the Whigs, that of O'Donnel in effect praised the cast of mind of non-Radicals in England, and opposed potentially Socialist theories of egalitarianism. The non-revolutionary and inegalitarian characteristics of the Americans were high-lighted to this end,[5]

---

[1] Ibid. p. 468 [O'Donnel].

[2] Ibid. p. 468. Cf. Tocqueville: 'America is perhaps . . . the country of the whole world which contains the fewest germs of revolution.' O'Donnel, in making his theme striking, was less than fair to Tocqueville, who of course made a point of distinguishing French and American experience.

[3] Ibid. p. 469. This argument jostled a little uneasily with that other strand of conservative thought which insisted that the nobility provided a 'spiritual' counterbalance to 'the pursuit of everyday interests'.

[4] To illustrate his argument, O'Donnel pointed out the essential incompatibility between French and English genius. France could produce no demagogue with the qualities of Cobbett; Cartwright could not be compared with Lafayette. It was because Godwin's cast of mind was French, and Mme de Staël's essentially English, that they were not appreciated in their home countries.

[5] Associated with this theme was the argument that freedom was more cherished in countries with an empiricist tradition. Freedom, it was contended, was an essentially pragmatic attitude; unlike equality, it referred to no abstract ideal but existed only in practice and experience; it was by its nature an exercise in compromise.

although five years earlier O'Donnel had accepted Tocqueville's view about the existence of equality in the United States. Such conclusions were partly arrived at by undeniable distortion or rejection of some of Tocqueville's theses, by ignoring some of his important qualifications.[1] His thesis that egalitarian societies must predominate in Western Europe and America was repudiated. Faced with working-class movements in Britain and the Continent, the Tories had to concede Tocqueville's point about the aggrandizement of popular power in the civilized nations. They agreed that the masses would have to be conciliated, politically and socially. But to reason from this to an entire and inescapable remoulding of mankind was, they thought, 'preposterous, false and pernicious'. The English, and the Americans, were empirically-minded people, who rejected absolutes in favour of concrete solutions to situations as they arose. They would certainly come to profoundly less radical conclusions. Again, as in the case of Mill and the Whigs, ideas about America were assimilated to the dominant gradualist ethos of the age.

[1] Tocqueville, for example, was much more aware of the fact that divergent national conditions shaped democracy than *Blackwood's* allowed. He realized the importance of gradualism in English development and wrote for instance of British customary law that 'it has given that nation what one might call its taste for precedents, that is to say, a certain turn of mind which leads men to try and find out not what is reasonable in itself, but what is done, not what is just, but ancient, not general theories but particular facts . . . habits bred from customary law . . . have proved strong allies of aristocratic institutions.' This he wrote in his journal during his American tour; see Tocqueville, *Journey to America*, ed. J. P. Mayer (London, 1959), p. 16.

CHAPTER VI

CONCLUSION

THE PRECEDING chapters have shown that the English image of America
changed continually in response to the political interests, the political
philosophy, and the disposition of English observers. Image and reality
merged or collided according to the needs of the English situation.
Without doubt, as Anglo-American historians have effectively demonstrated, the implications of the American democratic experiment were a
challenge to established modes of thought. But what seems to have been
less clearly recognized is the capacity of nineteenth-century Englishmen,
in an age of British supremacy in the world, to accommodate the facts
about America within their own characteristic framework of values.
Very often this was in effect to reduce the threat to tradition, or to the
Victorian social balance.

Each political group had its own favourite stereotype. America was
the ideal, the Utopia attained, the conscience of Radical Britain, offering
an interpretation of the present and a prophecy about the future. It
seemed to vindicate the Radical's faith in mankind, and in environment
as a condition for endless improvement. The English Left of the time
found deep satisfaction in such qualities, despite some stirrings of doubt
as the full face of America was brought to light. In the van of intellectual
Radicalism, Bentham and his followers saw the Republic through
doctrinaire spectacles, as the exemplification of utilitarian theory; and
until their political platform had been either attained or outmoded, they
ignored contradictory evidence. The Whigs were fondest of discovering
in the new world a vindication of the glorious principles of 1688. At the
same time the Tories preferred to find there the *reductio ad absurdum* of
Whiggism. Middle-class liberals who read John Stuart Mill and Tocqueville imagined America to justify the supremacy of the middle class in
Britain. The manufacturers and capitalists (or their apologists) praised
America's *laissez faire*. On the other hand, the landed Tories and Old
Whigs attacked America's materialist culture and low popular standards
with a view to discrediting both political democracy and *laissez faire*.
On transatlantic evidence, they pleaded for the continuance of aristo-
cratic rule and aristocratic culture in Britain.

Contemporary American history was only too frequently presented so as to further party-political purposes, with assertions and counter-assertions constantly in play. One party upheld the purity of American politics, while the other depicted them as a sink of depravity. Radicals defended the character and ability of public men in the Union, but Tories described Jacksonian politicians as inexpert, venal, and subservient to the vulgar masses. Quite disparate meanings were attached to the careers of America's great men. Jefferson was portrayed by the Radical and Benthamite press more or less as he is portrayed to this day in popular American legend—that is as a social rebel wedded to extreme democratic principles. But the English Whigs pictured Jefferson as a very Whiggish democrat who repudiated revolution and discouraged social conflict, who was not optimistic about mankind outside America, and who believed in checking the rule of the people where the people were not to be trusted. Alexander Hamilton, for his part, received the abuse of all true Radicals and the laurels of the conservative-minded.

An episode such as the affair of Jackson and the Bank of the United States was certain to meet with a mixed reception. A left-of-the-road Benthamite like H. S. Chapman depicted Jackson as the people's choice, energetically smashing the oligarchic ambitions of the eastern monied interests by destroying their 'monster monopoly', Biddle's Bank. The classical Whig economists were more impressed by the Bank's stabilizing influence—as advocates of a centralized currency, linked to gold, they had less sympathy with the 'easy credit' men who supported Jackson, and they censured his aggressive policy as unwise and unsettling. Entrenched conservative opinion tended to dismiss the whole unsavoury affair as a domestic squabble typical of democracies. (In the same fashion the landed gentry, at the time of the panic of 1837, professed indifference to the plight of London merchant bankers who had been rash enough to lend money to demagogues.)

Even when there was agreement about the facts, there was dispute about causes, or else separate value judgments were made. Most observers agreed, for instance, that America's mass culture was mediocre and materialist. Conservatives found democratic causes for mediocrity and ascribed materialism to the commercial ethic. In so doing, however, they risked inconsistency, for the first charge depended upon the concept of America as an egalitarian, levelling democracy, while the second depended upon the concept of an inegalitarian, capitalist society. Radicals, for their part, found natural causes for mediocrity and were undismayed by materialism that resulted in overall prosperity. Most liberals deplored the predicament of the individual as a cog in a giant mass machine, and argued that subservience to mobs lowered the standards of political morality. But utilitarian thinkers, and also those who placed less emphasis upon the values of individualism, found compensations in the vision of a higher comfort and culture for the labouring masses under democracy.

The capacity of Englishmen for fitting facts about the United States to their existing values could, and did, have radical as well as conservative bearings. In the important instance of moderate and Tory opinion, however, the effect was to soften the impact of the American challenge to the political *status quo* established in 1832. When Alexis de Tocqueville visited England in 1833, he saw a country agitated by the throes of the Reform movement and, as he supposed, on the verge of a democratic revolution. Yet on his last visit in 1857 'he expressed his astonishment at finding the country so little changed after all, and that in spite of the Reform Bill and the incidents of twenty years, it was still just the same old England'.[1] This was indeed the supreme paradox of the age. In twenty years revolutionary Radicalism, Chartism, and Utopian Socialism had petered out. Despite the expectations of 1831, the age of *Sturm und Drang* had become the age of Victorian balance. By the fifties gradualism and pragmatism had become the chief characteristic of English social and political development.

Those who repudiated complacency and gradualism continued to use American arguments to favour immediate and far-reaching changes in England. Before 1832 they had been encouraged to do so by the Benthamites and, somewhat less wholeheartedly, by the liberal Whigs, both of whom perceived the value of American propaganda in the battle for the Bill (and in the case of the Benthamites, for something more). Opposition to this Radical standpoint in this early period had come mainly from the Tories and the more traditional Whigs. After 1832, however, there was built up a coherent body of moderate, middle-of-the-way opinion about America which was perceptively different from the idealist and strongly reformist approach of the strictly Radical Left. The effect—and the point must be made emphatically—was to favour pragmatic national solutions to political problems rather than thoroughgoing doctrinaire solutions based on comparison.

This development was made possible by many factors, the most fundamental in my view (although certainly not the only consideration) being a series of political realignments which followed the resolution of frustrations crowning the success of 1832. The new situation encouraged a rethinking about America, founded on accumulating knowledge and

---

[1] Reeve in *ER*, Vol. 122, Oct. 1865, p. 475 (Posthumous Writings of Tocqueville).

hastened by the fresh insights of thinkers such as Tocqueville. Extremist views persisted, also feeding upon the new literature. One symptom of the so-called conservative reaction in the thirties was jaundiced anti-Americanism, showing itself in a greater readiness to listen to criticisms of demagoguery, corruption, and 'tyranny of the majority'. America's cultural mediocrity, her vulgarity, all evidence of internal turmoil and sectionalism, negro slavery, Anglophobia and expansionism—all were attributed to the evil effects of universal suffrage. A more balanced approach was characteristic of centre opinion.

The Benthamites, the liberal Whigs and liberal Tories, the manufacturers and free traders, and the dissenters remained essentially pro-American; but they admired the economic and social system of the United States, her society of opportunity, rather than her democratic suffrages and supposed political Radicalism. Any honeymoon with Radicalism having now passed, they favoured interpretations of America which were both pro-American and anti-democratic. They favoured the 'propitious circumstances' doctrine, which discovered non-political causes for American success. They accepted the idea that property was safe, that democracy could be undangerous in continental North America, where men were either capitalists or expectant capitalists; but they denied that Radical principles could be safely applied to the industrial and over-populated countries of Europe. Those who insisted upon the Whiggish and conservative nature of some transatlantic institutions supplied a realistic corrective to the idealist impression of American politics. Whereas the Radicals pictured America as a nation of universal men, wedded to universal principles, the Whigs and Tories emphasized the Anglo-Saxon character of the people and attributed their successes to their pragmatic English instincts and traditions. Even Tocqueville's unsettling insistence upon the inevitability of democracy was cushioned: according to their likes, his British interpreters either denied the relevance of his thesis in arsitocratic England, or they equated the ideas of 'democracy' and 'rule by the commercial classes'. The most radical deduction that sprang from this style of thought was a recognition that immediate attention must be devoted to the problem of raising England's proletariat to the American standard of life and political responsibility.

Men of the centre in British politics, then, drew very limited and cautious lessons from the American example during an age that encouraged political caution. This is, in itself, a very important qualification to any brief that the 'American destiny' exerted a determining influence on the course of British history during the first half of the nineteenth century. As Lillibridge has shown, American propaganda was still widely

used by Radicals in an effort to attain the Charter in England—but surely
the crucial fact is that they failed signally to achieve their political
objectives. Indeed, there were intimations that the Radical image of
America, once so popular and useful, began to be less effective and to
have less appeal even amongst Radicals during the early Victorian age.
One reason seems to be that the Americophiles of this age—the Richard
Carliles, Henry Hetheringtons, etc.—although able men, lacked the status
of Paine, Godwin, Cobbett and the original 'United States lobby'. Again,
the opponents of the Radical tradition about America put their case with
vastly more force and reason in the 1830's and 1840's. As the Republic
experienced growing pains; as the reputation of Jacksonian democracy
suffered from increasing sectionalism, from slavery and economic crises;
as the anti-British policies of President Polk and his supporters became
known in England, even true Radicals began to have doubts. And, of
course, as mid-Victorian prosperity increased, the sharp edge of discontent
with the home country was dulled. Politically, any further extension of
the franchise was simply not practical politics between 1835 and 1850;
so that the American example, like the Charter itself, took on the
character of an unattainable panacea. There is yet another facet to consider. In the 1820's, political democracy in the American style had seemed
the answer to working-class problems, which were nevertheless essentially
economic problems. However, as Chartism progressed, the real aims of
many Chartists went beyond the mere attaining of the vote and political
equality, to the attaining of economic justice. And, as Mill and almost all
commentators emphasized, the Americans repudiated anything resem-
bling economic communism; they had a healthy middle-class respect for
property. Hence, for those extremists who were also the activists of the
Left, admiration of American democracy, like admiration for the formal
principles of the Charter, became less than wholehearted. Here the seeds
were sown for the later Socialist disillusionment with America in the
age of Carnegie and Rockefeller. It was perhaps only because thinkers did
not explore more deeply the basic schism between 'political' and 'economic' democracy that the Radical myth about the United States survived
as long as it did. Tocqueville was aware of the problem, but even he did
not incorporate it very explicitly into his early writings.

   This, indeed, was the age of mounting evidence that America exhibited
a middle-class, rather than a working-class, millennium; a paradise of
laissez faire and individual opportunities rather than of collectivism. This
was the vision that united very large numbers of Englishmen in admiration. The emigration statistics provide compelling evidence that the
doctrine of economic individualism, as exemplified in the new world,

was by no means entirely anathema to the English labouring and artisan classes. But to justify that principle as the backbone of English, as well as of American, progress was without doubt a much less attractive task (although one enthusiastically tackled by Cobden and a host of others, including, in the present day, such eminent scholars as Professor Ashton). Blake's 'dark, satanic mills', whether justifiably or not, haunted men's imaginations. Despite the free traders, English working-men often shared with the Tory landed gentry feelings of recoil from new economic and social forms, and looked back nostalgically to an era of rural patriarchy. Thus the Tory attack upon an acquisitive and commercial civilization in the United States was a shrewd one, designed to attract working-class support against Cobden and his kind. Before 1832 America had appealed to Radicalism as an argument against aristocracy and Establishments, as a justification of the Enlightenment. This appeal was rooted in reformist psychology, and it persisted. It had, nevertheless, much more limited political value after 1832, when one school of Radical thought began to look upon the factory owners and industrialists as a more dangerous foe than the effete nobility.

APPENDIX

The United States in British Periodicals: 1815–60

HERE I simply wish to identify the authors of some of the more important articles on America (which were all, of course, anonymous) to be found in the leading political periodicals.

A few articles mentioned are well known (e.g. John Stuart Mill's reviews of Tocqueville's *Democracy in America*). There is published evidence available for many articles, but such evidence is unfortunately scattered and very often inaccessible outside the largest libraries. The following lists may therefore prove useful in drawing such diverse materials together.

The evidence for authorship given below is, in most cases, not exhaustive, except where there is some doubt or debate about the matter.

I should like to acknowledge the generous assistance given to me in deciding the authorship of a number of articles, indicated in the text, by Mrs. Ester Rhoads Houghton of the *Wellesley Index for Victorian Periodicals* (1824–1900), Wellesley College, Mass.

I. Articles Relevant to America in Benthamite Periodicals: 1824-40

Abbreviations: WR—Westminster Review; LR—London Review; L & WR—London and Westminster Review.

Periodical	Date	Vol.	No.	Art.	Title	Author	Authority for Assignment of Authorship
WR	Jan. 1824	1	1	1	'Men and Things in 1824'	W. J. Fox	Garnett,[1] Nesbitt,[2] p. 179.
WR	Jan. 1824	1	1	2	'Moore's Fables for the Holy Alliance'	Peregrine Bingham[3]	Mill's Autobiog.*
WR	Jan. 1824	1	1	11	'Periodical Literature—the Quarterly Review, No. 58'	James Mill (asst. by J. S. Mill)	Bain,[4] Mill's Autobiog.: pp. 77–9.*
WR	Oct. 1824	2	4	9	'Quarterly Review (No. 41, review of Fearon's Sketches of America, 1818.)'	James Mill	Mill's Autobiog.*
WR	Jan. 1826	5	9	9	'The United States'	John Neal	Neal.[5]*
WR	Jul. 1830	13	25	1	'The Ballot'	James Mill	Bain, Place MSS.*
WR	Oct. 1830	13	26	3	'Randolph's Memoir of Jefferson'	Thos. Love Peacock	Peacock.[6]*

[1] Richard Garnett, Life of William Johnson Fox (London, 1910).

[2] George L. Nesbitt, Benthamite Reviewing—the first twelve years of the Westminster Review: 1824–1836 (Columbia, 1934). Nesbitt gives a most useful list of contributors in the WR in an Appendix, pp. 177–83. He relies mainly upon information given in works by reliable biographers, or other good evidence (such as the Bentham and Place papers). There are, unfortunately, no existing editorial files of the WR for this period, and it is very difficult to identify the authors of many articles. In this reference Nesbitt has cited Garnett's book for evidence of Fox's authorship; and wherever Nesbitt also mentions the source given, an asterisk will be placed after it.

[3] Bingham, according to John Stuart Mill, was a barrister, a frequenter of Bentham and a friend of the Austins. He had 'adopted with great ardour Mr Bentham's philosophical opinions'. The Mills were 'extremely pleased' with Bingham's five articles in the first number of the review. See J. S. Mill, Autobiography (London, 1924), p. 80, hereafter cited as Mill's Autobiog. See also Nesbitt, p. 27.

[4] Alexander Bain, James Mill, a Biography (New York, 1882), p. 265.

[5] John Neal, Wandering Recollections of a Somewhat Busy Life (Boston, 1869). Neal, an American author, editor, and man of affairs, visited England in 1823 and wrote over two dozen articles on America for journals of all leanings. His purpose was to correct the 'insolent misrepresentation' of American affairs common in the English press, and he was remarkably successful in doing so. Neal, after spending some months in Bentham's household, finally returned to America in 1827, a spokesman for utilitarianism.

[6] Thomas Love Peacock, Works (London, 1924–31). Peacock was a novelist and poet. His connection with the WR arose out of his position as examiner at India House under James Mill. Not a utilitarian, he yet approved much in the Benthamite platform.

Periodica	Date	Vol.	No.	Art.	Title	Author	Authority for Assignment of Authorship
WR	Apr. 1831	14	28	11	'Parliamentary Reform'	Thomas Perronet Thompson[1]	Thompson.[2]
WR	Jul. 1832	17	33	16	'Prospects of Reform'	Thompson	Thompson.*
WR	Apr. 1833	18	36	4	'Stuart's Three Years in North America'	Thompson and collaborator	Thompson,[3] III, 416n. Houghton.
WR	Jan. 1834	20	39	13	'Prospects of the Coloured Races'	Thompson and collaborator	Thompson.[3] Houghton.
LR	Jul. 1835	2	3	7	'Mrs. Butler's Journal'	Charles Buller(?)	Houghton.[4]
LR	Jan. 1836	2	4	5	'State of Society in America'	John Stuart Mill	MacMinn.[5]
L & WR	Oct. 1837	(VI & 28)	(XI & 54)	3	'Miss Sedgwick's Works'	Harriet Martineau	Towers.[6]

[1] '. . . retired major, afterwards colonel, of dragoons, dabbler in mathematics, music, economics, and politics, as well as in journalism' (Nesbit, p. 27). In 1828 he became owner of the WR.

[2] Thomas Perronet Thompson, Exercises, Political and Others, 6 vols. (London, 1842). The article is reprinted herein.

[3] In the review of Stuart, Thompson wrote the section beginning on p. 339 with the words 'Washington the capital . . .' and continuing to p. 353. His co-author has not been identified, but he also collaborated with Thompson in article 13, 'Prospects of the Coloured Races', in Jan. 1834. (I am indebted for this information to Mrs. Houghton of the Wellesley Index to Victorian Periodicals; as also for information on the ascription of article XI, Jan. 1824, to James Mill, and evidence on article 7, July 1835, LR, and article 6, Jan. 1838, L & WR. This source is cited hereafter as 'Houghton'.)

[4] The article is possibly Buller's, because of the signature (–) which is believed to have been used by Buller. Professor Francis Mineka, now editing J. S. Mill's letters, also attributes this article to Buller, on the basis—it is believed—of a manuscript letter from Mill to Falconer, 3.10.1835, indicating that Buller had an article in this issue, but not specifying which.

[5] MacMinn, Hainds, and McCrimmon, Bibliography of Published Writings of J. S. Mill in Northwestern University Studies in the Humanities, No. 12 (1945).

[6] The article is signed H.M., initials used by Martineau in the L & WR (Nesbit, p. 172). The identification is confirmed in a letter of J. S. Mill to John Robertson (his assistant editor in the L & WR) of 12.7.37, quoted in C. M. D. Towers, 'J. S. Mill and the London & Westminster Review', Atlantic Monthly, LXIX [Jan. 1892] 59, hereafter cited as 'Towers'. Mill, although not on good terms with Martineau, thought her article on Sedgwick 'unobjectionable'.

Periodical	Date	Vol.	No.	Art.	Title	Author	Authority for Assignment of Authorship
L & WR	Jan. 1838	(VI & 28)	(XII & 55)	6	'Martineau's Western Travel'	W. E. Hickson(?)	Initials.[1]
L & WR	Dec. 1838	32	1	1	'The Martyr Age of the United States'	Harriet Martineau	Towers.[2] Martineau.[3]
L & WR	Mar. 1840	33	2	4	'Emerson's Works—American Philosophy'	Richard Monckton Milnes	Pope-Hennessy,[4] et al.

[1] The article is signed W.H., which may mean Hickson, who wrote for the review. However, he used a variety of initials (including W.E.H.), so the ascription is doubtful. The L & W was turned over to Hickson by Mill in 1840, and he retained it (under various names) until the 1850's, when it was sold to John Chapman.

[2] In a letter to Robertson of 2.10.38, Mill wrote of 'H.M.'s' intention to write upon American slavery (and H.M. stood for Martineau in all their correspondence); 'but it must be a condition', he added, 'that she shall not be sentimental, which she has more tendency to than any other writer we have' (Towers, p. 67). Mill had in 1837 privately criticized Martineau to Robertson, observing that, whilst she tried hard for philosophy, she 'had not an opinion that you may not drive a coach and six through'. (Towers, p. 63; letter to Robertson, 28.9.37.)

[3] The article was reprinted as Martineau's under the title *The Martyr Age of the United States* (N.Y. & Boston, 1839; Newcastle, 1840).

[4] J. Pope-Hennessy, *Monckton Milnes: The Years of Promise* (London, 1950) I, p. 115. Pope-Hennessy based his identifications upon the papers of Milnes. See also T. W. Reid, *Life, Letters, etc. of Richard Monckton Milnes*, 2 vols. (London, 1891) I, 239–40. There is also, according to the Wellesley Index, a letter from Mill to Milnes, which supports Milne's authorship, in private possession.

208

2. Articles upon America in the 'Edinburgh Review': 1820–1860

Date	No.	Art.	Title	Author	Authority for Assignment of Authorship
May 1820	66	6	Dispositions of England and America (review of Walsh, *Appeal from the Judgments of Gt. Britain, etc.* London, 1819.)	Francis Jeffrey	Copinger,[1] p. 31.
Jan 1820	65	3	Seybert's *Statistical Annals of the U.S.*	Sydney Smith	Cockburn.[2] reprinted in Smith, *Works* (Lond., 1848)
Jul. 1824	80	7	America (review of Duncan's *Travels* . . . and Hodgson's *Letters from N. America*.)	Sydney Smith	Copinger, p. 31. Smith, *Works*.
Oct. 1829	99	7	American Literature—Dr. Channing (review of W. E. Channing, *Sermons and Tracts*, repr. London, 1829.)	William Hazlitt	Copinger, p. 43. Reprinted in Hazlitt, *Works*.
Jun. 1829	98	9	U.S.A. (review of Fenimore Cooper, *Notions of the Americans*, Lond., 1828, and Basil Hall, *Travels in N. America, etc.*, Edin., 1829.)	William Empson	Copinger, p. 42. Johnson,[3] p. 50. Napier Papers.[4]
Jul. 1830	102	9	Jefferson's Memoirs and Correspondence (review of *Memoirs, Corresp., etc., of Thomas Jefferson*, 4 vols., 1829.)	Empson	Johnson, p. 41. Napier Papers.[5]

[1] W. A. Copinger, *On the Authorship of the first 100 Numbers of the 'Edinburgh Review'* (Manchester, 1895). *Edinburgh Review* is hereafter abbreviated to *ER*.

[2] Lord Cockburn, *Life and Correspondence of Francis Jeffrey* (London, 1852), I, 419.

[3] L. G. Johnson, 'On Some Authors of *Edinburgh Review* Articles, 1830–49', *Library*, 5th Ser., VIII (Mar., 1952), 38–50. Johnson assigns authorship for a number of years on the basis of annotations in a set of *Edinburgh Reviews* owned by William Empson's brother. Empson, who succeeded Macvey Napier as editor of the *ER*, was Jeffrey's son-in-law, Professor at Haileybury and a close friend of Macaulay and Malthus. Empson was regarded as the journal's expert on American affairs during the 'twenties and 'thirties.

[4] Br. Mus. Add. MSS., 34614–34624; including letters to Macvey Napier as editor of the *ER*, 1829–47 (hereafter 'Napier Papers'). Empson's authorship in this case is confirmed from Add. MSS., 34614, fols. 144–5, 150–1, 152–3.

[5] Add. MSS., 34614. fol. 356.

Date	No.	Art.	Title	Author	Authority for Assignment of Authorship
Jul. 1832	110	8	America and her Detractors	Empson	Napier Corresp.,[1] p. 128. Johnson, p. 43.
			(review of Mrs. F. Trollope, *Domestic Manners of the Americans*, 1832; G. T. Vigne, *Six Months in America*, 1832; W. G. Ouseley, *Remarks on Statistics, etc. . . . of the U.S.*, 1832.)		
Jul. 1832	110	11	Dumont's Recollection of Mirabeau	Thos. Babington Macaulay	Johnson, p. 43. Reprinted in Macaulay, *Essays*.
Oct. 1832	111	11	Working and Prospects of Reform	Henry Brougham	Aspinall,[2] p. 260. Napier Corresp., pp. 131-2.
Jan. 1833	112	8	Sarran's *La Fayette*	Empson	Napier Papers.[3]
			(review of B. Sarran, *La Fayette et la Révolution de 1830*)		
Jan. 1833	112	7	Stuart on America	J. R. McCulloch	Fetter,[4] p. 255.
			(review of Jas. Stuart's *3 Years in N. America*)		
Jul. 1833	116	9	Diplomat's Narrative of Residence in London	Empson	Johnson, p. 43.
			(review of R. Rush, *Narrative of a Residence at the Court of London, 1817-25*, London, 1833.)		
Apr. 1836	125	11	Walsh's Contemporary History	Empson	Napier Corresp., p. 177.
			(review of Sir J. Walsh, *Chapters on Contemporary History* 1836, 3rd ed.)		

[1] *Selections from the Correspondence of the late Macvey Napier, Esq.*, ed. by his son (London, 1879)—hereafter 'Napier Corresp.'

[2] A. Aspinall, *Lord Brougham and the Whig Party* (Manchester, 1927). Aspinall based his ascriptions upon information, supplied by Longmans, Green & Co., publishers of the ER. This firm's files on this topic to 1847 were unfortunately destroyed by bombing during World War II.

[3] Empson wrote to Napier (7.11.32)—'I have only lately been reading Sarran's Memoir of Lafayette: I am much disposed to send you a short paper on the case which it makes out against Republics from the feeling of France.' This describes accurately the content of the article. See also Add. MSS. 34, 615, fols. 435-6.

[4] F. W. Fetter, 'The Authorship of Economic Articles in the *Edinburgh Review*, 1802-47', in *J. of Pol. Econ.*, LXI, No. 3, Jun. 1953. Fetter's authority for identification of McCulloch's articles is H. G. Reid's biographical notice of McCulloch in the 1869 edition of McCulloch's *Dictionary of Commerce and Commercial Navigation*. (Reid's information was derived from lists prepared by the economist, see Fetter, p. 249.)

Date	No.	Art.	Title	Author	Authority for Assignment of Authorship
Apr. 1836	125	6	American Slavery (review of Congregationalist pamphlet on *Slavery*, Glasgow, 1836.)	Brougham	Aspinall, p. 260. Napier Papers.[1]
Jul. 1837	132	7	Newspaper Literature (review of A. Fonblanque, *England Under Seven Administrations*, London, 1837.)	Empson	Napier Corresp., p. 200. Johnson, p. 45. Napier Papers (34, 618, ff. 13–14).
Jul. 1837	132	12	State of Parties	Empson	Napier Corresp., p. 197.
Jul. 1837	132	9	Cause and Consequences of the Crisis in American Trade	McCulloch	Johnson, p. 45. Fetter, p. 256.
Oct. 1837	131	8	Tucker's Life of Jefferson (review of Prof. G. Tucker, *Life of Thos. Jefferson . . . etc*, 2 vols, New York, 1837.)	Brougham	Napier Corresp., p. 207.
Apr. 1839	137	9	False Taste—Dr. Channing (review of W. E. Channing, *Remarks on the Character and Writing of John Milton*, 1838.)	Brougham	Aspinall, p. 260. Napier Papers.[1]
Oct. 1839	141	5	Marryat's Diary in America (review of Capt. Marryat, *A Diary in America*, 3 vols, 1839.)	Empson	Aspinall, p. 261. Napier Papers.[1]
Jul. 1840	144	7	Foreign Policy of the Govt.	Spring Rice (Lord Monteagle)	Napier Corresp., pp. 303–4, 307. Cockburn MSS.[2]

[1] B.M. Add. MSS., 34, 628.

[2] Cockburn prepared a list of *Edinburgh Review* authors on the authority of the editor, or of the authors, or of 'undisputed notoriety' frequently corroborated by other works. It is now in the possession of the Earl of Rosebery, but Dr. E. Schneider of Temple University has a copy and kindly forwarded information from it to the writer.

Date	No.	Art.	Title	Author	Authority for Assignment of Authorship
Apr. 1841	147	10	Texas and its Recognition	Charles Buller	Napier Papers.[1]
Jul. 1841	148	6	State of Massachusetts	Geo. Combe	Napier Papers.[2] Gibbon.[2]
Apr. 1842	151	1	France, America and Britain	Nassau Wm. Senior	Napier Corresp., p. 384. Senior, Essays.[3]
Jan. 1843	154	8	Dickens's American Notes	James Spedding	Spedding,[4] pp. 240–276.
Jul. 1843	157	6	Mexico	Herman Merivale	Chas. Merivale.[5]
Oct. 1843	158	8	Bentham (review of J. Bowring, ed., *Memoirs of Jeremy Bentham . . . etc.*, Edin., 1842–3.)	Wm. Empson	Napier Corresp., p. 438.
Jan. 1845	163	1	Brougham's Political Philosophy (review of Henry Brougham, *Political Philosophy*, 3 vols., 1842–4.)	N. W. Senior	Napier Corresp., p. 462. Senior, *Essays*.
Apr. 1845	164	8	The Churches and the Three Kingdoms (review of Thos. Arnold, *Fragment on the Church*, 1844.)	Wm. Empson	Napier Corresp., p. 486.
Jul. 1845	165	8	The Oregon Question	N. W. Senior	Napier Corresp., pp. 497, 500–1, 532. Senior, *Essays*.

[1] Add. MSS., 34, 621, fols. 523–5, 586–8.

[2] Add. MSS., 34, 621, fol. 564 and 34, 623, fols. 373–7. See also Chas. Gibbon, *Life of Geo. Combe* (London, 1878), II, 127–8. Combe was a well-known Scottish educational reformer.

[3] N. W. Senior, *Historical and Philosophical Essays* (London, 1865). Some of his most important ER articles are reprinted here.

[4] Jas. Spedding, *Reviews and Discussions* (London, 1879); includes his *Edinburgh Review* articles and an account of the controversy which his review of the *American Notes* provoked with Dickens (p. 270n).

[5] Charles Merivale, D.D., Dean of Ely, 'Herman Merivale, C.B.', *Report and Transactions of the Devonshire Soc. for the Advancement of Science, Lit., and Art*, XVI (1884), 579–580. There is a list of Merivale's articles here.

Date	No.	Art.	Title	Author	Authority for Assignment of Authorship
Jan. 1846	167	5	Lyell's *Travels in N. America* (review of Chas. Lyell, *Travels in N. America . . . etc.*, 2 vols., 1845.)	Hernan Merivale	Napier Corresp., p. 519.
Jan. 1846	167	6	European and American State Confederacies	N. W. Senior	ER, Oct. 1902, p. 300. Napier Corresp., p. 519. Senior, *Essays.*
Jan. 1847	171	4	Bancroft's History of the U.S.	John Arthur Roebuck	Cockburn MSS. Napier Papers (34, 624, fols. 387–8).
Oct. 1847	174	4	Macgregor's American Commerce	Merivale	Chas. Merivale.
Oct. 1850	188	2	Lyell's 2nd Visit to the U.S.	Spedding	Longmans' List.[1]
Oct. 1850	188	8	Difficulties of Republican France	William Rathbone Greg	Longmans' List. Greg, *Essays.*[2]
Apr. 1852	194	7	Mallet du Pan	Merivale	Longmans' List.
Oct. 1852	196	7	Representative Reform	W. R. Greg	Longmans' List. Greg, *Essays.*
Jul. 1853	199	6	Popular Education in the U.S.	Elias Hasket Derby[3]	Longmans' List.
Oct. 1853	200	7	Newspaper Stamp	Alexander Russell	Longmans' List.
Oct. 1853	200	9	Parliamentary Purification	W. R. Greg	Longmans' List. Hayward Corresp.,[4] I, 194.

[1] Longmans, Green Co. have records relating to authorship of *ER* articles from 1847, and have generously supplied information to me.
[2] W. R. Greg, *Essays on Political and Social Science*, 2 vols. (London, 1853). The article is reprinted here.
[3] 1803–1880, Boston lawyer.
[4] *Selection from the Correspondence of Abraham Hayward*, ed. H. E. Carlyle (London, 1886).

Date	Vol.	No.	Art.	Title	Author	Authority for Assignment of Authorship
Jul. 1854	203	8		European Emigration to the U.S.	—. Davis[1]	Longmans' List.
Apr. 1855	206	1		Slavery in U.S. (review of Stowe)	Senior (and Davis)	Senior, *Slavery*.[2] Levy,[3] pp. 316, 416. Longmans' List.
Oct. 1856	212	10		Political Crisis in U.S.	Wm. Henry Hurlbert[4]	Longmans' List.
Jul. 1857	215	4		Representative Reform	Greg	Longmans' List.
Jan. 1859	221	9		History and Prospects of Parliamentary Reform	Geo. Cornewall Lewis	Laughton,[5] II, 401. Longmans' List.

[1] Longmans gives the name 'Davis' or 'Davies'. Probably John Chandler Bancroft Davis, 1822–1907, a New York lawyer, Sec. of the American Legation in Gt. Britain (1849–1852), and American Correspondent to the *Times* 1854–1861. Longmans credits Davis with assisting Senior (Davis received £20, Senior £32 for the article). Davis' sentiments were abolitionist and pro-North.

[2] Senior, *American Slavery; reprinted with additions from the Edinburgh Review* (London, 1856).

[3] S. Leon Levy, *Nassau W. Senior, etc.* (Boston, 1943).

[4] 1827–1895, New York journalist. Hurlbert, like Davis, imparted abolitionist flavour to his article, which was well-received in Whig and liberal quarters.

[5] J. K. Laughton, *Memoirs of the Life and Correspondence of Henry Reeve* (London, 1898).

3. Articles with Relevance to the United States in Tory Periodicals: 1819–1852

I. Quarterly Review: (QR)

Date	Vol.	No.	Art.	Title	Author	Authority for Assignment of Authorship
Jan. 1819	21	41	1	Bristed—Statistical View of America	Wm. Jacob[1]	Murray List.[2] Shines, p. 65.[3] Fetter II, p. 159.[4]
Jan. 1819	21	41	7	Fearon's Sketches of America	Sir John Barrow[5]	Murray List. Shines, p. 65. Fetter II, p. 159.
July 1820	23	46	12	New Churches	Robert Southey	Murray List. Shines, p. 71. Smiles II, 109.[6]
July 1823	29	58	3	Faux—Memorable Days in America	Barrow and Wm. Gifford	Murray List. Shines, p. 85. Fetter II, p. 160. Smiles II, 157.

[1] 1762(?)–1851; Tory pamphleteer, writer, and M.P. (Sussex, 1808–12). Comptroller of corn returns for the Board of Trade until 1842, Jacob was a staunch defender of the Corn Laws.

[2] Authors of QR articles are entered in the *Contributors Book* at the London office of John Murray, publishers. Entries are based on correspondence held. I have consulted a number of bibliographical works which made use of the 'Murray List' among other sources and reference is made to these for further details.

[3] Hill Shine and H. C. Shine, *The QR under Gifford: identification of contributors, 1809–1824* (N. Carolina, 1949). This gives a full account of all available evidence upon authorship until 1824.

[4] Frank W. Fetter, 'Economic Articles in the QR and their Authors, 1809–1852', *J. Pol. Econ.*, LXVI (Feb. 1958), 47–64; and LXVI (Apr. 1958), 154–170. Hereafter cited as 'Fetter II', to distinguish from his 1953 article referred to in an earlier section. Fetter uses the Murray List and other sources.

[5] 1764–1848; regular contributor to the QR after 1812; 2nd Secretary to the Admiralty (1807–45), patron of maritime exploration and a staunch defender of King, Lords and Commons.

[6] Samuel Smiles, *A Publisher and his Friends: Memoirs and Correspondence of John Murray*. 2 vols. London, 1891.

Date	Vol.	No.	Art.	Title	Author	Authority for Assignment of Authorship
Oct. 1823	30	59	1	Dwight—Travels in N. Eng.	Southey	Murray List. Shines, p. 86. Fetter II, p. 160.
Dec. 1824	31	61	1	Travels in Brazil	Jacob	Murray List.
Mar. 1826	33	66	6	Political Importance of our American Colonies	Barrow	Murray List.
Jan. 1828	37	73	8	United States	Barrow	Fetter II, p. 161. Murray List.
Jan. 1829	39	77	7	Commerce of U.S. and W. Indies	Jacob	Fetter II, p. 162. Murray List.
Nov. 1829	41	82	6	Travels in N. America	Barrow	Fetter II, p. 163. Murray List. Brightfield PMLA.[1]
May 1830	43	85	7	Political Conditions and Prospects of France	Richard Chenevix[2]	Murray List. Fetter II, p. 163.
Apr. 1831	45	89	7	Reform in Parliament	John Fullarton?	Frazer's Magazine.[3] Houghton.
Jan. 1832	46	92	9	Progress of Misgovernment	John Wilson Croker	Brightfield biog.[4]
Mar. 1832	47	93	2	Domestic Manners of the Americans	Basil Hall	Murray List. Brightfield PMLA.
Oct. 1832	48	95	7	Flint's 10 Years in the Valley of the Mississippi	John Gibson Lockhart	Murray List. Brightfield PMLA.

[1] Myron F. Brightfield, 'Lockhart's *Quarterly* Contributors', *PMLA*, LIX (June 1944), 491–512. This article indentifies authors of all literary articles in the QR under Lockhart's editorship (1826–53). It uses the Murray List, biographical material and collected works.

[2] 1774–1830, Irish chemist, who specialized on France for the QR.

[3] Doubtful ascription. Fullarton, formerly a medical officer in India, was known to have written political articles for the QR during 1831 [see *DNB*, and Geo. Boyle, *Recollections* (London, 1895), p. 58]. *Fraser's Mag.* (Vol. 3, May 1831, p. 525) attributes this article to Fullarton; but the publisher's list, which is not always correct, gives as the entry for this article '?John Miller'.

[4] Myron F. Brightfield, *John Wilson Croker* (California 1940). A list of Croker's numerous articles written for the QR is given on pp. 453–9. It is based mainly upon the 'Murray List' but one or two ascriptions conflict with other sources. Hereafter cited as 'Brightfield biog.'

Date	Vol.	No.	Art.	Title	Author	Authority for Assignment of Authorship
Dec. 1832	48	96	9	Mr. Ouseley on the U.S.A.	Jacob	Murray List. Brightfield *PMLA*.
Apr. 1833	49	97	7	Russell on the Causes of the French Revolution	Lord Mahon (Philip Henry Stanhope)	Murray List. Brightfield *PMLA*. *Hist. Essays*,[1] p. 272.
Mar. 1834	51	101	6	Life of Dr. Adam Clarke	J. J. Blunt	Murray List. *Blunt Essays*.[2]
Feb. 1835	53	105	7	The Church and the Voluntary System	Henry Hart Milman[3]	Murray List. Brightfield *PMLA*.
Apr. 1835	53	106	1	M. Beaumont on the Americans	Lockhart	Murray List. Brightfield *PMLA*.
Apr. 1835	53	106	10	Essays of Fisher Ames	Croker	Murray List. Brightfield biog.
July 1835	54	107	2	Journal of Fanny Kemble	Croker	Murray List. Brightfield biog.
Dec. 1835	55	109	2	Foreign Poor Laws	George Poulett Scrope[4]	Murray List. Fetter II.
Apr. 1837	58	116	8	Chevalier and Cooper on Europe and America	Francis Egerton[5]	Murray List. Brightfield *PMLA*.
Oct. 1837	59	118	2	Cooper's England	Croker	Murray List. Brightfield biog.

[1] Lord Mahon, *Historical Essays: contributed to the QR* (Lond. 1861).

[2] The article is reprinted in John James Blunt, *Essays Contributed to QR* (Lond., 1860). Blunt (1794–1855) was an Anglican divine, the author of the *History of the Christian Church during the 1st Three Centuries* (1856).

[3] 1791–1868; Dean of St. Paul's, eminent commentator on early Christianity, editor of Gibbon.

[4] 1797–1876; geologist, economist and Tory M.P. Scrope in this article described the unpleasant American workhouses, and did not want them copied in Britain (p. 49).

[5] 1800–57; a liberal Tory of the Canning School, free trader, and a well-known literary figure.

Date	Vol.	No.	Art.	Title	Author	Authority for Assignment of Authorship
Apr. 1838	61	122	3	Texas	Benjamin Bussy Thatcher(?)	Napier Papers.[1]
Apr. 1838	61	122	10	The Ballot	Croker	Murray List.
						Brightfield biog.
June 1838	62	123	6	Atlantic Steam Navigation	Thatcher(?)	Am. Dict. Biog.[1]
Jan. 1839	63	125	1	Railroads in Ireland	Sir Francis Bond Head[2]	Murray List.
						Fetter II, p. 166.
Oct. 1839	64	128	2	Travels in North America	Lockhart	Murray List.
						Brightfield *PMLA*.
Dec. 1840	67	133	1	American Orators and Statesmen	Abraham Hayward	Murray List.
						Brightfield *PMLA*.
						Hayward, *Letters* I, 79.[3]
Mar. 1841	67	134	8	U.S. Boundary Question	Croker	Murray List.
						Brightfield biog.
June 1841	68	135	2	Foster's Notes on the U.S.	Lockhart	Murray List.
						Brightfield *PMLA*.
Sept. 1841	68	136	1	Buckingham and Combe on the U.S.	Lockhart	Murray List.
						Brightfield *PMLA*.

[1] It seems likely that Thatcher, who was in England in 1838, was the author. Thatcher in the same year offered an article on Texas to the *ER* (see Add MSS. 34, 619, ff. 70–71) but it was rejected. The article in the QR is written from an American and abolitionist viewpoint consistent with Thatcher's opinions. The *Am. Dict. of Biog.* attributes an article, 'Atlantic Steam Navigation', QR, June 1838, to Thatcher. Murray's list gives no information on either 'Texas' or 'Steam Navigation' (information from Wellesley Index).

[2] 1793–1875; soldier, traveller, assistant poor-law commissioner, Lt.-Governor Upper Canada. The article is strongly anti-American and anti-democratic.

[3] *Selection from the Correspondence of Abraham Hayward*, ed. H. E. Carlyle, 2 vols. (Lond., 1886). Hayward (1801–84) was a liberal Tory who became a Peelite in 1846; an essayist and a man of letters, he contributed to the QR, *Fraser's, ER* and other journals. Hayward was a friend and correspondent of Chas. Sumner and Joseph Story. The article relies upon an essay by Edward Everett in the *N. Am. Rev.* for its political analysis; see Sumner to Hayward 31.8.1840, ibid., I, 78–80. Hayward also incorporated some of Sumner's criticisms about the 'Log Cabin and Cider' campaign of Harrison. Although Hayward was critical of American oratory, he had a high opinion of leading Americans: Fisher Ames was 'the American Burke', Marshall the 'Lord Stowell of the U.S.'; Hamilton America's 'most consummate' statesman; the Adamses, Washington, Patrick Henry, Clay, Webster and others were, some for the first time, given due credit in a Tory journal.

Date	Vol.	No.	Art.	Title	Author	Authority for Assignment of Authorship
Sept. 1841	68	136	7	Letters of Mrs. Adams	Croker	Murray List. Brightfield biog.
Dec. 1841	69	137	8	Letters of John Adams	Croker	Murray List. Brightfield biog.
Mar. 1843	71	142	10	Dickens's American Notes	Croker	Murray List. Brightfield biog.
Mar. 1843	71	142	12	Treaty of Washington	Croker	Murray List. Brightfield biog.
June 1845	76	151	2	Census of 1841	George Taylor	Surtees.[1]
Mar. 1846	77	154	8	The Oregon Question	Croker	Murray List. Brightfield biog.
Sept. 1846	78	156	9	Close of Peel's Administration	Croker[2]	Murray List. Brightfield biog.
June 1849	85	169	6	Lyell's 2nd Visit to U.S.	Milman	Murray List, Brightfield *PMLA*.
June 1849	85	169	8	Democracy	Croker	Murray List. Brightfield biog.
Jan. 1851	89	177	3	Recent Travellers in N. America	Robert Hogarth Patterson[3]	Murray List. Brightfield *PMLA*.
Mar. 1852	90	180	8	California vs. Free Trade	David Trivena Coulton[4]	Murray List. Fetter II, p. 169.
Dec. 1852	92	183	2	Life and Letters of Mr. Justice Story	Sir John Taylor Coleridge	Murray List.

[1] Geo. Taylor, *A Memoir of Robert Surtees* (Lond., 1852), p. xiv. Taylor (1771–1851) was Secretary of Commission of the Inquiry into Poor Laws in 1832 and an occasional contributor to QR on political economy, statistics, literature and political history (ibid.).

[2] According to the Murray list, the article was a composite affair; written by Croker, with additions by Lord Brougham, Edward Stanley (afterwards Lord Derby) and Ashburton; Wellington read it in proof. (See QR, Vol. 210, No. 419, Apr. 1909, p. 767n.) The article maintains the prophecy that Repeal of the Corn Laws would cause England 'to glide, by due course of law . . . into a national bankruptcy, and a republic of the American fashion' (p. 578).

[3] 1821–1886; journalist, writer; contributed to QR and *Blackwood's* and enjoyed a reputation as a financial expert.

[4] 1810–1857; journalist.

II. *Blackwoods:*

Date	Vol.	Title	Author	Authority for Assignment of Authorship
May 1824	15	Sketches of 5 American Presidents	John Neal	Strout,[1] p. 120.
Oct. 1824– Feb. 1825	16/17	American Writers (Series)	John Neal	Strout. Neal.[2]
Dec. 1824	16	Summary View of America	John Neal	Strout, p. 126.
Sept. 1825	18	The Nobility	David Robinson	Strout, p. 133.
Sept. 1825	18	North American Politics	John Neal	Strout, p. 133.
Oct. 1827	22	The Faction	Robinson	Publisher's List.[3]
Nov. 1828	24	Notes on U.S.A.	Robinson	Publisher's List.
Sept. 1833	34	America No. I	Archibald Alison	Alison, *Autobiog.*[4] I, 326.
Oct. 1833	34	America No. II	John Wilson	Publisher's list.
Sept. 1835	38	Whither are we Tending?	Alison	Alison, *Autobiog.* I, 363.
Dec. 1841	50	The United States	Geo. Croly[5]	Publisher's list.
Feb. 1842	51	American Sympathisers (with Irish Repeal)	Croly	Publisher's list.
Apr. 1846	59	How they manage Matters in 'the Model Republic'	Mr. Gardner[6]	Publisher's list.
Sept. 1846	60	Mexico	Croly	Publisher's list.

[1] A. L. Strout, *A Bibliography of Articles in Blackwood's Magazine, 1817–1825* (Lubbock, Texas, 1959). A very large number of *Blackwood's* articles are still unfortunately anonymous.

[2] John Neal, *Wandering Recollections of a Somewhat Busy Life* (Bost., 1869).

[3] Mrs. Houghton has kindly supplied information about entries in the publisher's list.

[4] Sir Archibald Alison, *Some Account of My Life and Writings: an Autobiography*, ed. Lady Alison (2 vols. Edinburgh, 1883). Alison (1792–1867), historian and lawyer, opposed the 'growing tyranny of democratic opinions' from American and French example.

[5] 1780–1860; author and divine; Irish Anglican minister and a leading contributor to *Blackwood's* in the 1830's and 1840's. Croly had immeasurable disdain for American democracy and the climate of American politics. He was bitterly opposed to American expansionism and was particularly incensed by the sympathy of Americans for Irish nationalism.

[6] No biographical information available.

Some Leading Articles on Alexis de Tocqueville: 1836–1865

1. *British and Foreign Review*, Vol. 2, No. 3 (1836), 'Tocqueville's Democracy in America', by Henry Reeve and Gilbert Ainslie Young. See J. K. Laughton, *Memoirs of Life and Correspondence of Henry Reeve* (London, 1898), I. 57–8, 62.
2. *Edinburgh Review*, Vol. 72, No. 145 (Oct. 1840), 'Tocqueville', by John Stuart Mill; reprinted in Mill, *Dissertations and Discussions*, Vol. 2 (London, 1859). See also Cockburn MSS., and B.M. Add. MSS., 34, 621, fos. 131–3.
3. *Edinburgh Review*, Vol. 113, No. 230 (Apr. 1861), 'Remains of Tocqueville', by Henry Reeve. See *Longman's List*. Also reprinted in Reeve, *Royal and Republican France*, Vol. 2 (London, 1872).
4. *Edinburgh Review*, Vol. 122, No. 250 (Oct. 1865), 'Posthumous Writings of Tocqueville', by Henry Reeve. See *Longman's List*, and reprinted in *Royal and Republican France*.
5. *London Review*, Vol. 26 (Oct. 1835), 'Tocqueville on Democracy in America', by J. S. Mill. See MacMinn, Hainds and McCrimmon, *Bibliography of the Published Writings of John Stuart Mill*, in *Northwestern University Studies in the Humanities*, *No. 12* (Evanston, 1945). There is evidence that various people aided Mill: Faucher, Blanco White, and Nassau Senior.
6. *Quarterly Review*, Vol. 57, No. 113 (Sept. 1836), 'Tocqueville', by Basil Hall. See *Murray List*, and Tocqueville, *Oeuvres Complètes: édition définitive*, ed. J. P. Mayer (Paris, 1954), VI. pt. i, 300.
7. *Quarterly Review*, Vol. 110, No. 200 (Oct. 1861), 'Alexis de Tocqueville', by Richard Monckton Milnes. See *Murray List*, and T. W. Reid, *Life, Letters and Friendships of Richard Monckton Milnes, etc.* (London, 1891), II, 63–4, 76.
8. *Blackwood's*, Vol. 37 (May 1835), 'Democracy in America', by Mr. O'Donnel (no biographical details available). See publisher's list.
9. *Blackwood's*, Vol. 61 (May 1847), 'M. de Tocqueville', by Archibald Alison. See publisher's list; also Alison, *Some Account of My Life and Writings, etc.* (Edinburgh, 1883), I, 554.
10. *Blackwood's*, Vol. 48 (Oct. 1840), 'Democracy in America', by O'Donnel. See publisher's list.

BIBLIOGRAPHY

THIS study relies heavily upon periodical literature, and some justification may be thought necessary. The periodicals were very probably the main intellectual inspiration to the parties, and to their supporters particularly, in an age when party organizations were still embryonic, and when no attempt was made to set up separate information centres. To attempt to study Whig opinion, for example, without consulting the *Edinburgh Review* would be like trying to guess at Labour policy today without having access to the *New Statesman*, and with no Transport House. Parliamentary comment is very useful at times, but it was sporadic on America, and was often so propagandist and vague as to be of limited importance. The daily newspapers were also polemical, and contained few serious discussions of American politics. Manuscript material is sometimes quite illuminating on Anglo-American links, and on the conscious propaganda use made of the American example; but, in truth, the new world occupies a very marginal place in most letters of the time. Letters, moreover, are rarely the vehicle for serious theoretical discussions. Pamphlets and books are very valuable for this purpose, and the following list includes those with more significant references to America:

I. *Primary Sources*

Manuscript Material in the British Museum

> The Bentham Correspondence
> The Cobden Papers
> The Gladstone Papers
> The Napier Papers
> The Place Papers

Periodicals

> *Blackwood's Edinburgh Magazine*
> *The British and Foreign Review*
> *The Edinburgh Review*
> *Fraser's Magazine*
> *The Jurist, or Quarterly Journal of Jurisprudence*
> *The London Review*
> *The London and Westminster Review*
> *The Monthly Repository*
> *The Parliamentary History and Review*
> *The Quarterly Review*

Tait's Edinburgh Magazine
The Westminster Review

Weeklies and Dailies

The Examiner
John Bull
Pamphlets for the People
The Morning Chronicle
The Standard
The Times

Hansard's *Parliamentary Debates* (1820–1850, new and third series).

Books and Pamphlets

Abdy, Edward S., *Journal of a Residence and Tour in the United States, etc.*, London, 1835.

Alison, Archibald, *Some Account of My Life and Writings: an Autobiography*, ed. by his daughter-in-law, Lady Alison, Edinburgh, 1883.
   Essays: Political, Historical and Miscellaneous, Edinburgh, 1850.

Barrow, Sir John, *An Autobiographical Memoir, etc.*, London, 1847.

Beaumont, Gustave de, *Marie*, Paris, 1835.

Bentham, Jeremy, *The Works of Jeremy Bentham, published under the Superintendence of . . . John Bowring*, London, 1838–43.

Beresford-Hope, A. J., *England, the North and the South, etc.*, London, 1862.

Birbeck, Morris, *Letters from Illinois*, London, 1818.
   Notes on a Journey in America, etc., London, 1818.

Blunt, Rev. J. J,, *Essays Contributed to the Quarterly Review*, London, 1860.

Bright, John, *The American Question*, London, 1865.
   Speeches on Public Policy, ed. J. E. Thorold Rogers, London, 1868.

Bristed, John, *Resources of the United States of America, etc.*, London, 1818.

Brougham, Henry, Lord, *Aristocracy, Democracy and Mixed Monarchy*, London, 1844.
   Collected Essays from the Edinburgh Review, London, 1856.
   Life and Times, etc., London, 1871.

Buckingham, James Silk, *America, Historical, Statistics and Descriptive*, London, 1841.

Butler, Frances Ann, *Journal*, London, 1835.

Canning, George, *Speeches*, ed. R. Therry, 3rd ed., London, 1836.

Carlyle, Thomas, *Latter Day Pamphlets*, London, 1872.
   Correspondence of Thomas Carlyle and Ralph Waldo Emerson: 1834–1872, ed. C. E. Norton, London, 1883.

Chevalier, Michel, *Society, Manners and Politics in the United States, etc.*, trans. T. G. Bradford, Boston, 1839.

Citizen of the United States, *Vindiciae Americanae . . . Letter . . . to Sir Robert Peel in refutation of the calumnious attacks on America and her citizens*, London, undated (mid-1830's).

16

Cobden, Richard, *England, Ireland and America*, London, 1835.
  Speeches on Questions of Public Policy, etc., ed. J. Bright and J. E. Thorold Rogers, London, 1870.
  The American Diaries of Richard Cobden, ed. E. H. Cawley, Princeton, 1952.
Cockburn, Lord, *Memorials of His Time*, London, 1856.
  Journal, London, 1874.
Combe, George, *Notes on the United States of North America*, Edinburgh, 1841.
Cooper, James Fenimore, *Residence in France, etc.*, Paris, 1836.
  England, with Sketches of Society in the Metropolis, London, 1837.
Croker, John Wilson, *The Croker Papers*, ed. L. T. Jennings, London, 1884.
Crombie, Rev. A., *Letter to Henry William Tancred . . . on the Ballot*, London, 1837.
  Letter to George Grote . . . on the Ballot, London, 1838.
Disraeli, Benjamin, *Vindication of the English Constitution, etc.*, London, 1835, reprinted in William Hutcheson, ed., *Whigs and Whiggism, etc.*, London, 1913.
  Parliamentary Reform: Speeches by Disraeli, ed. Montagu Corry, London, 1867.
Drummond, Henry, *Speeches in Parliament and Some Miscellaneous Pamphlets, etc.*, ed. Lord Lovaine, London, 1860.
  Letter to John Bright on his plan for turning the English monarchy into a democracy, London, 1858.
Dwight, Timothy, *Remarks on the Review of Inchiquin's Letters, etc.*, Boston, 1815.
Ewbank, Henry, ed., *The Influences of Democracy on the Liberty, Property and the Happiness of Society, etc.*, by Fisher Ames, London, 1835.
Faux, William, *Memorable Days in America*, London, 1823.
Fearon, Henry B., *Sketches of America, etc.*, London, 1818.
Fonblanque, Albany, *Life and Labours of Albany Fonblanque*, ed. E. B. Fonblanque, London, 1874.
Foster, Sir Augustus J., *Notes on the United States*, London, 1841.
Fox, Caroline, *Memories of Old Friends*, ed. H. N. Pym, Philadelphia, 1882.
Gladstone, W. E., *Gleanings of Past Years*, London, 1879.
Godley, John Robert, *Letters from America*, London, 1844.
Graham, Sir James, *Life and Letters, etc.*, ed. C. S. Parker, London, 1907.
Grattan, Thomas Colley, *England and the Disrupted States of America*, London, 1861.
Greg, William Rathbone, *Essays on Political and Social Science*, London, 1853.
Grote, George, *Statement on the Question of Parliamentary Reform, with a reply to the objections of the Edinburgh Review, etc.*, London, 1821.
  Essentials of Parliamentary Reform, London, 1831.
  Minor Works of George Grote, ed. Alexander Bain, London, 1873.
Grote, Harriet, *The Personal Life of George Grote*, London, 1873.
Hall, Basil, *Travels in North America, etc.*, London, 1829.
Hamilton, Thomas, *Men and Manners in America*, 3rd ed., Edinburgh, 1843.
Hayward, Abraham, *Biographical and Critical Essays*, London, 1858.
  Selection from the Correspondence of Abraham Hayward, ed. H. E. Carlyle, London, 1886.
Hodgson, Adam, *Letters from North America*, London, 1824.

Jeffrey, Francis, *Life and Correspondence of Francis Jeffrey*, ed. Lord Cockburn, London, 1852.

Latrobe, Charles J., *The Rambler in North America, 1832–1833*, New York, 1835.

Lockhart, John Gibson, *Life and Letters, etc.*, ed. Andrew Lang, London, 1897.

Lorimer, Rev. J. G., *The Past and Present Condition of Religion and Morality in the U.S.A.: an Argument not for Voluntary but for Established Churches*, London, 1833.
Church Establishments Defended, London, 1834.

Lewis, Sir George Cornewall, *Letters*, ed. by his brother, London, 1870.

Lieber, Francis, *The Stranger in America*, London, 1835.

Lyell, Sir Charles, *Travels in North America*, London, 1845.
Second Visit to the United States, London, 1849.

Lytton, Edward Bulwer, *England and the English*, Paris, 1834.

Macaulay, Thomas Babington, *Life and Letters*, ed. Sir Otto Trevelyan, New York, 1877 (II, Appendix).

McCulloch, J. R., *Descriptive and Statistical Account of the British Empire*, London, 1847.

Mackay, Alexander, *The Western World*, London, 1847.

Mackintosh, Sir James, *Miscellaneous Works*, ed. R. J. Mackintosh, Philadelphia, 1847.
Memoirs of the Life of . . . Mackintosh, ed. R. J. Mackintosh, Boston, 1853.

Marryat, Frederick, *A Diary in America*, London, 1839.

Martineau, Harriet, *Society in America*, London, 1837.
Retrospect of Western Travel, London, 1838.
The Martyr Age of the United States, Newcastle, 1840.

Merivale, Herman, *Lectures on Colonization and Colonies*, London, 1841.

Mill, James, *Essay on Government*, introd. Sir E. Barker, London, 1937.

Mill, John Stuart, *Autobiography*, introd. H. J. Laski, London, 1924.
Spirit of the Age, ed. F. A. Hayek, Chicago, 1942.
Dissertations and Discussions, London, 1859.
Letters of John Stuart Mill, ed. H. S. R. Eliot, London, 1910.

Murray, Charles A., *Travels in North America*, London, 1839.

Napier, Macvey, *Selections from the Correspondence of the late Macvey Napier*, ed. by his son, London, 1877.

Neal, John, *Wandering Recollections of a Somewhat Busy Life*, Boston, 1869.

Ouseley, William Gore, *Remarks on the Statistics and Political Institutions of the United States, etc.*, London, 1832.

Peel, Sir Robert, *Correct Report of Sir Robert Peel's Speeches at Glasgow, Jan. 1837*, London, 1837.
Sir Robert Peel from his Private Papers, ed. C. S. Parker, London, 1899.

Reed, Andrew, and James Matheson, *Narrative of a Visit to the American Churches, etc.*, London, 1835.

Reeve, Henry, *Royal and Republican France*, London, 1872.
Letters of Charles Greville and Henry Reeve, 1836–1865, ed. A. H. Johnson, London, 1924.

Roebuck, John Arthur, *Life and Letters*, ed. R. E. Leader, London, 1897.

Ryle, Thomas, *American Liberty and Government Questioned*, London, 1855.

Senior, Nassau William, *Correspondence and Conversations of Alexis de Tocqueville with Nassau William Senior, 1834–1859*, ed. M. C. M. Simpson, London, 1872.

Historical and Philosophical Essays, London, 1865.

American Slavery, London, 1856.

Shirreff, Patrick, *A Tour through North America*, Edinburgh, 1835.

Smith, Rev. Sydney, *The Ballot*, London, 1839.

Works, London, 1848.

Southey, Robert, *Sir Thomas More: or Colloquies on the Progress and Prospects of Society*, London, 1829.

Essays, Moral and Political, London, 1832.

Life and Correspondence of Robert Southey, ed. C. C. Southey, New York, 1851.

Spedding, James, *Reviews and Discussions*, London, 1879.

Stanhope, Philip Henry (Lord Mahon), *Historical Essays: contributed to the Quarterly Review*, London, 1861.

Stanley, Edward, *Journal of a Tour in America: 1824–1825*, privately printed, London, 1930.

Stephen, Leslie, et al., *Essays in Reform*, London, 1867.

Stuart, James, *Three Years in North America*, Edinburgh, 1833.

Thompson, Thomas Perronet, *Exercises, Political and Others*, London, 1842.

Catechism on the Ballot, London, 1862.

Tocqueville, Alexis de, *Democracy in America*, trans. Henry Reeve, London, 1836.

Democracy in America, ed. E. Phillips Bradley, New York, 1945.

Tocqueville, Alexis de, *Oeuvres Complètes, etc.*, ed. Gustave de Beaumont, Paris, 1864–1867.

Oeuvres Complètes: édition définitive, ed. J. P. Mayer. Vol. VI, *Correspondance Anglaise*, Paris, 1954.

Letters, Memorials, Remains, ed. M. C. M. Simpson, London, 1861.

Recollections, ed. J. P. Mayer, London, 1948.

Journeys to England and Ireland, ed. J. P. Mayer, London, 1958.

Journey to America, ed. J. P. Mayer, London, 1959.

Tracts Relating to Elections (Miscellaneous pamphlets, British Library of Political and Economic Science, OW 1831/2).

Tremenheere, Hugh S., *Notes . . . made during a Tour in the United States and Canada*, London, 1852.

The Constitution of the United States Compared with our own, London, 1854.

Trollope, Frances M., *Domestic Manners of the Americans*, London, 1832.

Tudor, Henry, *Narrative of a Tour in North America, etc.*, London, 1834.

Vigne, Godfrey T., *Six Months in America*, London, 1832.

Wakefield, Edward Gibbon, *England and America: a Comparison of the Social and Political State of Both Nations*, New York, 1834.

Walsh, Robert, *An Appeal from the Judgments of Great Britain respecting the United States of America, etc.*, Philadelphia, 1819.

[Wright, Frances], *Views of Society and Manners in America, etc.*, London, 1821.

II. *Selected Secondary Sources*

Adams, E. D., 'The Point of View of the British Traveller in America', *Pol. Science Quart.*, XXIX (1914), 244–64.

Adams, H. B., 'Jared Sparks and Alexis de Tocqueville', *Johns Hopkins University Studies in Historical and Political Science*, Series XVI (1898).

Adams, K. M., 'How the Benthamites Became Democrats', *J. of Social Philosophy and Jurisprudence*, VII (Jan. 1942), 161–71.

Allen, H. C., *Great Britain and the United States, 1783–1952*, London, 1954.

—— ed., *British Essays in American History*, London, 1957.

Andrews, Alexander, *History of British Journalism, etc.*, London, 1859.

Aspinall, A., *Lord Brougham and the Whig Party*, London, 1927.

Bagehot, Walter, *Literary Studies*, London, 1879.

—— *Works* (Vol. 9), London, 1915.

Bagehot, Walter, *Biographical Studies*, ed. R. H. Hutton, London, 1889.

Bain, Alexander, *James Mill: a Biography*, New York, 1882.

Beatty, Richard Croom, *Lord Macaulay: Victorian Liberal*, Oklahoma, 1938.

Benns, F. Lee, *The American Struggle for the British West Indian Carrying Trade, 1815–1830*, Indiana, 1930.

Berger, Max, *The British Traveller in America, 1836–1860*, New York, 1943.

—— 'American Slavery as seen by English Visitors, 1836–1860', *J. Negro History*, XXX.

Blagden, C., '*Edinburgh Review* Authors 1830–1849', *Library*, 5th Ser., VII (1952), 212–14.

Bowley, M., *Nassau Senior and Classical Economics*, London, 1937.

Brebner, J. B., *North Atlantic Triangle*, London, 1945.

Brightfield, Myron F., *John Wilson Croker*, California, 1940.

—— 'Lockhart's *Quarterly* Contributors', *PMLA*, LIX (June 1944), 491–512.

Britton, K., *John Stuart Mill*, London, 1953.

Bryce, Lord, 'Predictions of Hamilton and Tocqueville', *Johns Hopkins University Studies in Historical and Political Science*, IX, 1887 (Series V).

—— 'The United States Constitution as seen in the Past', *Studies in Jurisprudence*, New York, 1901.

Buckley, J. K., *Joseph Parkes of Birmingham, etc.*, London, 1926.

Burn, W. L. *The Age of Equipoise—a Study of the Mid-Victorian Generation*, London, 1964.

Burns, J. H., 'John Stuart Mill and Democracy, 1829–1861', *Pol. Studies*, V (June and Oct. 1957).

Carrington, C. E., *John Robert Godley of Canterbury*, Christchurch, 1950.

Cecil, Lady Gwendolen, *Life of Robert Marquis of Salisbury*, Vol. 1, *1830–1861*, London, 1921.

Clark, R. B., *William Gifford, Tory Satirist, Critic and Editor*, New York, 1930.

Clive, J., *Scotch Reviewers: The Edinburgh Review, 1802–1815*, London, 1957.

Clive, J., and B. Bailyn, 'England's Cultural Provinces: Scotland and America', *William and Mary Quarterly*, 3rd Ser., XI (Apr. 1954), 200ff.

Commager, Henry Steele, ed., *America in Perspective*, New York, 1947.

Copinger, W. A., *Authorship of the first hundred numbers of the Edinburgh Review*, Manchester, 1895.

Cowherd, R. G., *The Politics of English Dissent, 1815–1848*, London, 1956.

Dicey, A. V., *Law and Opinion in England*, London, 1905.

'Alexis de Tocqueville', *National Review*, XXI (Mar.–Aug. 1893), 771–84.

Douglas, Sir George, *The Blackwood Group*, London, 1897.

Drescher, Seymour, *Tocqueville and England*, Cambridge, Harvard University Press, 1964.

Edwards, H. W. J., ed., *The Radical Tory: Disraeli's Political Development illustrated from his original writings and speeches*, London, 1937.

Elwin, M., 'Founder of the Quarterly Review: John Murray II', *Quarterly Review*, CCLXXXI (Jul. 1943), 1–15.

Engel-Janosi, F., 'New Tocqueville Material . . .', *Four Studies in French Romantic Historical Writing*, Ch. V.

Erickson, A. B., *The Public Career of Sir James Graham*, Oxford, 1952.

Fawcett, Mrs., *Life of Sir William Molesworth*, London, 1903.

Fetter, Frank W., 'Authorship of Economic Articles in the *Edinburgh Review*, 1802–1847', *J. Pol. Econ.*, LXI (June 1953).

'Economic Articles in the *Quarterly Review* and their Authors, 1809–1852', *J. Pol. Econ.*, LXVI (Feb. 1958), 47–64; and LXVI (Apr. 1958), 154–170.

'Authorship of Articles in the *Edinburgh Review*', *Bull. Instit. Hist. Research*, XXX (1957).

Ffrench, Y., *Transatlantic Exchanges: Anglo-U.S. Opinion in the Nineteenth Century*, London, 1951.

Fraiberg, Louis, 'The *Westminster Review* and American Literature, 1824–1885', *Am. Lit.*, XXIV (Nov. 1952), 310–29.

Graham, Walter, *English Literary Periodicals*, New York, 1930.

'Southey as Tory Reviewer', *Philological Quart.*, II (1923), 97–111.

Guedalla, P., *Palmerston*, London, 1926.

Halévy, Élie, *Growth of Philosophic Radicalism*, London, 1928.

Hawkins, R. L., 'Unpublished Letters of Alexis de Tocqueville', *Romanic Review*, XIX (1929), 195ff.

History of the Times: Vol. 2, *Thunderer in the Making: 1841–1894*, London, 1945–48.

Hodder, Edwin, *Life and Work of the 7th Earl of Shaftesbury*, London, 1887.

Johnson, A. H., 'Correspondence of Tocqueville and Reeve', *Edinburgh Review*, CCXXXVIII (Oct. 1923), 287ff.

Johnson, L. G., 'On Some Authors of *Edinburgh Review* Articles, 1830–1849', *Library*, 5th Ser., VIII (Mar. 1952), 38–50.

Jones, W. J., 'British Conservatives and the American Civil War', *Am. Hist. Rev.*, LVIII (Apr. 1953), 527–43.

Kaderly, N. L., 'Southey and the *Quarterly Review*', *Mod. Lang. Notes*, LXX (Apr. 1955), 261–3.

Kern, J. D., E. Schneider and I. Griggs, 'Lockhart to Croker on the *Quarterly*', *PMLA*, LX (1945), 175–98.

'Brougham's Early Contributions to the *Edinburgh Review:* a new list', *Mod. Philology*, XLII (1945).

'Early Edinburgh Reviewers', *Mod. Philology*, XLIII (1946).

Klingberg, F. J., *The Anti-Slavery Movement in England*, New Haven, 1926.

'Harriet Beecher Stowe and Social Reform in England', *Am. Hist. Rev.*, XLIII (Apr. 1938).

Kraus, M., *The Atlantic Civilization: Eighteenth Century Origins*, New York, 1949.

Laski, Harold J., 'Alexis de Tocqueville and Democracy', in F. J. C. Hearnshaw, ed., *Social and Political Ideas of Some Representative Thinkers of the Victorian Age*, London, 1935.

Laughton, J. K., *Memoirs of the Life and Correspondence of Henry Reeve*, London, 1898.

Levy, S. Leon, *Nassau W. Senior: The Prophet of Modern Capitalism*, Boston, 1943.

Lewis, G. K., 'A Forgotten Classic of English Life and Government (Lytton's *England and the English)*', *Canadian J. Economics and Pol. Sc.*, XIX (Aug. 1953), 377ff.

Lillibridge, G. D., *Beacon of Freedom: The Impact of American Democracy upon Great Britain, 1830–1870*, Pennsylvania, 1954.

Lively, Jack, *The Social and Political Thought of Alexis de Tocqueville*, Oxford, 1962. (The best single work to date on this topic.)

Lodge, Henry Cabot, *One Hundred Years Peace*, New York, 1913.

Lytton, Earl of, *Life of Edward Bulwer, 1st Lord Lytton*, London, 1913.

Magnus, Philip, *Gladstone: a Biography*, London, 1954.

Mayer, J. P., 'Unpublished Letters of John Stuart Mill to Alexis de Tocqueville', *Times Lit. Supp.*, 1 Sept. 1950.

'Alexis de Tocqueville and John Stuart Mill', *Listener*, March 1950.

'Tocqueville as Political Sociologist', *Pol. Studies*, II (1953).

Mayer, J. P., *Alexis de Tocqueville: Prophet of the Mass Age*, New York, 1940.

Merk, F., 'British Party Politics and Oregon', *Am. Hist. Rev.*, XXXVII (July 1932).

Mesick, J. L., *The English Traveller in America, 1785–1835*, New York, 1922.

Monypenny, W. F., and G. E. Buckle, *Life of Benjamin Disraeli, Earl of Beaconsfield*, London, 1910–1920.

Morley, John, *Life of Gladstone*, London, 1903.

Life of Richard Cobden, London, 1896.

Mueller, I., *John Stuart Mill and French Thought*, New York, 1956.

Nesbitt, George, *Benthamite Reviewing: The First Twelve Years of the Westminster Review, 1824–1836*, New York, 1934.

Nevins, A., ed., *America Through British Eyes*, New York, 1948.

Oliphant, Mrs., *William Blackwood and his Sons*, Edinburgh, 1897.

Packe, M. St. John, *Life of John Stuart Mill*, London, 1954.

Palmer, P. A., 'Benthamism in England and America', *Am. Pol. Sc. Rev.*, XXXV (Oct. 1941).

Peardon, Thomas P., 'Bentham's Ideal Republic', *Canadian J. Econ. and Pol. Sc.*, XVII (May 1951), 184–203.

Pelling, Henry, *America and the British Left*, London, 1956.

Pierson, C. W., *Tocqueville and Beaumont in America*, New York, 1938.

Plamenatz, John, *The English Utilitarians*, London, 1949.

Pope-Hennessy, J., *Monckton Milnes: The Years of Promise*, London, 1950.

Reid, S. J., *Life of Lord Durham*, London, 1906.

Roberts, David, 'Tory Paternalism and Social Reform in Early Victorian England',
   Am. Hist. Rev., LXIII (1958).

Salomon, A., 'Tocqueville, Moralist and Sociologist', *Social Research*, II (Nov. 1935).
   'Tocqueville's Philosophy of Freedom', *Review of Politics*, I (Oct. 1939), 400–32.

Schapiro, J. S., 'Tocqueville: Pioneer of Democratic Liberalism in France', *Pol.
   Sc. Quart.*, LVII (Dec. 1942).

Shepperson, W. S., *British Emigration to North America: Projects and Opinions in the
   Early Victorian Period*, Oxford, 1957.

Shine, Hill, and H. C. Shine, *The Quarterly Review under Gifford: identification of
   contributors, 1809–1824*, North Carolina, 1949.

Smiles, Samuel, *A Publisher and his Friends: Memoirs and Correspondence of John
   Murray*, London, 1891.

Smith, L., 'Tocqueville and Public Administration', *Pub. Admin. Rev.*, II (1942),
   221–39.

Stephen, Leslie, *The English Utilitarians*, New York, 1900.

Swann, Elsie, *Christopher North: John Wilson*, London, 1934.

Taylor, Clare, 'Notes on American Negro Reformers in Victorian Britain',
   Bulletin of the British Assoc. for American Studies, New Ser., No. 2 (Mar. 1961),
   40–51.

Temperley, H., *The Foreign Policy of George Canning, 1822–1827*, London, 1925.

Thistlethwaite, Frank, *The Anglo-American Connection in the Early Nineteenth
   Century*, Philadelphia, 1959.
   'America and Two Nations of Englishmen', *Virg. Quart. Rev.*, XXXI (Autumn
   1955), 505–525.

Thrall, M. M. H., *Rebellious Frasers, etc.*, New York, 1934.

Towers, C. M. D., 'John Stuart Mill and the *London and Westminster Review*',
   Atlantic Monthly, LXIX (Jan. 1892).

Tuckermann, H. T., *America and her Commentators, etc.*, New York, 1864.

Turner, R. E., *James Silk Buckingham, 1786–1855*, London, 1934.

Wallas, Graham, *Life of Francis Place, 1771–1854*, London, 1925.

Watkin, Sir Edward, *Alderman Cobden of Manchester, etc.*, London, 1891.

Webb, R. K., *The British Working Class Reader, 1790–1848*, London, 1955.
   Harriet Martineau: a Radical Victorian, London, 1960.

Wheeler, Paul Mowbray, *America Through British Eyes: A Study of the Attitude of
   The Edinburgh Review toward the United States of America from 1802 until 1861*,
   South Carolina, 1935 (lithoprint).

Whibley, Charles, *Lord John Manners and his Friends*, Edinburgh, 1925.

Williamson, Clinton, 'Bentham Looks at America', *Pol. Sc. Quart.*, LXX (Dec.
   1955), 543–51.

Willson, Beckles, *America's Ambassadors to England, 1785–1928*, London, 1928.

Yonge, C. D., *Life and Administration of . . . the 2nd Earl of Liverpool*, London, 1868.

Zemach, A., 'Tocqueville in England', *Rev. of Politics*, XIII (July 1951), 329ff.

INDEX

Abdy, E. S., 63, 110, 122, 130
Acquisitiveness in U.S., *see* Materialism in U.S.
Acton, Lord, 55
Adams, Charles Francis, 139
Adams, E. D., 70
Adams, H. B., 191
Adams, John, 1, 12, 47, 105, 107, 119, 121, 126, 138, 139, 146
Adams, W. Bridges, 27, 126
Addison, J., 103
Alison, Archibald, 116–19, 193
Alman, M., *see* Crick, B. R., and Alman, M.
Ambrister, 99
American Constitution, *see* Constitution, American
American Declaration of Independence: Bentham on, 1, 20; Brougham on, 77
Ames, Fisher, 98, 111, 118, 139, 140
Anglicanism, *see* Church of England
Anglophobia, 5–7, 9, 142, 202
Annual elections, *see* Parliamentary reform
Anti-Americanism, 29, 69, 94, 102, 107, 110–12, 118, 128, 202
Anti-Corn-Law League, 58, 84
Anti-State Church Conference (1844), 158
Arbuthnot, 99, 126
Ashburton, Lord, 130
Ashley, Lord (7th Earl of Shaftesbury), 165
Ashton, Prof. T. S., 204
Austin, John, 49, 168

Bacon, Francis, 22, 78
Bagehot, Walter, 45, 82, 149
Bain, Alexander, 41
Baines, E., 158
Ballot, *see* Parliamentary reform
Balzac, Honoré de, 169
Bancroft, George, 91
Bank of U.S., 57, 64, 112, 200
Bannatyne, Dugald, 114, 115, 127, 129
Barbarism in U.S., 55, 76–77, 100, 202, *see also* Culture, Literature, Manners
Barrow, John, 30, 99, 101, 102, 103, 106, 107, 126, 128, 133, 137, 161, 163
Bassett, J. S., 12
Beaumont, Gustave de, 97, 110, 129, 137, 162, 191
Beccaria, Marchese di, 48
Benns, F. Lee, 107
Bentham, Jeremy; and culture, 34; and law reform, 12–13, 27, 48–51; and parliamentary reform, 14–17, 40–48; as a democrat,

14–15, 20–21, 36–37, 48, 172; as a 'Philo-Yankee', 11–12, 16, 17, 36, 58; as a Republican, 15–19; influence on English politics, 13–21, 24, 25, 26, 36, 61, 105; political philosophy of, 14–21, 36–37, 48, 60, 62, 100, 125, 149, 150
Benthamism and Benthamites: *see also* Bentham, Jeremy; Benthamite Radicalism, American democratic influence on, 13, 16, 17, 19, 28–29, 36, 37–38, 40, 52, 57, 58–59, 60–61, 202; and American liberalism, 19–21; and Bentham, J., 11–22; and economic policy, 38; and education, 29, 56, 57; and emigration, 35, 38; and the Establishment, 36–38, 109–110; and Jefferson, 291; and law reform, 48–51; and parliamentary reform, 40–48, 57, 126–7, 184; and property rights, 24–26; and republicanism, 38–39; and Tocqueville, 170; and the *Westminster Reveiw*, 12, 13, 26–35; as a middle-class movement, 8, 36, 52, 109–10; defence of America, 29–35; development of, 35–36, 37, 52–68; 'orthodox', 53–56, 57, 60–61; as proselytes, 170; subjectivity of, 21, 28, 29–30, 40, 52, 199–200
Beresford-Hope, Alexander, 128
Bi-cameralism, 21, 47, 139, 144–7
Biddle, Nicholas, 57, 64, 112
Biddle's Bank, *see* Bank of U.S.
Bingham, P., 27, 32
Birkbeck, Morris, 101, 102, 108
Birsted, John, 157
Black, John, 27
Blackstone, 18, 49, 149
Blackwood, William, 113
Blackwood's, 84, 113, 116, 139, 192, 193–8
Blake, W., 204
Blunt, J. J., 112, 158
Bowen, Francis, 188
Bowring, J., 12, 58, 168
Bradley, E. P., 188
Bribery at Elections, Select Committee on (1835), 169, 191
Bright, J., 5, 85
Brightfield, M. F., 119
Brougham, Henry, 49, 50, 51, 73, 74, 76, 77, 79, 82, 91, 145, 169, 187
Brown, 103
Buckingham, James Silk, 105
Buckley, J. K., 41, 50
Buena Vista, 151
Buller, Charles, 59, 131, 168